Europe and the Occupation of Palestinian Territories Since 1967

Focusing on key countries and topics, this book looks at Europe's involvement in the occupation of Palestinian territories.

What has been Europe's role in the occupation of Palestinian territories since 1967? How have European actors responded, countered and/or supported the occupation? The international context of this exceptionally long occupation shows a complex web of denunciations, but also and especially complicit engagements and indifference. The book looks at the perspective of international law, before analysing the European Union and key European countries (France, Germany, Norway, Sweden, United Kingdom). It also embraces different perspectives, from the debate on campus to the role of European multinational companies to the conceptual approach of the World Bank. While much of the literature focuses on Israel, Palestine and the United States, this volume by leading experts adds a very important piece to the puzzle: the European dimension.

The chapters in this book were originally published as a special issue of the journal, *Global Affairs*.

Federica Bicchi is Associate Professor in International Relations of Europe in the Department of International Relations, London School of Economics, UK.

Europe and the Occupation of Palestinian Territories Since 1967

Edited by
Federica Bicchi

LONDON AND NEW YORK

First published 2021
by Routledge
2 Park Square, Milton Park, Abingdon, Oxon, OX14 4RN

and by Routledge
52 Vanderbilt Avenue, New York, NY 10017

Routledge is an imprint of the Taylor & Francis Group, an informa business

© 2021 European International Studies Association

All rights reserved. No part of this book may be reprinted or reproduced or utilised in any form or by any electronic, mechanical, or other means, now known or hereafter invented, including photocopying and recording, or in any information storage or retrieval system, without permission in writing from the publishers.

Trademark notice: Product or corporate names may be trademarks or registered trademarks, and are used only for identification and explanation without intent to infringe.

British Library Cataloguing-in-Publication Data
A catalogue record for this book is available from the British Library

ISBN13: 978-0-367-54226-9

Typeset in Minion Pro
by codeMantra

Publisher's Note
The publisher accepts responsibility for any inconsistencies that may have arisen during the conversion of this book from journal articles to book chapters, namely the inclusion of journal terminology.

Disclaimer
Every effort has been made to contact copyright holders for their permission to reprint material in this book. The publishers would be grateful to hear from any copyright holder who is not here acknowledged and will undertake to rectify any errors or omissions in future editions of this book.

Printed in the United Kingdom
by Henry Ling Limited

Contents

Citation Information vii
Notes on Contributors ix

1 Introduction 1
   Federica Bicchi

2 Can an Occupation Become Unlawful? Third party responsibilities and
   Israeli practices in the Palestinian territories 4
   Michael Lynk

3 Non-Recognition à la European Union: Reflections on the
   Revisions to EU-Israeli Relations and the Obligation of
   Non-Recognition in International Law 19
   Valentina Azarova

4 France and the Israeli occupation: Talking the talk, but not walking the walk? 34
   Benedetta Voltolini

5 Germany and the Israeli Occupation: Torn Between Special Relationship
   and Two-State-Commitment 47
   Jan Busse

6 The debate about the occupation of Palestinian territories on UK campuses:
   from politicisation to re-writing the rules 59
   Federica Bicchi

7 Swedish recognition of Palestine: politics, law, and prospects for peace 71
   Jacob Eriksson

8 The angel in disguise? Norway's complicity in Israel's continued
   colonisation of Palestinian territories 82
   Michelle Pace

9	Missing the train. International governance gaps and the Jerusalem Light Railway *Mary Martin*	94
10	OECD principals or World Bank guidance? EU development aid in the occupied Palestinian territories *Jeremy Wildeman*	108
	Index	123

Citation Information

The chapters in this book were originally published in the *Global Affairs*, volume 4, issue 1 (September 2018). When citing this material, please use the original page numbering for each article, as follows:

Chapter 1
The Occupation of Palestinian territories since 1967: an analysis of Europe's role
Federica Bicchi
Global Affairs, volume 4, issue 1 (September 2018) pp. 3–5

Chapter 2
The challenge for Europe: making international law work for Middle East peace
Michael Lynk
Global Affairs, volume 4, issue 1 (September 2018) pp. 7–21

Chapter 3
The secret life of non-recognition: EU-Israel relations and the obligation of non-recognition in international law
Valentina Azarova
Global Affairs, volume 4, issue 1 (September 2018) pp. 23–37

Chapter 4
France and the Israeli occupation: talking the talk, but not walking the walk?
Benedetta Voltolini
Global Affairs, volume 4, issue 1 (September 2018) pp. 51–63

Chapter 5
Germany and the Israeli occupation: the interplay of international commitments and domestic dynamics
Jan Busse
Global Affairs, volume 4, issue 1 (September 2018) pp. 77–88

Chapter 6
The debate about the occupation of Palestinian territories on UK campuses, from politicization to re-writing the rules
Federica Bicchi
Global Affairs, volume 4, issue 1 (September 2018) pp. 89–100

Chapter 7
Swedish recognition of Palestine: politics, law, and prospects for peace
Jacob Eriksson
Global Affairs, volume 4, issue 1 (September 2018) pp. 39–49

Chapter 8
Norway's ambiguous approach towards Israel and Palestine
Michelle Pace
Global Affairs, volume 4, issue 1 (September 2018) pp. 65–76

Chapter 9
Missing the train. International governance gaps and the Jerusalem Light Railway
Mary Martin
Global Affairs, volume 4, issue 1 (September 2018) pp. 101–114

Chapter 10
EU Development aid in the occupied Palestinian territory, between aid effectiveness and World Bank guidance
Jeremy Wildeman
Global Affairs, volume 4, issue 1 (September 2018) pp. 115–128

For any permission-related enquiries please visit:
http://www.tandfonline.com/page/help/permissions

Contributors

Valentina Azarova Center for Global Public Law, Koç University Law School, Istanbul, Turkey.

Federica Bicchi Department of International Relations, London School of Economics, UK.

Jan Busse Institute of Political Science, Bundeswehr University Munich, Neubiberg, Germany.

Jacob Eriksson Department of Politics, University of York, York, UK.

Michael Lynk Faculty of Law, Western University, London, Canada. UN Special Rapporteur for the situation of human rights in the Palestinian territories.

Mary Martin London School of Economics, London, UK.

Michelle Pace Department of Social Sciences and Business, Roskilde University, Denmark.

Benedetta Voltolini Department of European and International Studies, King's College London, London, UK..

Jeremy Wildeman Department of Social and Policy Sciences, University of Bath, UK.

Introduction

Federica Bicchi

The issue at stake

50+ years of Israeli occupation of Palestinian territories have not existed in a vacuum. While much of the scholarly attention has scrutinized dynamics on the ground, the international context within which the occupation has persisted deserves equal scrutiny beyond the traditional reference to US foreign policy, because the sustainability of regional phenomena depends also on the international context within which they are embedded. This forum focuses on European actors and how they have interacted with the occupation, through an analysis of legal, political and socio-economic practices. It shows that the Israeli-Palestinian conflict has been played out not only in the foreign policies of European countries and organizations, but also and increasingly in their domestic politics, policies and debates. The aim of this brief introduction is to highlight the main points and anticipate some of the key themes that weave the collection together, in terms of substance and scope.

First, an analysis of the occupation's international context requires an engagement with international law, which might sound painful to the ears of political scientists or policy-makers, but at times of global contestation of the liberal order it is essential to remind ourselves how internationally agreed principles apply to this specific instance. This collection is based on the premise that all European countries have agreed that Israel is an occupying power, a position that the state of Israel formally rejects but all articles included here explore. In fact, as argued by the contribution of the UN Special Rapporteur, Michael Lynk, international law presents us with a paradox. While much of it has developed in response to the Israeli occupation of Palestinian territories, it has had seemingly little direct impact on the conflict itself. This points to a potential avenue for the Europeans' action, if they are to be true to their hard-won liberal sensibilities and contribute to a compassionate resolution of the Arab-Israeli conflict, namely to re-assess the legality of Israel's occupant status and give meaning to law through their actions. Moreover, international law has evolved and has codified the need for third parties to avoid de facto recognizing illegal situations. Azarova shows how this is particularly important for the European Union (EU), as it needs to ensure consistency between international law, EU law and domestic implementation within member states of EU related rules. The revisions to EU-Israeli relations that the EU has promoted in recent years should be read (also) in this light. Recognition is a theme that marks the most visible European action in current times, namely

Sweden's recognition of Palestine in 2014. As Eriksson recounts, the decision was a divisive one, but also marked the continuity of Sweden's position on the conflict and it showed the current relevance of politics in law-related decisions.

A second crucial theme of the collection highlights the extent to which member states have outsourced to international organizations (and to the EU in particular) the responsibility to act on their stance about the occupation, while maintaining a softer line vis à vis Israel at the governmental level in bilateral relations, and how this puts governments often at odds with parts of their own citizens. As shown by Voltolini, France is a case in point, given that it has used considerable political capital on the international scene to champion the Palestinians' right to self-determination and condemn Israel's occupation of the occupied Palestinian territory (OPT), by for instance promoting the EU policy of differentiation between Israel inside the Green Line and Israeli settlements. However, France's bilateral relations and the government's line on the domestic scene in the last decade have tended to skirt the issue's implications, in order not to upset an increasingly warm bilateral relationship. In the analysis of Pace, Norway too aims to maintain excellent relations with both the Palestinians and with Israel, even when the majority of its population, which largely supports the EU differentiation policy, would suggest a tougher stance. The tension between governments and public opinion in Europe is further brought to the fore in the analysis of Germany and of the UK. There is a clear discrepancy between, on the one hand, the German government's commitment and special responsibility towards Israel and, on the other, the Germans' critical attitude towards Israel, as analysed by Busse. Criticism in Germany does not take the form of support of the Boycott, Divest and Sanction (BDS) movement, though, which is instead a major issue in the UK domestic debates. As Bicchi shows through the analysis of debates on UK campuses, the conflict is played inside the UK predominantly as a domestic issue, despite its international ramifications, and in London much of "who can say what" about the conflict is once again debated and ultimately decided.

A last theme running across this collection pertains to the socio-economic dimension of the Europeans' attitude towards the occupation. Often mentioned as a possible way forward, the "economic peace" option has clear limits. In particular, Martin shows how European governments and the EU have been slow to tackle corporate responsibility of European private actors on the ground, while European companies have often been swift to exploit economic opportunities. A governance gap remains, despite the UN Guiding Principles on Business and Human Rights agreed in 2011 – another avenue that European governments could explore, following in the path of civil society. In his exploration of public aid to the OPT, Wildeman argues that the Europeans' traditional role as "payers" has largely adhered to the model provided by the World Bank. But the World Bank has increasingly avoided any reference to the occupation, thus countering the principles that the Europeans have codified in relation to the conflict.

Therefore, this forum presents a conversation between scholars belonging to different disciplines with a view to assess European practices in this case of prolonged occupation. The analysis is thus not addressing Israeli occupation per se or the Israeli-Palestinian conflict or the impact of European practices thereupon. Rather, it focuses on the international context in which such an occupation is situated and specifically on the ways in which European actors relate to the occupation, recognize it or resist it. Ultimately, the picture that emerges is of a group of countries quick to condemn internationally, but in practice helping at a bilateral level to normalize the occupation against the will of parts of their population.

Would the picture have changed had a broader set of European countries been included? It would have been interesting to examine countries from Central and Eastern Europe, or from Southern Europe, in order to assess the range of variation. "New" EU member states, in particular, project an image that is intentionally different from the position of "older" member states, and it would have been interesting to check the substance below the surface. However, not only pragmatic considerations had to be taken into account, but also part of the rationale for this collection was exactly to probe how countries tradionally condemning the occupation at the international level behave in practice, and to highlight the tensions in these actors' practices. Future research will then be able to compare practices across different groups of European countries, as well as across different occupations – and continue the scholarly conversation and the political debate.

As the anniversaries of the 1967 war and of the Balfour Declaration are beyond us, it seems that the contradictions implicit in the conflict will continue to mark the Europeans' action for the time to come. Hopefully, this set of contributions will help in clarifying the terms of the debate.

Disclosure statement

No potential conflict of interest was reported by the author.

Can an Occupation Become Unlawful? Third party responsibilities and Israeli practices in the Palestinian territories

Michael Lynk

ABSTRACT
No modern conflict has contributed so much to the development of international law as the Israeli–Palestinian conflict yet, paradoxically, no conflict has so undercut the efficacy of law by its political marginalization of a rights-based framework throughout the Oslo peace process. International law has a potentially redemptive role to play in securing a just and lasting peace in Israel/Palestine, but its absence in the formative agreements of the Oslo process – supported by the international mediating powers and the occupying power – has contributed mightily to the failures of the past quarter-century. Europe has played a muffled role during this process, advocating for the principles of international law – such as the illegality of the Israeli settlements and the annexation of East Jerusalem – yet unwilling to enforce these principles through the adoption of political measures against Israeli policy in the occupied Palestinian territory. As Israel's prolonged role as belligerent occupier crosses a bright red line into illegality, the importance of Europe taking an effective stand to end the occupation assumes an increasingly greater significance.

Introduction

The role of international law in the Israeli-Palestinian conflict embodies a fateful and troubling paradox. On the one hand, this conflict, more than any other since the end of the Second World War, has contributed immensely to the progressive development of international rule-making. Many of the core principles on public international law – the laws of war, the interrelationship between international humanitarian and human rights law, the rights of refugees, the centrality of self-determination, the meaning of terrorism, the scourge of demographic engineering, and the inadmissibility of the acquisition of territory by war, among others – have been significantly shaped, enriched and deepened by the norms established through the copious UN resolutions, diplomatic statements, legal commentaries and judicial pronouncements on the many features of the conflict (Akram, 2011). The leading tomes on the law of occupation are drenched with examples from Israel's 50-year-old rule over the Palestinian territory (Benvenesti, 2004; Gross, 2017).

Yet, at the same time, the efficacy of law has suffered mightily because the most powerful actors involved in the management of the Israeli-Palestinian conflict have consistently marginalized international law as a political and diplomatic touchstone when constituting the negotiation principles for the quarter-century-long peace process. Since the establishment of the Oslo process in 1993, the major agreements and declarations on the conflict have been conspicuously silent on the many cornerstone legal obligations pertaining to the conflict. To be sure, there are regular references in these documents to United Nations Security Council (UNSC) resolutions 242 (1967) and 338 (1973) and, after 2002, to the two-state vision first endorsed by UNSC resolution 1397 (2002), all of which are based on the amorphous concept of land-for-peace. However, we would look in vain through the leading peace process proclamations – the 1993 Oslo Accord (Peters & Newman, 2013a, pp. 412–420), the 1995 Oslo II Accord (Peters & Newman, 2013b, pp. 421–439), the 2000 Clinton Parameters (Peters & Newman, 2013c, pp. 440–444), the 2003 Roadmap (Peters & Newman, 2013d, pp. 445–450), the 2006 Quartet Principles (Peters & Newman, 2013e, pp. 451–452), the 2007 Annapolis Joint Understanding (Government of the State of Israel and the Palestine Liberation Organization (PLO), 2007), and the three Security Council resolutions on the vision for two states (UNSC Res. 1397 (2002); UNSC Res. 1515 (2003b); UNSC Res. 1850 (2008)) – for any mention of the more exacting legal principles established by multiple United Nations resolutions. These legal principles include the existence of the occupation and the unequal dynamics between occupier and occupied, the unlawful annexation of East Jerusalem, the illegality of the Israeli settlements, the rights of the Palestinian refugees, the application of human rights law and the unlawful location of the Israeli-built wall.[1] In the hands of Israel and the countries and international bodies leading the peace process – the United States, the European Union, the United Nations and Russia – these pre-established legal rights have been recast as issues for further negotiations between the two unequal parties rather than irreducible principles by which to frame the process.

This is no oversight. As Professor Kattan (2009) has succinctly stated: "the problem is not international law *per se*, but its lack of enforcement; that in the Middle East, international law is closer to power than to justice." In this conflict, the occupying power has insisted that international law should have no role, the international mediating powers have shown no great interest in infusing the substantive obligations under international law into the foundational peace process documents, and the occupied people have no real power to demand the application of a rights-based approach. Thus, the tragedy has become that, for all of the substantive body of international law generated by the conflict over the past seven decades, the actual victims in Palestine and Israel have seen precious few of the benefits and protections promised by the international community.

Continuing to marginalize the substantive principles of international law will not bring peace to the Israeli-Palestinian conflict any closer. As a political undertaking, international law provides a baseline for negotiations by acting as the indispensable foundation for state leaders and diplomatic representatives to actually honour and enforce what they have endorsed and rhetorically support. As a moral vision, it has the potential to mobilizes the vital energy of NGOs and civil society to articulate the principles of humanitarian protection and human rights as a persuasive campaign tool. And as legal principles, the equitable obligations of international law are, in the absence of a functioning peace process, a productive basis for politics-by-other-means aimed at enforcing humanitarian and human rights norms through global tribunals (such as the International Court of Justice (ICJ) and the International Criminal Court (ICC)), domestic courts and the forums of the United Nations.

International law possesses the untapped capacity to ameliorate the unequal playing field between the parties to this conflict, so that the grossly asymmetrical bargaining power that presently exists between Israel and the Palestinians will not continue to distort the negotiating process and lead predictably to yet more peace-process failures. To be sure, international law alone will not bring about a just and durable peace in the Middle East – that also requires engaged policy and political will – but its deliberate and unprincipled exclusion from the various stages of the Oslo process over the past 25 years has contributed mightily to the quagmire that the Israeli-Palestinian conflict is in today.

Europe and the peace process assumption

Europe has played a muffled role in advancing the place of international law in the efforts to resolve the Israeli-Palestinian conflict. To its credit, the (then nine member) European Community stated in its 1980 *Venice Declaration* that the Palestinians have a right to self-determination, the Israeli settlements are illegal, Israel has a right to live in security, the occupation must end, and Jerusalem's status cannot be unilaterally altered (European Council, 1980). But by 1999, in an era of misplaced optimism, the enlarged European Union in the *Berlin Declaration*, while calling for a "democratic, viable and peaceful sovereign Palestinian state" and cautioning against "any activity contrary to international law, including all settlement activity", was emphasizing the land-for-peace formula without linking it to any substantive legal criteria (Berlin, European Council, 1999). In its most recent comprehensive statement, the Council of the EU in 2016 warned against the erosion of the two-state solution through "facts on the ground", repeated its position that the Israeli settlements are illegal, and sought an end to the occupation through the negotiation by the parties of all permanent status issues, but with no insistence that the peace negotiations be grounded in the rights-based approach established through the body of United Nations resolutions (Council of the European Union, 2016).

While European diplomats in Jerusalem and Ramallah have acted as compelling witnesses to the deepening occupation,[2] and the European Union has initiated admirable steps to differentiate between Israel and its activities beyond the 1967 Green Line (Lovatt & Toaldo, 2015), Europe has more often adopted risk avoidance as its primary stance towards the conflict (Hollis, 2013). For many European aid donors to the Palestinians, it has been easier to rebuild a demolished school or replace confiscated solar panels for the third time than to confront Israel for perpetuating the occupation (European Court of Auditors, 2017). As Miguel Moratinos, the former EU Special Envoy for the Middle East Peace Process, has lamented: "We Europeans excel at declarations ... it is compensation for our scarcity of action" (Bouris, 2014).

The land-for-peace and the two-state mantras that are regularly invoked by the European Union and the international community have become hollow invocations in the face of the entrenched occupation. The two-state solution, which was created as a plausible roadmap for a lasting peace, has become in recent years a recipe for international inertia, a fig-leaf formula to proclaim at summits as a substitute for taking any consequential action to bring the occupation to an end. As the Middle East peace process – the *Jarndyce v. Jarndyce* of international diplomacy – has become emptied of energy and ideas, the relentless facts on the ground are establishing their own reality.

In 2017 alone, the Israeli settlement enterprise witnessed the greatest number of construction starts since 2000 (Peace Now, 2017), the Knesset adopted legislation both to retroactively legalize a number of unauthorized outposts (Fisher, 2017) and to legitimize the confiscation of private Palestinian land in the West Bank for Jewish settlements (Association for Civil Rights in Jerusalem, December, 2017), Israel consolidated its presence in Area C (which makes up 60% of the West Bank) as a hinterland for permanent Jewish settlement (B'Tselem, November, 2017b), the Knesset came very close to enacting legislation that would formally annex several major West Bank settlement blocs to Jerusalem (Eldar, 2017), and the acute humanitarian crisis in Gaza instigated by the decade-long Israeli blockade deteriorated even further (UN, July, 2017). Even as the character of the occupation is being inexorably transformed into a *de facto* annexation (11.11.11, June, 2017) and influential media organs are acknowledging the shallow last breaths of the two-state solution (New York Times, 2018), Europe and the international community have continued to play diplomatic checkers while Israel has been playing chess.

The Israeli political leadership's uninhibited willingness over the past few years to express out loud what its actions have been proclaiming for years is overturning the core assumption – that the Israeli occupation is unsustainable – that has guided European and American policy for the past 25 years (Levy, 2017). Prime Minister Netanyahu has stated that the most he would yield to the Palestinians is a "state minus", with all the settlement blocs and the Jordan Valley remaining in Israel's possession (The Times of Israel, 2017). Many of his cabinet ministers have been even blunter.[3] Here might be a good time to revisit Oslo's assumption of unsustainability, which is premised on the supposedly irreducible fact that Israel has no demographic or political choice but to withdraw from all or most of the occupied territory and allow a sovereign Palestinian state to emerge if it is to preserve its Jewish character and democratic values (US Department of State, 2016).

This working assumption has been left behind by the galloping realities of the occupation. It fails to account for the creative thinking among the ascendant Israeli right that it can comfortably live with models of permanent rule over the Palestinians that would deny them citizenship and democratic rights (Fleisher, 2017). It overlooks the striking degree of control that Israel exercises over the Palestinians as it confines them to smaller, denser and more fragmented islands of land through its sophisticated security network of walls, checkpoints, control over the population registry and overwhelming military superiority (Shafir, 2017). It overestimates the willingness of the Oslo sponsors – particularly Europe, Israel's largest trading partner, and America, its military and diplomatic patron – to challenge Israel with meaningful consequences should it retreat, as it has, from any lingering commitment to a genuine two-state formula (Thrall, 2017). It disregards Oslo's escape clauses that have allowed Israel to pocket the cost-free features of the occupation – the large amounts of European and international aid to fund the Palestinians, and the annual $3 billion (US) military aid package from the United States – while continuing to thicken its presence throughout the West Bank and East Jerusalem and also blockading Gaza (Shafir, 2017). And it begs the question as to whether a genuine two-state solution was ever possible in the absence of the international community's political will to enforce the clear obligations and prohibitions of international law that could have stemmed Israel's revanchism over the past half century.[4]

Back to the future: international law as a way forward

In June 1980, the United Nations Security Council – sufficiently alarmed by the duration and harshness of the thirteen-year-old occupation and Israel's defiance of prior resolutions on Jerusalem and the nascent settlements – adopted Resolution 476 (UNSC, June, 1980). The resolution re-affirmed " ... the *overwhelming necessity* to end the *prolonged occupation* of Arab territories ... by Israel" and to "*strongly deplore* the *continuing refusal* of Israel to comply with the relevant resolutions of the Security Council and the General Assembly."

If Israel's occupation of the Palestinian territory by 1980 was already prolonged and already a matter of overwhelming necessity to end, and Israel had already demonstrated by 1980 its aversion to comply with the explicit directions of the international community, how should we characterize the occupation in 2018? The prevailing approach of the international community has been to treat Israel as the lawful occupant of the Palestinian territory, albeit one that has engaged in a number of grave breaches of international law, including the settlement enterprise (UNSC, 2016), the construction of the Wall (ICJ, 2004), the annexation of East Jerusalem (UNSC, 1980) and the systematic violations of Palestinian human rights (UNGA, 2017). A restatement of the occupation's character has been long overdue. While the "lawful occupant" approach may have been the appropriate diplomatic and legal portrayal of the occupation in its early years, it has since become wholly inadequate both as an accurate legal characterization of what the Israeli occupation has become and as a viable political, diplomatic and legal catalyst to compel Israel to completely and finally terminate the occupation in accordance with its international legal obligations.

Some Israeli international law scholars have argued that an occupying power can cross the tipping point into illegality if its rule over an occupied territory has become an acquisitive mission contrary to the governing rules of international humanitarian law. Professor Benvenesti (2004) has written that: " ... it would seem that an occupant that in bad faith stalls efforts for a peaceful ending to its rule would be considered an aggressor and its rule would be tainted with illegality". Professors Ben-Naftali, Gross, and Michaeli (2005) take a more expansive view, arguing that a violation of any of the fundamental legal principles of occupation – listed below – "renders an occupation illegal *per se*". Professor Gross (2017) has extended this argument more recently to emphasize the importance of analyzing whether an indefinite or permanent occupation has become illegal, so as to counter: " ... the risk of occupation becoming conquest or a new form of colonialism while hiding behind an imagined temporality".

Whether an occupying power can cross a red line into illegality is not a question that can be answered by a literal reading of the principal instruments of international humanitarian law, including the 1907 *Hague Regulations*, the 1949 *Fourth Geneva Convention* and the *1977 Additional Protocol to the Geneva Conventions* (Victims of International Armed Conflicts, 1977). On this question, these instruments are silent. However, a purposive reading of these instruments, together with the foundations of international humanitarian law, led inexorably to the conclusion that an occupying power whose intent is to turn occupation into conquest becomes an illegal occupant.

In my October 2017 report as Special Rapporteur to the United Nations General Assembly (Lynk, 2017), I argue that a four-part test can be derived from the leading principles of the law of occupation to determine whether the status of an occupying power has become illegal. An occupying power that violated any one of the elements of this test would be in breach of the principle underlying the foundation of the modern world order: that states cannot engage in conquest. Any country that would seek to transform an occupation into a claim of sovereignty is in violation of its fundamental obligations under international humanitarian law and would acquire the status of an illegal occupant.[5]

The four elements of the test are as follows:

(i) An Occupying Power cannot annex any of the Occupied Territory

In the modern world, an occupying power cannot, under any circumstances, acquire the right to conquer, annex or gain sovereign title over any part of the territory under its occupation. Leading public international law scholars have endorsed the "no-annexation" principle as a binding legal doctrine.[6] Beginning with UNSC resolution 242 in November 1967, the Security Council has endorsed the principle of "the inadmissibility of the acquisition of territory" by war or by force on at least nine occasions (UNSC, S/RES/242 (1967); S/RES/252 (1968), S/RES/267 (1969), S/RES/298 (1971); S/RES/476 (1980); S/RES/478 (1980); S/RES/497 (1981); S/RES/2334 (2016)). The International Court of Justice held in 2004 that the: " ... illegality of territorial acquisition resulting from the threat or use of force" has acquired the status of customary international law. This absolute rule against the acquisition of territory by force makes no distinction as to whether the territory was occupied through a war of self-defence or a war of aggression; annexation is prohibited in both circumstances (Korman, 1996).

Israel's *de jure* annexation of East Jerusalem in 1967 (by a Cabinet decision) and 1980 (by a Knesset vote) is, *ipso facto*, a grave breach of the laws of occupation. Shortly after the Knesset vote, the United Nations Security Council in August 1980 censured Israel "in the strongest terms" for the Knesset vote, affirmed that Israel's actions were in breach of international law, and that Israel's annexation of Jerusalem was "null and void" and "must be rescinded forthwith (UNSC, August, 1980)." Israel remains non-compliant with all of the United Nations' resolutions on the annexation of Jerusalem, there are presently about 210,000 Israeli settlers living in East Jerusalem and Prime Minister Netanyahu has stated that Israel intends to keep all of Jerusalem permanently.[7]

Beyond Jerusalem, Israel has been energetically erasing the differences between its pre-1967 border and its settlement enterprise in the occupied West Bank (Dajani, 2017). The ICJ, in its 2004 *Wall Advisory Opinion,* warned that the reality of the Wall and the settlement regime was constituting a *fait accompli* and a *de facto* annexation (ICJ, 2004). In the West Bank, Israel exercises complete control over Area C (which makes up 60% of the West Bank), where its 420,000 settlers live in approximately 225 settlements. The settlers live under Israeli law in Jewish-only settlements, drive on Israeli-only roads, and benefit greatly from the enormous sums of public money spent by Israel on entrenching, defending and expanding the settlements. The only credible explanation for Israel's continuation of the occupation, and the increasing density of its settlement regime, is to enshrine its sovereign claim over part or all of the Palestinian territory, a colonial ambition *par excellence*.

Israel's predominant reply-arguments are that it has a superior title to East Jerusalem and the West Bank because they were acquired in a defensive war and because Jordan was never the true sovereign at the time of the 1967 war (Blum, 1968; Shamgar, 1971). In response, the absolute rule against the acquisition of territory by force makes no distinction as to whether the territory was occupied through a war of self-defence or a war of aggression; annexation is prohibited in both circumstances (Korman, 1996). And, as the International Committee of the Red Cross (2016b) has recently stated, in its authoritative commentary on the laws of occupation, the legal status of occupation does not require the existence of a prior legitimate sovereign over the territory in question.

(ii) An Occupation is inherently temporary, and the Occupying Power must seek to end the occupation as soon as reasonably possible.

Occupation is by definition a temporary and exceptional situation where the occupying power assumes the role of a *de facto* administrator of the territory until conditions allow for the return of the territory to the sovereign, which is the people of the territory (Pictet, 1958). Because of the absolute prohibition against the acquisition of territory by force, the occupying power is prohibited from ruling the territory on a permanent or even an indefinite basis (Gross, 2017). While the laws of occupation do not set out a specific length of time for the lawful duration of an occupation, the purposive conclusion to be drawn is that the territory is to be returned to the sovereign power in as reasonable and expeditious a time period as possible, so as to honour the right to self-determination (UNSC, 2003a). Indeed, the longer the occupation, the greater the justification that the occupying power must satisfy to defend its continuing presence in the occupied territory.

The duration of the 50-year-old Israeli occupation is without precedent or parallel in today's world. Modern occupations that have broadly adhered to the strict principles of temporariness, non-annexation, trusteeship and good faith have not exceeded 10 years, including the American occupation of Japan, the Allied occupation of western Germany and the American-led coalition's occupation of Iraq. Every Israeli government since 1967 has pursued the continuous growth of the settlements, and the scale of the financial, military and political resources committed to the enterprise belies any intention to make the occupation temporary. Israel can offer no compelling reason for the extraordinary length of the occupation that would be consistent with its obligation to end its rule as soon as reasonably possible. As Professor Shafir (2017) has observed: "temporariness remains an Israeli subterfuge for creating permanent facts on the ground", with Israel able to employ a seemingly indeterminate nature of the occupation's end-point to create a "permanent temporariness" that intentionally forestalls any meaningful exercise of self-determination by the Palestinians.

(iii) During the Occupation, the Occupying Power is to act in the best interests of the people under Occupation

The occupying power, throughout the duration of an occupation, is required to govern in the best interests of the people under occupation, subject only to the legitimate security requirements of the occupying military authority. This principle has been likened to a trust or fiduciary relationship in domestic and international law, where the dominant authority is required to act in the interests of the protected person or entity above all else (Gross, 2017). The 1907 *Hague Regulations,* the 1949 *Fourth Geneva Convention* and modern body of international human rights instruments are sated with provisions which protect the lives, property, natural resources, institutions, civil life, fundamental human rights and latent sovereignty of the people under occupation, while curbing the security powers of the occupying power to those genuinely required to safely administer the occupation. Accordingly, the occupying power is prohibited from administering the occupation in a self-serving or avaricious manner and it must act in a manner consistent with its trustee responsibilities.

The pervasive barriers and restrictions in the civil and commercial life of the Palestinians have created a shattered territorial space, resulting in a highly dependent and strangled economy, mounting impoverishment, daily impositions and indignities, and receding hope for a reversal of fortune for the foreseeable future (UNCTAD, 2016). According to the World Bank (2013) and the United Nations (2016), the Palestinians in the West Bank endure distinctly inferior civil, legal and social conditions compared to Israeli settlers; they suffer from significant restrictions on their freedom of movement and a denial to access to water and natural resources; Israel has imposed a deeply discriminatory land planning and housing permit system; and a number of West Bank communities live under the threat of forcible transfer and land confiscation (B'Tselem, 2016).

Living conditions in Gaza – particularly after a decade of a suffocating economic and travel blockade imposed by Israel that has sealed its land and sea frontiers and its air space – are particularly bleak. More than 60 per cent of the population in Gaza is reliant upon humanitarian aid; it is unable to secure more than 40 per cent of the electrical power that it requires; it will soon exhaust its sources of safe drinking water; and, virtually unique in the world, its gross domestic product is actually lower than it was in 2006 (UN, July, 2017). As for East Jerusalem, the occupation has increasingly detached it from its traditional national, economic, cultural and family connections with the West Bank because of the Wall, the rings of settlements and a discriminatory travel permit regime. Its economy has become depleted, it is neglected by the Jerusalem Municipality in terms of services and infrastructure, and East Jerusalemites have only a small land base to build housing.

On the probative evidence, Israel has ruled the Palestinian territory as an internal colony, deeply committed to exploiting its land and resources, and profoundly indifferent to the rights and best interests of the protected people under occupation, contrary to its obligations.

(iv) The Occupying Power must act in good faith

The principle of good faith has been called the "cardinal rule of treaty interpretation" in the international legal system, and has become an integral part of virtually all legal relationships in modern international law (Bjorge, 2014). The principle requires states to carry out their duties and obligations in an honest, loyal, reasonable, diligent and fair manner, and with the aim of fulfilling the purposes of the legal responsibility, including an agreement or treaty (UNCTAD, 2013). Conversely, the good faith principle also prohibits states from participating in acts that would defeat the object and purpose of the obligation, or engaging in any abuse of rights that would mask an illegal act or the evasion of the undertaking (Reinhold, 2013). Accordingly, an occupying power is required to govern the territory in good faith, which can be measured by its compliance with the following two obligations: (i) its conformity with the specific precepts of international humanitarian law and international human rights law applicable to an occupation; and (ii) its conformity with any specific directions issued by the United Nations or other authoritative bodies pertaining to the occupation.[8]

Israel has been deemed to be in breach of many of the leading precepts of international humanitarian and human rights law throughout the occupation. Its settlement enterprise has been repeatedly characterized as illegal by the United Nations Security Council.[9] The prohibited use of collective punishment has been regularly employed by Israel through the demolition of Palestinian homes of families related to those suspected of terrorism or security breaches, and by extended closures of Palestinian communities (B'Tselem, 2017a). Freedom of movement is impaired through a complex system of administrative, bureaucratic and physical constraints that affects virtually every aspect of daily life for the Palestinians (United Nations Office for the High Commissioner for Human Rights, 2016). And above all, the entrenched and unaccountable occupation – through its denial of territorial integrity, genuine self-governance, a sustainable economy and a viable path to independence – substantively violates, if not undermines, the right of the Palestinians to self-determination, the platform human right that enables the realization of many other rights.

Since 1967, the Security Council has adopted, in clear and direct language, more than 40 resolutions critical of Israel's occupation of the Palestinian territory. They have dealt with the settlements, the annexation of Jerusalem, the denial of Palestinian human rights and the refusal of Israel to abide by the *Fourth Geneva Convention*.[10] Several hundred similar resolutions have been adopted by the UN General Assembly and the Human Rights Council. In the face of the persistent Israeli refusal to adopt and apply any of these resolutions, the Security Council has "strongly deplored the continued refusal of Israel, the occupying power, to comply with the relevant resolutions of the Security Council and the General Assembly" (UNSC, 1980, 1980). Yet, immediately following the Security Council's adoption of Resolution 2334 in December 2016 condemning the settlement enterprise and Israel's failure to apply the *Fourth Geneva Convention*, Prime Minister Netanyahu dismissed the resolution as "delusional" and "part of the swan song of the old world," and announced that Israel would not abide by it (Kershner, 2016).

Europe and international law

Europe's contemporary liberal sensibilities have been hard won. Modern international law arose in large part because of the tragic history of Europe's twentieth century, where much blood was spilt both on its soil and on those of its colonies. And because of the Holocaust and Europe's colonial history in Palestine and the Levant, the continent retains a special responsibility for actively seeking a compassionate resolution to the Middle East conflict (Judt & Snyder, 2012; Shlaim, 2014).

By the application of any one of the four core principles of the laws of occupation discussed above, there is a compelling argument that Israel has crossed the tipping point. The first step for Europe is to acknowledge the solidity of the legal framework respecting the Israeli occupation, and work within that framework to support the political and judicial assessment of Israel's "illegal occupant" status, which would likely be determined by the UN General Assembly and the International Court of Justice. Should the conclusion of these forums be that Israel is indeed occupying the Palestinian territory unlawfully, then Europe and the international community would then take the necessary steps to bring Israel's illegal occupant status to a resolute and timely conclusion.[11] The obligation upon the international community would involve both the observation of negative duties to not encourage or assist Israel respecting its violations, and the taking of affirmative steps to bring such violations to an end (ICRC, 2016a; UNSC, 2008, 2003, 2002, 1973, 1967).

The next step would be to create, and select from, a policy menu of escalating political and diplomatic options for imposing genuine costs on Israel for its rejectionism (should Israel actually change course and genuinely respond to measures to end the occupation, it should be appropriately rewarded.) Given the role of Europe as Israel's principal trading partner (40 per cent of Israel's exports are destined for the European market (European Commission, 2018)), its political capacity to effect change is not inconsiderable. While Europe cannot impose a peace agreement upon the parties, it is in the position of being able to help shape the conditions – through creative policy, strategic pressure and inspired diplomacy – that would reverse the entrenchment of the occupation. Despite Israel's ongoing record of non-compliance with the directions of the international community, it has rarely paid a meaningful price for its defiance. Indeed, where the international community has employed sanction or conditions in this conflict, they have been largely directed towards the Palestinians (i.e. after the 2006 parliamentary elections; after the Palestinian Authority joined a variety of international organizations; and to require the Palestinian Authority to recognize Israel as a Jewish state). Daniel Levy, an Anglo-Israeli political analyst, has observed that: "Nothing is likely to change in Israel until its public feels that impunity for occupations and settlements is eroding" (Black, 2014).

Finding a path that encourages non-violent steps which pushes the conflict in a productive direction should be the policy's focus. The menu of available conditions and sanctions is broad. Non-recognition of the prevailing features of the occupation – Jerusalem's annexation, the settlements, the location of the Wall, the *de facto* annexation steps in Area C and the blockade of Gaza – must continue and deepen. As for affirmative steps, these could include the imposition of visas for foreign travel by Israelis; a comprehensive import ban on settlement products; legal liability for Israeli and foreign companies, organizations and individuals that invest or operate in furtherance of the occupation; a review of existing trade, cultural and economic agreements with Israel; and penalties for Israel to compensate for its destruction of humanitarian projects in the oPt. Diplomatically, Europe could initiate or support efforts to strengthen the institutional capacity of the Palestinians to rule themselves; it should speak out clearly and firmly against the deepening occupation; it must insist that Israel's ongoing obligations under international humanitarian and human rights law remain in full force; and it should be guided in its actions by international law.[12]

Could it be too much to hope that the judicious application of international law led by Europe – and particularly a finding of illegality by the United Nations General Assembly and the ICJ, leading to an international resolve to apply effective pressure points on Israel – would hasten the end of the Israeli occupation and the achievement of Palestinian independence? Could this be done without the needless consumption of more bloodshed and the further erosion of faith in the efficacy of international law and our international institutions? Could this be an answer to the bitter smile of history?

Notes

1. Among the key UN resolutions on these issues are: UNSC Res. 446 (1979) (occupation); UNSC Res. 465 (1980) (settlements); UNSC Res. 478 (1980) (Jerusalem); UNGA Res. 194 (1948) (refugees); and UNGA Res. ES-10/15 (2004) (the wall).
2. As an example, see: Office of the European Union Representative (2017, December 15), Six-Month Report on Israeli Settlements (January-June 2017).
3. See Science Minister Ofir Akunis in December 2017: "Two states for two peoples is a concept that has disappeared from the world" (Ben Zion, 2018) while Jerusalem Minister Ze'ev Elkin said in November 2017: "Halas ['enough' in Arabic] with the story of two states. There is no other option but the state of Israel, certainly between the Jordan [River] to the [Mediterranean] sea there will be one state," 'We must plan for a million settlers in the West" (Middle East Monitor, 2017).
4. Dean Rusk, U.S. Secretary of State in the 1960s, presciently, if optimistically, stated shortly after the June 1967 war that: "Israel's keeping territory would create a revanchism for the rest of the twentieth century," (Gorenberg, 2006, p. 55).
5. Advisory Opinion on Namibia issued by the International Court of Justice: Legal Consequences for States of the Continued Presence of South Africa in Namibia (South West Africa), notwithstanding Security Council Resolution 276 (1970), Advisory Opinion, I.C.J. Reports 1971, p. 16.
6. As one example, see Malcom Shaw: "It is, however, clear today that the acquisition of territory by force alone is illegal under international law." (International Law (8th ed.), 2017, p. 372).
7. Prime Minister Netanyahu in 2015: "Forty-eight years ago, the division of Jerusalem was ended, and we returned to be united … We will keep Jerusalem united under Israeli authority." (Liebermann, 2015).
8. Article 25 of the Charter of the United Nations stipulates that: "The Members of the United Nations agree to accept and carry out the decisions of the Security Council in accordance with the present Charter."
9. UNSC Res. 2334 (2016) is the latest of seven Security Council resolutions since 1979 affirming the illegality of the settlements.
10. Supra, note 1.
11. Common Article 1 of the four Geneva Conventions stipulates that all parties "undertake to respect and to ensure respect for the present Convention in all circumstances." Also see UNSC Res. 681 (1990) and Wall Advisory Opinion, at para. 159.
12. For a rich review of Europe's policy options, see Dajani and Lovatt (2017).

Disclosure statement

No potential conflict of interest was reported by the author.

References

11.11.11. (2017, June). *Report: Occup'Annexation: The shift from occupation to annexation in Palestine.*

Akram, S. (2011). *International Law and the Israeli-Palestinian conflict: A rights-based approach to Middle East peace.* London: Routledge.

Association for Civil Rights in Jerusalem. (2017, December). *Situation Report: The state of human rights in Israel and the occupied Palestinian territories.*

Ben-Naftali, O., Gross, A., & Michaeli, K. (2005). Illegal occupation: Framing the occupied Palestinian territory. *Berkeley Journal of International Law, 23*(3), 551–614.

Benvenesti, E. (2004). *The international Law of occupation.* Princeton, NJ: Princeton University Press.

Ben Zion, I. (2018, January 1). *Israel's Likud party members call for annexing settlements.* Retrieved from National Post: http://nationalpost.com/pmn/news-pmn/israels-likud-party-members-vote-to-annex-settlements

Berlin European Council. (1999, March 24-25). *Presidency Conclusions.*

Bjorge, E. (2014). *The evolutionary interpretation of treaties.* Oxford: Oxford University Press.

Black, I. (2014, December 11). French and Irish parliaments call for recognition of Palestinian state. *The Guardian.*

Blum, Y. (1968). The missing reversioner: Reflections on the status of Judea and Samaria. *Israel Law Review, 3*(2), 279–301.

Bouris, D. (2014). *The European Union and occupied Palestinian territories: State-building without a state.* London: Routledge.

B'Tselem. (2016). Editorial: Expel and exploit: The Israeli practice of taking over rural Palestinian land. *B'Tselem.*

B'Tselem. (2017a, November). Editorial: Home demolitions as collective punishment. *B'Tselem.*

B'Tselem. (2017b, November). *Planning policy in the West Bank.* Retrieved from B'Tselem: https://www.btselem.org/planning_and_building

Council of the European Union. (2016, January 18). *Council conclusions on the middle east peace Process.*

Dajani, O. (2017). Israel's creeping annexation. *American Journal of International Law Unbound, 111,* 51–56.

Dajani, O., & Lovatt, H. (2017, July 26). *Rethinking oslo: How Europe can promote peace in Israel-Palestine.* Retrieved from European Council on Foreign Relations: http://www.ecfr.eu/page/-/ECFR226_-_RETHINKING_OSLO_-_HOW_EUROPE_CAN_PROMOTE_PEACE_IN_ISRAEL-PALESTINE.pdf

Editorial New York Times. (2018, January 5). Editorial: Israel digs a grave for the two-state solution. *New York Times.*

Editorial The Times of Israel. (2017, January 22). Netanyahu says Palestinians can have a 'state minus'. *The Times of Israel.*

Eldar, S. (2017, October 30). US pressure kills "Greater Jerusalem bill". *Al-Monitor.*

European Council. (1980, June 13). *Venice declaration.* Retrieved from https://eeas.europa.eu/archives/docs/mepp/docs/venice_declaration_1980_en.pdf

European Court of Auditors. (2017). *Follow-up of the court's recommendations made in its special report on EU direct financial support to the Palestinian Authority.* SR No. 14/2013, European Court of Auditors.

Fisher, I. (2017, February 6). Israel passes provocative law to retroactively legalize settlements. *New York Times.*

Fleisher, Y. (2017, February 14). A settler's view of Israel's future. *New York Times.*

Geneva Convention (Fourth). (1949, August 12). Relative to the protection of civilian persons in time of war.

Gorenberg, G. (2006). *The accidental empire: Israel and the birth of the settlements, 1967–1977.* New York, NY: Henry Holt and Co.

Government of the State of Israel and the Palestine Liberation Organization (PLO). (2007, November 27). *Annapolis conference joint understanding and statements, joint understanding on negotiations*. Retrieved from https://peacemaker.un.org/sites/peacemaker.un.org/files/IsraelOPt_JointUnderstandingOnNegotiations2007.pdf

Gross, A. (2017). *The writing on the wall: Rethinking the international Law of occupation*. Cambridge: Cambridge University Press.

Hague Convention (IV). (1907, October 18). Respecting the laws and customs of war on land and its annex. *Regulations Concerning the Laws and Customs of War on Land*.

Hollis, R. (2013). Europe. *The Routledge handbook on the Israeli-Palestinian conflict*, 336–345.

International Committee of the Red Cross. (2016a). *Commentary on the first Geneva Convention*.

International Committee of the Red Cross. (2016b). Note 178, Article 323, Commentary of 2016 / Convention (I) for the Amelioration of the Condition of the Wounded and Sick in Armed Forces in the Field. Geneva, 12 August 1949. Retrieved from ICRC: https://ihl-databases.icrc.org/applic/ihl/ihl.nsf/Comment.xsp?action=openDocument&documentId=BE2D518CF5DE54EAC1257F7D0036B518#178_B

International Court of Justice. (1971). *Advisory opinion, legal consequences for states of the continued presence of South Africa in Namibia (South West Africa), notwithstanding Security Council Resolution 276 (1970)*. ICJ Reports.

International Court of Justice. (2004, July 9). Advisory opinion concerning legal consequences of the construction of a wall in the occupied Palestinian Territory. *I.C.J Reports* 2004.

Judt, T., & Snyder, T. (2012). *Thinking the twentieth century*. New York, NY: Penguin.

Kattan, V. (2009). *From coexistence to conquest: International Law and the origins of the Arab-Israeli conflict, 1891-1949*. London: Pluto Press.

Kershner, I. (2016, December 24). Netanyahu promises retribution for 'Biased' U.N. resolution. *New York Times*.

Korman, S. (1996). *The right of conquest: The acquisition of territory by force in international Law and practice*. Oxford: Oxford University Press.

Levy, D. (2017, August 24). Has Netanyahu defeated the Palestinians? *The National Interest*.

Liebermann, O. (2015, May 18). *Benjamin Netanyahu: Jerusalem will remain united city*. Retrieved from CNN: https://edition.cnn.com/2015/05/17/middleeast/israel-netanyahu-united-jerusalem/index.html

Lovatt, H., & Toaldo, M. (2015). *EU differentiation and Israeli settlements*. London: European Council on Foreign Relations.

Lynk, M. (2017). *Report of the special rapporteur on the situation of human rights in the Palestinian territories occupied since 1967, A/72/556*.

Middle East Monitor. (2017, November 15). *Israel minister: We must plan for a million settlers in the West Bank*. Retrieved from Middle East Monitor: https://www.middleeastmonitor.com/20171115-israel-minister-we-must-plan-for-a-million-settlers-in-the-west-bank/

Office of the European Union Representative. (2017, December 15). *Six month report on Israeli settlements (January - June 2017)*. Retrieved from https://eeas.europa.eu/delegations/palestine-occupied-palestinian-territory-west-bank-and-gaza-strip_en/37466/Six-Month%20Report%20on%20Israeli%20settlements%20in%20the%20occupied%20West%20Bank,%20including%20East%20Jerusalem%20%28%20January%20-%20June%20

Peace Now. (2017, November). *Escalation in Israel's settlement policy: The creation of De-Facto Annexation*. Retrieved from Peace Now: https://peacenow.org/entry.php?id=25999#.WlaGonly670

Peters, J., & Newman, D. (2013a). Declaration of principles on interim self-government arrangements. In J. Peters & D. Newman. *The Routledge hazndbook on the Israeli-Palestinian conflict* (pp. 412–420). London: Routledge.

Peters, J., & Newman, D. (2013b). Israeli-Palestinian interim agreement on the west bank and the Gaza strip. In J. Peters & D. Newman. *The Routledge handbook on the Israeli-Palestinian conflict* (pp. 421–439). London: Routledge.

Peters, J., & Newman, D. (2013c). President W.J. Clinton: Proposal on Israeli-Palestinian peace. In J. Peters & D. Newman. *The Routledge handbook on the Israeli-Palestinian conflict* (pp. 440–444). London: Routledge.

Peters, J., & Newman, D. (2013d). A performance-based roadmap to a permanent Two-state solution to the Israeli-Palestinian conflict. In J. Peters & D. Newman. *The Routledge handbook on the Israeli-Palestinian conflict* (pp. 445–450). London: Routledge.

Peters, J., & Newman, D. (2013e). Statement by the Middle East quartet. In J. Peters & D. Newman. *The Routledge handbook on the Israeli-Palestinian conflict* (pp. 451-452). London: Routledge.

Pictet, J. (1958). *Commentary: IV Geneva convention relative to the protection of civilian persons in time of War*. Geneva: ICRC.

Protocol Additional to the Geneva Conventions of 12 August 1949, and relating to the Protection of Victims of International Armed Conflicts (Protocol I). (1977, June 8).

Reinhold, S. (2013). Good faith in international Law. 2 UCL Journal of Law and Jurisprudence 40–63.

Shafir, G. (2017). *A half century of occupation Israel, Palestine, and the world's most intractable conflict*. Oakland: University of California Press.

Shamgar, M. (1971). The observance of international law in the administered territories. *Israel Yearbook on Human Rights*.

Shaw, M. (2017). *International Law* (8th ed.). Cambridge: Cambridge University Press.

Shlaim, A. (2014). *The iron wall: Israel and the Arab world* (2nd ed.). New York, NY: W.W Norton & Co. Inc.

Thrall, N. (2017). *The only language they understand*. New York, NY: Henry Holt and Company.

United Nations. (2016). *Occupied Palestinian territory - fragmented lives: Humanitarian overview*. Jerusalem: Office for the Coordination of humanitarian Affairs.

United Nations. (2017, July). *Gaza: Ten years later (July 2017)*.

United Nations Conference on Trade and Development. (2013). *The Palestinian economy in East Jerusalem: Enduring annexation, isolation and disintegration*. Geneva: Author.

United Nations Conference on Trade and Development. (2016). *Developments in the economy of the occupied Palestinian territory*. Geneva: Author.

United Nations General Assembly. (1948, December 11). Progress report of the United Nations Mediator. A/RES194 (III).

United Nations General Assembly. (2004, august 2). Advisory opinion of the International Court of Justice on the Legal Consequences of the Construction of a Wall in the Occupied Palestinian Territory, including in and around East Jerusalem. A/RES/ES-10/15.

United Nations General Assembly. (2017, December 7). Israeli practices affecting the human rights of the Palestinian people in the occupied Palestinian territory, including East Jerusalem. *A/RES/72/87*.

United Nations Office for the High Commissioner for Human Rights. (2016). *Freedom of movement*.

United Nations Security Council. (1967, November 22). Middle East. *S/RES/242 (1967)*.

United Nations Security Council. (1968, May 21). Middle East. *S/RES/252 (1968)*.

United Nations Security Council. (1969, July 3). Middle East. *S/RES/267 (1969)*.

United Nations Security Council. (1971, September 25). Middle East. *S/RES/298 (1971)*.

United Nations Security Council. (1973, October 22). Cease-fire in Middle East. *S/RES/242 (1973)*.

United Nations Security Council. (1979, March 22). Territories occupuied by Israel. S/RES/446 (1979).

United Nations Security Council. (1980, August 20). Territories occupied by Israel. *S/RES/478 (1980)*.

United Nations Security Council. (1980, June 30). Territories occupied by Israel. *S/RES/476 (1980)*.

United Nations Security Council. (1981, December 17). Israel-Syrian Arab Republic. *S/RES/497 (1981)*.

United Nations Security Council. (1990, December 20). Territories occupied by Israel. S/RES/681 (1990).

United Nations Security Council. (2002, March 12). Middle East, including the Palestinian question. *S/RES/1397 (2002)*.

United Nations Security Council. (2003a, May 22). Situation between Iraq and Kuwait. *S/RES/1483 (2003)*.

United Nations Security Council. (2003b, November 19). Middle East, including the Palestinian question. *S/RES/1515 (2003)*.

United Nations Security Council. (2008, December 16). Middle East, including the Palestinian question. *S/RES/1850 (2008)*.

United Nations Security Council. (2016, December 23). The situation in the Middle East, including the Palestinian question. *S/RES/2334 (2016)*.

US Department of State. (2016, December 28). *John Kerry, remarks on Middle East Peace*. Retrieved from US Department of State: https://2009-2017.state.gov

Website European Commission. (2018). *Trade, policy, countries and regions: Israel.* Retrieved from ec.europa.eu: https://ec.europa.eu/trade/policy/countries-and-regions/countries/israel

World Bank. (2013). *Area C and the future of the Palestinian economy*. Washington, DC: World Bank Group.

Non-Recognition à la European Union: Reflections on the Revisions to EU-Israeli Relations and the Obligation of Non-Recognition in International Law

Valentina Azarova[†]

ABSTRACT
The European Union (EU) is undertaking a prolonged, slow-burning revision of its relations with Israel, driven by the need to avoid recognition of an illegal situation. This article reviews these ongoing developments from the perspective of international law. As compared with the EU's response to the annexation of Crimea by imposing sanctions on Russia, its measures vis-à-vis Israel aim at protecting the EU internal legal and political order from the illegal situation created by Israel's institutional practice with regards to the Palestinian territory. The EU's approach to non-recognition is a rule-based cornerstone of its external relations law and foreign policy, and provides insights on the otherwise opaque workings of this obligation in international law and the transnational legal enforcement process in which it manifests.

Introduction

For decades, the EU has maintained firm public policy positions and commitments on the unlawful status of Israel's claims to sovereignty over territory across the "Green Line" that it has occupied since 1967. But the EU had structured its relations with Israel haphazardly in this regard, without taking heed of the incompatibility of its own positions with the domestic laws and practice of the Israeli authorities. Israeli laws and practice have had a detrimental effect on the EU's ability to ensure the full and effective implementation of EU law consistent with its public policy positions and commitments on Israel's status in the Palestinian territory. The host of revisions being undertaken by the EU to its relations with Israeli entities, intended to correct this state of affairs, date back as far as the 1980s, but enjoyed particular public attention with the July 2013 publication of the EU's guidelines on Israel's participation in its research programme (Guidelines on the eligibility of Israeli entities and their activities in the territories occupied by Israel since June 1967 for grants, prizes and financial instruments funded by the EU from 2014 onwards, 2013).

These EU revisions have been discussed by political scientists who tend to view them solely as political responses to the policies of Israeli authorities (Gordon & Pardo, 2015). Such analyses seldom examine the legal form and rationale for the EU's special-

[†]Member of the ILA Recognition/Non-Recognition Committee.

purpose measures. In fact, international lawyers have criticized the EU for falling short of its obligations of non-recognition and non-assistance to Israel's serious breaches of peremptory norms under international law (Dubuisson, 2014; Moerenhout, 2012). As virtually no work has addressed the compatibility between, on the one hand, the EU's approach to the protection of its internal legal order, and on the other, the mandates of the obligation of non-recognition in international law, this essay aims to fill this gap. It analyses revisions to EU-Israeli relations as a case of compliance with international legal norms that have been internalized by a domestic (or supranational, in the EU's case) legal order. It highlights the stringency of this process and the relative immunity to political considerations of the institutional actors that implement it, while interrogating its restrictive purpose. The essay also uses this example to illuminate the contours of the obligation of non-recognition, as well as states' responsibilities, in international law.

The essay proceeds in three parts. First, it explores non-recognition according to international law, as well as related obligations (Section 1). Second, it shows that revisions to EU-Israeli relations, unlike the EU's restrictive measures towards Russia following its annexation of Crimea, are in fact driven by the imperative to ensure non-recognition of an "illegal situation," created in this case by the particular character of Israel's control and administration of Palestinian territory. This is a case of "EU internal legal necessity," as it has been put (Muller & Slominski, 2016; Nikolov, 2014) (Section 2). Third, the article explores the extent to which the international legal order relies on domestic regulatory processes to implement non-recognition in the context of specific dealings so as to ensure that the rights, titles, and entitlements constituted by an "illegal situation" do not "produc[e] legal effects at the international level and in the respective national systems" (Arangio-Ruiz, 1993, p. 29) (Section 3). The Conclusion reflects on the prospects of a more rigorous practice of non-recognition by states and international actors in the context of their bilateral dealings in the Israeli-Palestinian context and beyond.

The obligation of non-recognition in international law

After decades of negotiations, the obligation of non-recognition known to international lawyers was codified in 2001 in the International Law Commission's Articles on the Responsibility of States for Internationally Wrongful Acts (ARSIWA). Draft Article 41 (2) maintains that "No state shall recognize as lawful a situation created by a serious breach of an obligation arising under a peremptory norm of general international law."[1] The normative content and scope of the obligation are however not fully known, and have as yet, partly also for this reason, been fully internalized by the domestic systems of states and international actors alike. Despite having an object and purpose that is hardwired to the first principles of international law, as a law that governs relations between different domestic and internal legal orders, the states' practice of non-recognition is surprisingly underdetermined.

The object and purpose of non-recognition

As a matter of international law, the imperative of non-recognition is an automatic remedy for the most egregious acts known to international lawyers as violations of peremptory norms of international law, the perpetration of which often produces conditions and processes of structural violence.[2] In Article 41(2), 2001 ARSIWA explicitly extended the material scope of non-recognition beyond aggression and illegal territorial changes (Dawidowicz, 2010; League of Nations Covenant, 1924; Turns, 2003)[3] to include all serious breaches of the peremptory norms of international law, such as the flagrant denial of the right to self-determination of peoples, illegal use of force including territorial acquisition (Jennings, 1963; Wright, 1961), and the practice of systematic racial discrimination or slavery (Crawford, 2012a). The same obligation is expressly addressed to international organizations such as the EU in Article 42(2) of Draft Articles on the Responsibility of International Organisations 2011.

Therefore, the object of non-recognition is the specific category of internationally wrongful acts (the peremptory norms of international law), as well as the "illegal situations" they purport to constitute and benefit from – i.e. the rights, titles, and entitlements that may come into the hands of third parties. The principal objective of non-recognition measures is thus to guarantee the "non-admission" into the domestic orders of third states, of the elements of an illegal situation such as illegally constituted rights and titles predicated on violations of peremptory norms of international law, by ensuring that they do not "produc[e] legal effects at the international level and in the respective national systems" (Arangio-Ruiz, 1993; Krieger, 2018; Riphagen, 1980; Talmon, 2005). As a consequence, the non-recognising state's domestic regulatory authorities must ensure that they do not inappropriately rely on and extend comity to the practice of a wrongdoing authority, which would result in the state's treatment of such titles and rights as lawful and valid under its domestic law. The non-admission of such rights and titles is an *ipso jure* requirement of international law and a consequence of the objective illegality and thus invalidity of such rights and titles that a wrongdoing authority may claim to grant public and private actors under its jurisdiction (Crawford, 2012b; Morgenstern, 1951; Orakhelashvili, 2006). The juridical hermeneutic of non-recognition is prescribed by the general principle of *ex injuria jus non oritur*, according to which legal rights and benefits cannot derive from an illegal act (Dawidowicz, 2010; Lagerwall, 2016).

The restrictive measures adopted by a non-recognising third state, in most cases, target either the acts of a sovereign authority within its domestic jurisdiction or those of a de facto authority, in a domestic context or in occupied territory[4]. As widely affirmed by international legal experts, the very presence in the occupied territory of an occupying state that pursues its acquisition (in whole or in part), is, as Professor Lynk's contribution to this volume also observes, rendered unlawful by virtue of the consequences it attracts under the UN Charter prohibition on the use of force (Azarova, 2017; Bothe, 2017; Human Sciences Research Council of South Africa, 2009; Lynk, 2017). Peremptory norm violations common to Israel's occupation of Palestinian and Syrian territories, but also other ongoing cases of occupation and annexation, include violations of the intransgressible rules of international humanitarian law (IHL), the prohibition of aggression, and the right to self-determination of people (Gross, 2017; Wrange, 2015). As such, the effects of the specific acts and decisions of an occupying state that maintains its presence in the occupied territory with the aim of displacing the legitimate sovereign, appropriating and transferring property rights to its nationals, and changing the demographic character are invalid and must not be treated as lawful.[5]

States and international actors that wrongfully recognize such illegal situations as the settlements regime in the occupied Palestinian territory, by giving e.g. legal effect to rights and titles, contribute to the regime's consolidation and to the likelihood, frequency and severity of the human rights abuses and international law violations perpetrated as a result of its maintenance. In this sense, non-recognition might be said to resemble a form of complicity that is broader than the category of acts that constitute "state complicity," as it constitutes aid or assistance "given with a view to facilitating the commission of the wrongful act" and "the occurrence of the wrongful conduct" (Article 16 of ARSIWA, ILC, 2001). Non-recognition on the contrary has the forward-looking purpose of assisting the beneficiaries of a special protection regime to restore their rights, such as the category of rights afforded to "protected persons" subject to the control of an occupying power. The purpose of non-recognition is to correct a state of affairs in which a third state or an international actor would otherwise consolidate the legal claims furthered by an illegal situation by permitting perpetrators and their accomplices to enjoy and benefit from their wrongful acts, and contributing to the likelihood, frequency, and severity of such acts.

It is important to stress that the purpose of non-recognition is not to punish or coerce the wrongdoing authority into compliance, and that it is subject to crucial limitations. Foremost is the need to uphold the "basic rights of individuals," which may be harmed as a result of the suspension or severance of international co-operation. This is known as the "Namibia exception," coined by the ICJ in its Advisory Opinion on South Africa's presence in Namibia,[6] which affords (functional) recognition to a certain category of "beneficious" acts so as to avoid punitive overlay.

Although the termination of dealings with a partner country is neither an intended effect of non-recognition, nor is it, in most cases, politically desirable or legally practical, it may in some cases be necessary to guarantee non-recognition; that is if the non-recognising state cannot otherwise ensure that the wrongdoing authority undertake reforms of certain practices or otherwise exclude the situation constituted by its wrongful acts from a particular set of interstate dealings.[7] Considerations such as the embeddedness of the wrongful practice in the wrongdoing authority's laws and policies, and thus its susceptibility to reform, as well as the types of activities and actors that the "illegal situation" would affect on the non-recognising state's side, determine the process and implementing measures for ensuring non-recognition in the context of the parties' relations. While the implementation of non-recognition occurs principally in the context of interstate dealings, such measures often also indirectly affect activities and rights of private actors, such as businesses.

While having been overlooked by both international lawyers and political analysts, as the next section observes, the duty of non-recognition poses a demanding obligation to third parties to contribute to the maintenance of the international legal order by denying the effect of certain claims and situations across legal systems.

An underdetermined practice

While the duty of non-recognition is intuitively appealing, its application in practice is more complex, as the case under scrutiny here will show.

The provisions in ARSIWA, as international lawyers have observed, are far from clear about what states are expected to do in order to guarantee the non-recognition of a given "illegal situation" (Dawidowicz, 2010; Milano, 2014; Talmon, 2005). The documentation and understanding of the compliance dynamics of international law within domestic legal orders is wanting (Koh, 1997). The ARSIWA negotiations show that the codification of non-recognition, which resulted from decades of relatively tense negotiations, is driven by the deep-seated nature of this imperative within national systems.[8] The decision to include this norm in a first codification of secondary rules on the observance of international law by the ILC was perhaps rather intended to function as an aide-memoire. The fact that states do not actively invoke the international legal obligation of non-recognition to justify their decisions to revise relations with wrongdoing authorities means that non-recognition is a domestic practice. It also means that the true contribution of this potential rule of observance (and perhaps also mode of liability) to the international rule of law has been severely overlooked.

The indeterminacies concerning the scope of such measures have prompted criticisms by disenchanted scholars and practitioners taking aim at the patchwork nature of state practice and the perceived state of desuetude of this obligation of international law (Crawford, 2012a; Sassoli & Boutruche, 2016).[9] Talmon (2005) has called the obligation of non-recognition an obligation "without real substance," that offers little clarity either on the content of such measures, or on the processes for its regulation and enforcement. By ignoring the transnational legal process and the hybrid international/domestic law that is at work in the negotiations and conclusion of external relations, such critics however tend to misrepresent the origins and purpose of this obligation of international law (International Law Association (ILA), 2014; Bethlehem, 2012). The fact is that the understanding and potential of non-recognition as a domestic regulatory process that can generate peer enforcement remain underexplored both in scholarly works and in state practice (Cheng, 2012; ILA, 2014).[10]

EU law-based non-recognition, and EU-Israeli relations

EU-Israeli relations span some 60 areas of cooperation (including trade, research, social security, civil aviation, and data sharing), hundreds of bilateral agreements between Israel and individual member states (Rockwell & Shamas, 2007), and countless private transactions between businesses, financial institutions and charities. This provides us with an illustration of the challenges that derive from the principle of non-recognition, in a context characterized by a complex patchwork of shared and exclusive competences between the EU and its member states, as well as private actors. The EU has adhered early on to the principle of non-recognition. Moreover, in the case of the Israeli-Palestinian conflict, both the International Court of Justice (ICJ), in its 2004 Advisory Opinion on Israel's construction of a Wall in the occupied Palestinian territory, and the Security Council, in its Resolution 2334 (2016),[11] explicitly call for vigorous non-recognition of activities related to the settlements.[12] But the implementation of non-recognition has put the European legal system under pressure, as highlighted by the tension between, on the one hand, non-recognition of regular assessments of reliance on the partner country as part of the process of ensuring non-recognition of its unlawful acts and, on the other, processes of accommodation to which EU and Member States' domestic authorities turn when concluding bilateral relations.

The reassessment of EU bilateral relations and private dealings relations with Israel has been driven by the EU's need, internal to its legal order, to guarantee the non-recognition of certain internationally unlawful acts (Nikolov, 2014). These reviews have, as we consider next, been far from comprehensive, and have in many cases required instigation by independent external experts (Muller & Slominski, 2016).

Non-recognition as an imperative of EU law

The EU's commitment to non-recognition was affirmed during the Batinder Commission's proceedings on the falling apart of the former Yugoslavia, and refined during the ILC's drafting process of ARSIWA (Azarova, 2017). The process of non-recognition in EU law and policy, and the basis for the adoption of such measures in the context of the EU's external relations rely on two principles. The first is the requirement found in EU administrative law that EU institutions respect international law in the exercise of their powers. This principle is enshrined in the Lisbon Treaty of the European Union and has been upheld by the European Court of Justice's jurisprudence.[13] The second is the obligation incumbent upon all EU institutions under EU administrative law to protect the integrity and effectiveness of the EU's legal order by ensuring the "full and effective implementation" of EU law "consistently with EU public policy positions and commitments in international law" (Articles 3(5) and 21(3), TEU). EU institutions are thus required to actively monitor and scrutinize the legality of the institutional practices of its partner non-member countries to ensure that internationally wrongful acts are not treated as lawful by the EU's legal order (Koh, 1997).

The task of ensuring consistency between the EU policy positions and the implementation of EU law is entrusted to the European External Action Service (EEAS) (Shamas, 2007; von Bogdandy, 2011). The EEAS is tasked to ensure that the instruments that structure its bilateral dealings with third countries do not lead to the incorrect implementation of EU law because of a partner country's non-corresponding institutional practice or laws. To guarantee the non-admission into the EU legal order of acts it deems unlawful,[14] the EEAS relies on the positions adopted by the EU Council on the institutional practice of the third country to assess the effects of relations with that country on the EU's ability to ensure consistency and exclude internationally unlawful situations and facts from its internal domain.[15]

In fact, the EEAS is legally obliged to frame EU dealings with authorities engaged in internationally unlawful acts in such a way as not to give effect to the illegal situation created by these acts (Lovatt & Toaldo, 2015; Muller & Slominski, 2016; Nikolov, 2014). This also entails providing guidance to member states and EU institutions on the correct application of EU law to internationally wrongful "predicate facts" arising from within the jurisdiction of a partner country. Non-recognition, then, might consist of a variety of restrictive measures that are tailored to the specific case at hand.

The EU may therefore find itself in a position where it is required to ensure that specific authorities of its partner country are willing and able to either comply with specific legal criteria (even if only in the context of bilateral dealings with the EU) or to otherwise exclude elements of the illegal situation from a particular set of dealings. In such cases, the cooperation of the third country with such demands is a *sine qua non* for the EU's ability to guarantee non-recognition, as it is a matter of the EU's "internal legal necessity" (Nikolov, 2014). If the third country fails to shoulder the EU's demands by undertaking the special-purpose reforms and make appropriate adjustments to its institutional practice, or if the EEAS and Commission have no basis to believe, in good faith (O'Connor, 1991), that the necessary reforms and adjustments would be adopted (e.g. when the wrongdoing is sanctioned by the partner country's domestic laws), the EU may be obliged by its own law to abstain from or indeed severe such dealings.

While the EU law based imperative to ensure non-recognition appears to be a normatively rigid and deep-seated process for vetting partner countries practices at the stage of negotiations of a set of mutual dealings, its practice appears underdeveloped. Perhaps for this reason, the practice becomes susceptible to political and economic considerations, especially after an agreement is concluded and no formal avenue exists for reviewing such decisions. The (informal) process through which such revisions came about in the context of EU-Israeli relations, deserves separate treatment beyond the ambits of this brief essay. Critically, the correction process was driven by independent non-governmental experts that sought to expose the deficiencies in the way a particular set of dealings was constructed, and the effects produced by the EU's acquiescence to certain wrongdoing (Muller & Slominski, 2016; Voltolini, 2016). This experience has shown that the way to trigger the review and correction of such dealings is not only to highlight, but also to provide a granular account of the flaws in the EU's assessment of the third country's practice and the effects of the deficiently constructed dealing on EU law.

Non-recognition and EU-Israel relations

The EU's positions on the non-recognition of Israel's sovereignty over the territory it came to occupy in 1967 are not new. These positions, along with the need to ensure the non-recognition of Israel's internationally unlawful policies and practices, in the context of the EU's relations with Israel, date back to the 1980s, when they formed the groundwork for the 1986 EC-PLO Association Agreement (Bicchi & Voltolini, 2017; Muller & Slominski, 2016). Since before the ECJ's 2010 *Brita* judgment,[16] which ruled that products from settlements are not entitled to preferential treatment under the EU-Israel Association Agreement, the EU has reckoned with the fact that Israel self-defines its domestic jurisdiction to include large parts of the occupied Palestinian territory of the West Bank, where it implements a policy of *de facto* annexation, while having effectuated East Jerusalem's *de jure* annexation under Israeli law (Basic Law: Jerusalem, 1980; UN Security Council Resolution 478, 1980). The aim of these policies is to bring about the economic, social, political and legal integration within Israel proper of 250+ settlements illegally erected and maintained in occupied territory (ACRI, 2014; UN settlements fact-finding mission report, 2013).

In spite of this long standing awareness of Israel's wrongful practices, the prioritization of political interests led in the past to the EU's construction of its relations with Israel in a manner that mandates the EU to give legal effect to the illegal situation maintained by Israel's settlements regime and *de facto* annexation of Palestinian territory (Azarova, 2017). This has prompted the need to re-adjust EU practice. The most recent and overt series of adjustments to EU-Israeli relations came to light with the publication of the EU guidelines on the participation of Israeli entities in Horizon2020 in July 2013. These were preceded, in 2012, by the Foreign Affairs Council's conclusions affirming the EU's long-standing positions on the non-recognition of Israel's sovereignty over the Palestinian territory under its control, and commitments "to ensure continued, full and effective implementation of existing EU legislation and bilateral arrangements applicable to settlement products."[17] To this aim, the EU has to guarantee that "in line with international law - all agreements between the State of Israel and the EU must unequivocally and explicitly indicate their inapplicability to the territories occupied by Israel in 1967."[18]

The EU's release of its July 2013 guidelines excluding activities in Israeli settlements from being funded by the EU was perhaps the most public episode through which non-recognition was implemented. It entailed a special set of implementing rules for the EU financial legal instrument that enable Israel's participation in "Horizon 2020". The revisions came in response to the exposure, by independent experts, of an oversight in the terms and conditions for Israel's participation in the EU's research and development programme, which resulted in the eligibility to EU funding of Israeli entities based or operating in settlements (Bicchi & Voltolini, 2017; Muller & Slominski, 2016). To correct this oversight and the EU's inappropriate reliance on the non-corresponding definition of Israel's domestic jurisdiction, the EU amended the relevant EU financial instrument to explicitly exclude funding streams that extended beyond Israel's 1967 borders, but placed the burden of guaranteeing the full and effective implementation of this EU legislative instrument on both the Israeli government and all Israeli public and private grantees through a "Memorandum of Understanding". Recipient of funds are now required to accept a "declaration on honour" not to use their funding on settlement-related activities.

In a further example, the logic of the 2013 guidelines was matched in 2015 by the labelling guidelines, which were issued to ensure the implementation of EU consumer protection law requirements on "origin information" consistently with the EU's positions on the non-recognition of Israel's sovereignty beyond its 1967 borders. This implementing measure – issued in the form of an "Interpretative Notice on indication of origin of goods from the territories occupied by Israel since June 1967" – is narrowly concerned with ensuring the accurate designation of the "place of provenance" of goods produced in Israeli settlements in the West Bank and Golan Heights. The notice states that it "is without prejudice to other requirements established by Union legislation," and, it should be added, also to consequences of trade in goods originating from illicit economies in occupied territory under international law, which may require the adoption of restrictions on their importation.

A further set of non-recognition measures was adopted to accommodate Israel's participation in the EU's market for organic produce, as an equivalent certifier of such products. In 2008, Israel's ministry of agriculture committed to the implementation of a strict control system, with checks carried out at every stage of the organic supply chain. When evidence came to light that the ministry and its accredited control bodies were certifying settlement-based farms, and that their produce was being exported to the EU through exporters based in Israel, Israel's participation in this EU programme came under scrutiny. The EU proceeded to demand that the ministry restrict its scope of operations to the "Green Line," so as to enable the EU to fully and correctly implement EU laws on organic farming consistently with EU positions on the non-recognition of Israel's sovereignty over Palestinian territory (Bicchi & Voltolini, 2017; Ravid, 2015).

While most revisions to EU-Israeli relations have sought to address the Israeli authorities' non-corresponding self-definition of their domestic jurisdiction (to include entities and activities in occupied territory), the case of EUROPOL is a notable exception and it is still undergoing. In the negotiations of the EUROPOL-Israel operational cooperation agreement, the EU became aware that it will not be able to implement the agreement by processing and storing information transferred by Israel in conformity with the EU law requirements placed on EUROPOL (Council of the European Union, 2011; European Council on Foreign Relations, 2016). These concerns, which brought the negotiations to a halt, pertain to three aspects of Israel's practice: the extension of the executive jurisdiction of Israel's national police and internal security agency under Israeli domestic law to occupied territory; Israeli agencies' practice of obtaining information from protected persons from the occupied territory who have been unlawfully transferred and were being unlawfully detained inside Israel (Article 76, Fourth Geneva Convention, 1949); and the internationally unlawful interrogation techniques used by Israeli security agencies to obtain information particularly from members of the Palestinian population (Public Committee Against Torture in Israel, 2016). Critically, these practices do not correspond with the requirements now enshrined in the EUROPOL Regulation (2016/794, Article 23(9)) that "Any information which has clearly been obtained in obvious violation of human rights should not be processed."

This sample of cases casts some light on the complexity of the landscape of actors and processes involved in the review and correction of deficiently constructed dealings with third countries involved in the most serious abuses of international law. In a number of areas of cooperation with Israel and Israeli entities, such as social security cooperation and data protection (Annex in Nikolov, 2014), both the EU and member states jointly and separately incur liability for wrongfully "giving effect in their national systems" to the "illegal situation" maintained by Israel's internationally unlawful institutional practices related to the occupied Palestinian and Syrian territories. A number of such processes, each undertaken with respect to a specific dealing, remain underway, and have led the EU to expend much political capital and technical ingenuity. Despite there being some 60 areas of cooperation between the EU and Israel, only a number of these has come under review so far. In a few cases, the burden of guaranteeing non-recognition has been placed upon the Israeli authorities. Much remains to be done, not only in relations between the EU and Israel, but also in other cases, such as EU relations with Morocco (on which, see Kassoti, 2017).

EU non-recognition under international law and practice

The EU's practice illuminates the form, object and purpose of non-recognition and offers grounds for cautious optimism about its prospective implementation (Milano, 2014). Although the EU has not sought to justify its revisions to its relations with Israel with explicit reference to its obligation to ensure the non-recognition of the illegal situation maintained by Israel's unlawful practices, the compliance dynamics of the principle of consistency in EU law, based on the EU's positions on Israeli practice in international law, are arguably a construction of that principle that has been internalized by EU law, and inspired by the member states' legal traditions. This section considers some of the insights of this practice on the processes it drives, and the scope and purpose of the measures it generates.

First, it bears noting that the deep-seated nature of the EU imperative of non-recognition resonates with the logic of the secondary rules of international law. To put it differently, the international law obligation of non-recognition is the type of international norm that is reflected in an accumulated EU practice of consistency between the EU's policy positions, commitments and dealings with third countries. Therefore, the EU's commitment to non-recognition hinges on its internalization of international law in public policy positions, based on the determinations of international public authorities such as the Security Council and International Court of Justice.

For the EU, non-recognition is part of its external relations' law and practice. The EU's interaction with third countries manifests itself in a transnational legal process in which EU institutions interpret and apply international norms to third countries' practices, thus internalizing international law in its public policy (Koh, 1996). The aim is to use this position-taking to screen out internationally unlawfully practices from the realm of specific EU bilateral dealings. It is a process that occurs at the interface between the EU internal legal order and the international legality of its partner countries' institutional practices. In this sense, the domestic practice of non-recognition is a measure for the quality of a state's or international actor's commitment to and participation in the observance of international law.

The EU's practice of non-recognition is exemplary of the potential exigency and need for certainty in the result achieved through such processes of screening out and exclusion. Despite the relatively wide margin of appreciation that the EU has used in determining the manner, process and arrangement for guaranteeing non-recognition – and the loose timeframe and deferential approach it has taken to the revisions to its dealings with Israel in particular – the result of non-recognition was unequivocally upheld in many of the cases where the need for it was exposed. A failure to ensure non-recognition threatens a system's failure, which would in turn compromise the effectiveness and integrity of the EU's legal order. Thus, neither political backlash of the kind the EU faced from Israel, nor the EU's own political and economic interests in a given special relationship can sideline the urgency of this basic institutional need.

The cautious and deferential side of the EU's approach to non-recognition is also caused by the expectation that the termination of dealings is politically undesirable and harmful to both parties, as well as often legally challenging. To this end, non-recognition is a process that produces special-purpose measures that are discriminate and proportionate, and that are not intended to entail any punitive overlay. The severance or suspension of relations would be a political decision with punitive effect that would run counter to the EU's role as a global actor and deter the spread of the EU *acquis communautaire* through its bilateral dealings. Therefore, as the case of EU-Israeli relations demonstrates, the course of action for the implementation of such measures must be mutually agreed upon and expected to be voluntarily assumed by the third country.

Overall, the state of the EU's non-recognition practice, and in particular the capacity of EU institutions to ensure consistency of all EU dealings with its policy positions, remain so far underwhelming. The scope is far from coherent. Non-recognition measures have seldom directly targeted the rights and revenues accrued by private actors, through their involvement in the illicit economy of the Israeli settlements. In the absence of such measures, the state could find itself wrongfully extending recognition to the basis of rights and revenues gained by businesses via the business' home state authorities in the course of the application of domestic law to their overseas operations. Even though some 18 European governments issued advisories on the legal risks entailed by business activities in settlements (European Council on Foreign Relations, 2016), these have not been followed through with either implementing rules or compliance measures to protect the rights of investors, procurers and consumers in domestic law from the effects of such activities.

EU law based non-recognition is foremost a function of the integrity and effectiveness of the EU's internal legal order. By contrast to other unilateral responses by states to illegal acts such as the sanctions adopted by the EU and US in response to Russia's illegal annexation of Crimea, non-recognition is neither directed at the perpetrator nor intended to coerce its compliance (Crawford, 2012a; Raponi, 2015). Non-recognition is a reflexive self-serving consequence of a particular normative actor's need to protect its internal order and value system when confronted with the non-corresponding practice of another partner authority, placing places the EU in the position of a bystander enforcer or norm propagator (Bird, 2003; BrilMayer & Tesfelidet, 2010; Council of the European Union, 2011; Krieger, 2018).

Concluding remarks: the future of non-recognition in domestic and international law

The EU's limited non-recognition practice may not be a generalizable reference point on what non-recognition entails, but it does offer a unique insight into the "secret life" of non-recognition, which remains unknown also to international lawyers. The EU's practice is a reminder of the primary logic that underpins the object and purpose of non-recognition as a feature of solidarity in the global legal order, according to which states and international actors abstain from giving effect to invalid acts (Talmon, 2005). From the vantage point of international law, where non-recognition is often a call to arms by the Security Council, the rigidity of the EU's imperative of non-recognition may point to the kind of practice that international lawyers would like to consolidate.

The EU experience therefore shows the prospect and promise of a cohesive practice of non-recognition, by a host of third states and international actors vis-à-vis a particular wrongdoing authority, and reveals an often overlooked enforcement function of third states, which however that interstate dealings with a wrongdoing authority are correctly structured and implemented. This example also highlights the under-developed and piecemeal state of the processes for the implementation of non-recognition and their dependence on instigation by independent experts, which makes them more difficult to predict. In fact, most cases in which revisions to interstate dealings are needed to ensure non-recognition, under international and arguably also EU law, have not yet been addressed or in some cases even exposed.

Notes

1. Article 41(2) ILC Draft Articles on State Responsibility for Internationally Wrongful Acts (ARSIWA) 2001.
2. International Law Commission, Report on the Work of Its Fifty-Third Session. UN GAOR, 56th Session, Supplement No 10, 114, para. 5.
3. The pre-ARSIWA practice of non-recognition was preoccupied with aggression and territorial changes: 1970 Declaration on the Principles of International Law concerning Friendly Relations and Cooperation among States; 1970 Declaration on the Strengthening of International Security, the 1974 Definition of Aggression; and 1987 Declaration on the Enhancement of the Principle of Refraining from the Threat or Use of Force in International Relations.
4. See, e.g. the issuance of certificates of origin by a de facto entity: Case C-432/92 Anastosiou [1994] ECR I-3087.

5. In the case of an annexing state that extends its bilateral agreements to the annexed territory, non-recognition measures and processes are also mandated by the provisions of the 1969 Vienna Convention on the Law of Treaties that protect against attempts to erode the rights and obligations of third party sovereigns without their consent. See, Articles 17, 29 and 34, Vienna Convention on the Law of Treaties, 1969 and 1986. See its application in, *Council v. Front Polisario*, Judgment of the European Court of Justice, Grand Chamber Judgment, C-104/16 P, 21 December 2016, paras. 106.
6. ICJ Namibia para. 125 and p 166 (sep. op. Dillard), p. 149 (sep. op. Onyeama), pp. 134–137 (sep. op. Petren), p 219 (sep. op. De Castro), and p 297, para. 123 (sep. op. Fitzmaurice).
7. During the negotiations of ARSIWA, Western states in particular insisted that non-recognition would not entail a blanket ban on relations (Talmon, 2005).
8. Declaration of Guidelines on the Recognition of New States in Eastern Europe and in the Former Soviet Union, Adopted at an Extraordinary EPC Ministerial Meeting at Brussels on 16 December 1991; text in *European Journal of International Law* (1993).
9. See, e.g. the comments and observations submitted by the United Kingdom on Article 18 of the Draft Declaration on Rights and Duties of States, A/CN.4/2, 15 December 1948, 111; cited in Dawidowicz 2012, 679.
10. Articles 27 and 26 of the 1969 Vienna Convention on the Law of Treaties.
11. See, e.g. Secretary-General's Reporting to the Security Council on the implementation of Security Council Resoluton 2334 (2016), UN Doc. S/PV.7908, 24 March 2017 available at https://unispal.un.org/DPA/DPR/unispal.nsf/0/35B26C7B31ADDA1B852580F3006FB59A.
12. Advisory Opinion Concerning Legal Consequences of the Construction of a Wall in the Occupied Palestinian Territory, International Court of Justice (ICJ), 9 July 2004, paras. 157-9. Security Council Resolution 2334 (2016), adopted 23 December 2016, para. 5.
13. See, e.g. Anklagemyndigheden v Poulsen and Diva Navigation Corp. Case C-286/90 of 24 November 1992, para. 9.
14. Article 21(3), Treaty of the European Union. See, e.g. A Racke GmbH & Co. v Hauptzollamt Mainz, Case C-162/96 of 16 June 1998, ECR 1998, p. I-03655, para. 41.
15. See, e.g. Kaufring AG and Others v Commission of the European Communities, in joined cases, T-186/97 and T-147/99 of 10 May 2001, para. 272.
16. C-386/08 *Brita GmbH v Hauptzollamt Hamburg-Hafen*, Judgement of the Fourth Chamber, 25 February 2010.
17. Council Conclusions on the Middle East Peace Process, European Council, 20 July 2015, available at www.consilium.europa.eu/en/press/press-releases/2015/07/20-fac-mepp-conclusions/.
18. Council conclusions on the Middle East Peace Process, the European Council, 18 January 2016, available at www.consilium.europa.eu/en/press/press-releases/2016/01/18-fac-conclusions-mepp/.

Acknowledgements

This account of EU-Israeli relations is based on interviews with Brussels and Jerusalem based experts who have contributed to these developments, and in particular Charles Shamas, co-founder and senior partner at the Mattin Group, to whom I am hugely indebted. All errors are the author's own.

Disclosure statement

No potential conflict of interest was reported by the author.

Funding

This work was supported by Scientific and Technological Research Council of Turkey: [Grant Number 21514107-115.02-124017].

References

Association for Civil Rights in Israel (ACRI). (2014). *One rule, two legal systems: Israel's regime of laws in the west bank*. Retrieved from https://www.acri.org.il/en/2014/11/24/twosysreport/

Arangio-Ruiz, G. (1993). *Views of the fourth special Rapporteur on state responsibility. UN Doc. A/CN.4/469 and Add.1-2, Extract from the yearbook of the International Commission, Vol II(1) (1995).*

Azarova, V. (2017). *Israel's unlawfully prolonged occupation: Consequences under an integrated legal framework*. London: European Council on Foreign Relations.

Bethlehem, D. (2012). The secret life of international law. *Cambridge Journal of International and Comparative Law, 1*, 23–36.

Bicchi, F., & Voltolini, B. (2017). Europe, the green line and the issue of the Israeli-palestinian border: Closing the gap between discourse and practice? *Geopolitics, 23*(1), 124–146.

Bird, A. (2003). Third state responsibility for human rights violations. *European Journal of International Law, 21*, 883–900.

Bothe, M. (2017). *Expert opinion relating to the conduct of prolonged occupation in the occupied Palestinian territory*. Retrieved from Norwegian Refugee Council: https://www.nrc.no/resources/legal-opinions/expert-opinion-relating-to-the-conduct-of-prolonged-occupation-in-the-occupied-palestinian-territory/

BrilMayer, L., & Tesfelidet, Y. (2010). Third state responsibility and the enforcement of international law. *New York University Journal of International Law and Politics, 44*, 1–53.

Cheng, C. (2012). *When international law works*. Oxford: Oxford University Press.

Council of the European Union. (2011). *Tenth meeting of the EU-Israel Association Council with regard to the Europol-Israel Agreement*.

Crawford, J. (2012a). *Brownlie's principles of public international law*. Cambridge: Cambridge University Press.

Crawford, J. (2012b, January 24). *Third party obligations with respect to Israeli settlements in the occupied Palestinian territories*. Retrieved from tuc.org.uk: https://www.tuc.org.uk/sites/default/files/tucfiles/LegalOpinionIsraeliSettlements.pdf

Dawidowicz, M. (2010). The obligation of non-recognition of an unlawful situation. In J. Crawford (Ed.), *The law of international responsibility* (pp. 677–686). Oxford: Oxford University press.

Declaration of Guidelines on the Recognition of New States in Eastern Europe and in the Former Soviet Union, Adopted at an Extraordinary European Political Cooperation Ministerial Meeting. (1991, December 16). *Retrieved from the European Journal of International Law (1993)*.

Dubuisson, F. (2014). *The international obligations of the EU and its member states with regards to economic activities in settlements*. Brussels: Centre de Droit International de l'Université Libre de Bruxelles (ULB).

European Council on Foreign Relations. (2016, November 2). *EU member state business advisories on Israeli settlements*. Retrieved from www.ecfr.eu: https://www.ecfr.eu/article/eu_member_state_business_advisories_on_israel_settlements

Gordon, N., & Pardo, S. (2015). The European Union and Israel's occupation: Using technical customs rules as instruments of foreign policy. *The Middle East Journal, 69*, 74–90.

Gross, A. (2017). *The writing on the wall*. Cambridge: Cambridge University Press.

Guidelines on the eligibility of Israeli entities and their activities in the territories occupied by Israel since June 1967 for grants, prizes and financial instruments funded by the EU from

2014 onwards. (2013, July 19). Retrieved from http://eeas.europa.eu/archives/delegations/israel/documents/related-links/20130719_guidelines_on_eligibility_of_israeli_entities_en.pdf

Human Sciences Research Council of South Africa. (2009). *Occupation, colonialism, apartheid? A re-assessment of Israel's practices in the occupied Palestinian territories under international law*. Cape Town: Human Sciences Research Council of South Africa.

International Law Association Recognition / Non-Recognition in International Law Committee. (2014, August). *Report of the Seventy-Sixth Conference Held in Washington D.C.*

International Law Commission. (s.d.). *Report on the work of its fifty-third session*. Supplement n° 10, 114, para. 5, UN GAOR.

Jennings, R. (1963). *Territorial acquisition in international law*. Manchester: Manchester University Press.

Kassoti, E. (2017). The legality under international law of the EU's trade agreements covering occupied territories: A comparative study of Palestine and Western Sahara. *CLEER Paper Series, 3*.

Koh, H. (1996). Transnational legal process. *Nebraska Law Review, 75*, 181.

Koh, H. (1997). Why nations obey international law? *Yale Law Review, 108*, 2559–3659.

Krieger, H. (2018). Rights and duties of third parties in armed conflict. In E. Benvenisti, & G. Nolte (Eds.), *Community obligations in international law*. Oxford: Oxford University Press.

Lagerwall, A. (2016). *Le Principe Ex Injuria Jus Non Oriter en Droit International*. Brussels: Bruylant.

League of Nations Covenant. (1924). *Article 10*.

Lovatt, H., & Toaldo, M. (2015). *EU differentiation and Israeli settlements*. London: European Council on Foreign Relations.

Lynk, M. (2017, October 23). Report of the Special Rapporteur on the situation of human rights in the Palestinian territories occupied since 1967. *UN Doc. A/72/556*.

Milano, E. (2014). The non-recognition of Russia's annexation of Crimea: Three different legal approaches and one unanswered question. *Questions of International Law, 2*, 35–55.

Moerenhout, T. (2012). The obligation to withhold from trading in order not to recognize and assist settlements and their economic activity in occupied territories. *Journal of International Humanitarian Legal Studies, 3*, 344–385.

Morgenstern, F. (1951). Validity of the acts of the belligerent occupant. *British Yearbook of International Law, 28*, 291–322.

Muller, P., & Slominski, P. (2016). The role of law in EU foreign policy-making: Legal integrity, Legal Spillover, and the EU Policy of Differentiation towards Israel. *JCMS - Journal of Common Market Studies, 6*, 1–18.

Nikolov, K. (2014). Ashton's second hat: The EU funding guidelines on Israel as a post-Lisbon instrument of European foreign policy. *Diplomacy, 11*, 167–188.

O'Connor, J. (1991). *Good faith in international law*. Brookfield: Dartmouth Publishing Limited.

Orakhelashvili, A. (2006). *Peremptory norms of international law*. Oxford: Oxford University Press.

Public Committee Against Torture in Israel. (2016, March). *Independent report to the UN committee against torture towards the review the fifth periodic report on Israel*. Retrieved from www.omct.org: http://www.omct.org/files/2016/04/23728/pcati_cat_independent_submission_visual5B45D.pdf

Raponi, S. (2015). Is coercion necessary for law? The role of coercion in international and domestic law. *Washington University Jurisprudence Review, 8*, 35.

Ravid, B. (2015, June 07). *Israel launches intense efforts to halt EU directive to label settlement products*. Retrieved from www.haaretz.com: https://www.haaretz.com/israel-news/.premium-1.659946

Riphagen, W. (1980). Views of the third Special Rapporteur on the topic of State Responsibility. *32nd Session of the ILC, 2*, p. 117.

Rockwell, S., & Shamas, C. (2007, July). *Third annual review on human rights in EU-Israel relations accomodating to the 'special' case of Israel 2005–2006*. Retrieved from www.adalah.org: https://www.adalah.org/uploads/oldfiles/newsletter/eng/jul07/EMHRN-annual.pdf

Sassoli, M., & Boutruche, T. (2016). *Expert opinion on third states' obligations vis-à-vis IHL violations under international law, with a special focus on common article 1 to the 1949 Geneva conventions*. Oslo: Norwegian Refugee Council.

Shamas, C. (2007). *EU-third country contractual engagements under the European neighbourhood policy: Improving the EU's normative housekeeping through Ex-Ante conditionality and safeguard provisions.* (unpublished) Brussels.

Talmon, S. (2005). The duty not to recognize as lawful a situation created by the illegal use of force or other breaches of a Jus Cogens obligation: An obligation without real substance? Dans C. Tomuschat, & J. Thouvenin, *The fundamental rules of the international legal order* (pp. 99–126). The Hague: Martinus Nijhoff Publishers.

Turns, D. (2003). The stimson doctrine of non-recognition: Its historical genesis and influence on contemporary international law. *Chinese Journal of International Law, 2,* 105–143.

UN Settlements Fact-Finding Mission Report. (2013, 7 February). *Report of the independent international fact-finding mission to investigate the implications of the Israeli settlements on the civil, political, economic, social and cultural rights of the Palestinian people throughout the Occupied Palestinian Territory, including East Jerusalem* (Report No. A/HRC/22/63).

Voltolini, B. (2016). *Lobbying in EU foreign policy making: The case of the Israeli-Palestinian conflict.* London: Routledge.

von Bogdandy, A. (2011). Founding principles. In D. A. von Bogdandy, & J. Bast (Eds.), *Principles of European constitutional law* (pp. 11–54). London: Bloomsbury.

Wrange, P. (2015). *Occupation / annexation of a territory: Respect for international humanitarian law and human rights and consistent EU policy.* Retrieved from Directorate General for External Policies, European Parliament Think Tank: www.europarl.europa.eu/RegData/etaudes/STUD/2015/534995/EXPO_STU(2015)534995_E

Wright, Q. (1961). *The law on the elimination of war.* Manchester: Manchester University Press.

France and the Israeli occupation: Talking the talk, but not walking the walk?

Benedetta Voltolini

ABSTRACT
This article examines the rhetoric-practice gap in French foreign policy vis-à-vis Israel's occupation of the Palestinian territories. It shows that France has maintained a rather stable rhetorical position on the Israeli-Palestinian conflict and the Israeli occupation since 1967, based on the condemnation of Israeli settlements in these areas, and the recognition of the Palestinian right to self-determination which, over time, has been crystallised in the French support for the two-state solution. However, in practice France has fallen short of implementing and enforcing measures and policies aimed at the non-recognition of Israeli settlements. France tries to push for the two-state solution internationally, while adopting an accommodating approach towards the occupation when it comes to its bilateral relations with Israel.

Introduction

The Middle East has always played an important role in French foreign policy and the Israeli-Palestinian conflict has often been defined as "une passion française" (Sieffert, 2004). Not only does the situation in Israel and Palestine come high on the political agenda, but it has also had a great deal of resonance among French politicians, diplomats, intellectuals and public opinion (Benraad, 2014; Gresh & Aldeguer, 2017). This is not at all surprising, given the presence of important Jewish and Muslim communities in France, of a large French-speaking community in Israel, as well as French history, marked by its colonial past, the legacies of World War II and the collusion of the Vichy regime with the Nazi enterprise (Gresh & Aldeguer, 2017; Interview 1, 7).

French foreign policy vis-à-vis the Israeli-Palestinian conflict has been characterized by interweaving strands. On the one hand, since 1967 the French position vis-à-vis the Israeli-Palestinian conflict and the Israeli occupation of the West Bank, Gaza Strip, East Jerusalem and the Golan Heights has been rather stable, with minor adjustments over time. This stance is based on the condemnation of Israel's occupation and of the building of settlements in these areas, and on the recognition of the Palestinian right to self-determination which, over time, has crystallised in the French support for the two-state solution. This consistent and principled rhetoric has been strongly promoted internationally, both at the United Nations (UN) and within the European Union (EU), often leading to portraying France as a pro-Arab and pro-Palestinian actor. On the other hand, French-Israeli relations have fluctuated over time. Bilateral ties were strong during the IV République, cooled down in the early 1960s and became tense after 1967. Only in the mid-2000s diffidence and tensions were superseded in favour of a renewed rapprochement and a discourse of friendship, cooperation and alliance.

The tension between these two strands is partially solved by playing on different stages. At the international and European level France has been particularly active in carving out a role in support of the two-state solution and in favour of the Palestinian cause, while it has dealt with Israel mainly via bilateral ties. However, the mismatch between French rhetoric against Israeli occupation of the Palestinian territories and French practice vis-à-vis Israel remains. The implementation and enforcement of measures and policies aimed at the non-recognition of Israeli settlements are at best very partial. France tries to push for the two-state solution internationally, but it adopts a more accommodating approach towards the occupation when it comes to bilateral relations with Israel.

This article aims to provide the reader with a snapshot of this rhetoric-practice gap. First, it offers a historical overview of the French stance, detailing the two interwoven discursive strands mentioned above. In doing so, it highlights how France has maintained a stable position when it comes to the Palestinians and the condemnation of Israeli occupation, while developing since the mid-2000s a discourse leaning towards Israel. Second, it focuses on the partial implementation of its rhetorical stance against Israeli settlements, which leaves open the issue of (indirect) recognition of Israeli occupation (cf. Azarova, 2018). Finally, the conclusions suggest an explanation for the mismatch between France's rhetorical position and its partial implementation, briefly discussing how the Israeli-Palestinian conflict is turning into a domestic issue (cf. Bicchi, 2018 in this Special Issue).

France and Israel's occupation: resistance at the discursive level?

France's position vis-à-vis Israel and the Palestinians is marked by two interwoven discourses. On the one hand, French position vis-à-vis Israel has shifted over time, moving from a strong and almost unconditional alliance in the 1950s and early 1960s, through a phase of tense and distant relations in the following decades, to a renewed discourse of friendship since the mid-2000s. On the other hand, France's stance vis-à-vis the Israeli-Palestinian conflict emerged after the Six-Day war of 1967 and has remained relatively stable since then. This section shows how these two rhetorical positions have evolved and remained strongly interwoven, creating a discursive mismatch between an anti-occupation rhetoric and a more lenient and conciliatory stance towards Israel. The potential tensions emerging from these two strands are partially solved by carving out different roles for France on the national, EU and UN stages.

During the IV République, France was one of the closest allies of Israel. It recognized the newly created state and establish diplomatic relations in 1949. French-Israeli cooperation was very tight, ranging from scientific to military aspects (Vaïsse, 2009). In the 1950s, France was the main supplier of military equipment to Israel through a number of secret deals that included aircrafts, tanks and ammunitions (cf. Nouzille, 2018; Schillo, 2008). It also played a crucial role in Israel's acquisition of nuclear capabilities through the provision of know-how, material and technology. In a secret agreement signed in 1956 France committed to helping Israel build a nuclear reactor and to providing uranium. Nuclear capabilities were meant for civilian purposes, while military use was conditional upon consultation with, and agreement by, the French government (cf. Nouzille, 2018). At the time, France was the main ally of Israel and the Palestinian question was not yet perceived as a major issue.

However, this strong cooperation and almost unconditional friendship began to be questioned once Charles de Gaulle came to power in 1958. Although the General considered Israel as "our friend and our ally"[1] and military cooperation continued (e.g. 72 Mirage were delivered in 1961), he decided for the interruption of nuclear cooperation with foreign countries, including Israel, and for the reorientation of French foreign policy in the region. The end of the war in Algeria in 1962 created more room for manoeuvre for France and de Gaulle took up this opportunity to rebalance French policy with an opening and progressive relaunch of diplomatic relations with the Arab countries (Leveau, 2003; Vaïsse, 2009).

A more radical shift in the French-Israeli relationship took place in 1967, with the Six-Day war. De Gaulle had made clear that France would support Israel in case of aggression, but it would not intervene if Israel were to start the hostilities. In his view, Israel was not seriously threatened by its Arab neighbours, and a conflict would have further damaged the balance in the region, with the risk of a much larger war between the US and the USSR (cf. Bozo, 2012; Nouzille, 2018). Once Israel attacked its neighbouring countries, de Gaulle kept his promise by strongly condemning Israel's attack and its occupation of Palestinian territories. In line with this stance, France supported UNSC Resolution 242, refusing any *fait accompli* and requesting the withdrawal of Israel from the occupied territories.[2] Subsequent events continued to deteriorate the relations between France and Israel, leading to a cooling down of their bilateral ties.

At the same time as French-Israeli cooperation came to an end, French position vis-à-vis the Israeli-Palestinian conflict began to emerge, becoming the cornerstone of French diplomacy followed by all presidents. Following the 1967 war France was vocal in condemning Israel's occupation and pushing for the recognition of the Palestinian right to self-determination (including the establishment of a state) and of the PLO as representative of the Palestinian people.[3] It predominantly directed its diplomatic efforts at the European level, with the aim of aligning the then members of the European Economic Community (EEC) to its approach on the Palestinian question (cf. Allen & Pijpers, 1984; Miller, 2011). France thus succeded in shaping some European joint declarations, such as those in 1973, 1977 and the Venice declaration of 1980, when the then nine EEC members recognized the Palestinian right to self-determination and the need for the PLO to be associated with peace negotiations (Müller, 2012). In 1980 the Europeans also stated that Israel had to put an end to "the territorial occupation which it has maintained since the conflict in 1967" and that Israeli settlements in the "occupied Arab [sic] territories" were "illegal under international law".[4]

This position continued under François Mitterrand, who came to power in 1981 and was expected to give a more pro-Israel line to French foreign policy due to his personal sympathy for Israel. However, he maintained the established policy vis-à-vis the Israeli-Palestinian conflict and took "into full consideration the legitimacy of the Palestinian struggle" (Filiu, 2009, p. 40). During his visit to Israel in March 1982, the first of a French president of the V République, Mitterrand proclaimed that there was a strong friendship between the French and Israeli peoples, but he also argued in favour of the rights of the Palestinians to have a state (although he did not mention the issue of the settlements).[5] It was under Mitterrand that in 1989 the PLO liaison office was upgraded into the Official Delegation of Palestine, while Arafat was invited to Paris (cf. Filiu, 2009; Vaïsse, 2009).

Mitterrand's successors also maintained this established and principled position on the occupation and the two-state solution. In line with Gaullist policies, Jacques Chirac (1995–2007) pursued a balanced policy in the region, reinforcing ties with Arab countries and confirming French support for the Oslo peace process (Vaïsse, 2009). Similarly, Nicolas Sarkozy (2007–2012) and François Hollande (2012–2017) continued to resist Israel's occupation at the rhetorical level and expressed their support for the establishment of a Palestinian state. This was on display at the UN level, where France was able to show its commitment to the two-state solution and the condemnation of Israeli settlements. Paris voted in favour of Palestinian membership to the UNESCO in 2011,[6] Palestine's upgrade to a non-member observer state at the UN in November 2012[7] and the display of the Palestinian flag at the UN in September 2015.[8] More recently, it supported UN Security Council Resolution 2334 of 23 December 2016, in which the Security Council stated that settlements have no legal validity, are a flagrant violation under international law and a major obstacle to the two-state solution. It demanded for an immediate and complete cease of settlement activities, stated that it does not recognize any changes to the Green Line other than those agreed by Israelis and Palestinians, and calls upon all states to distinguish between Israel and the territories it occupied in 1967. Through its permanent representative at the UN, Ambassador François Delattre, France expressed full support for the resolution and saluted it as an important moment thanks to the clarity of the Council's position on the settlements' enterprise.[9]

In parallel to this discourse, however, a partial shift in the French position vis-à-vis Israel started to emerge under Chirac. While French-Israeli relations were at times tense during his mandates, he was the first President to recognize the responsibility of the French state during the Vichy regime for the crimes committed against the Jews. In 1996, during a visit to Israel, he stated that "France and Israel have a privileged relationship".[10] During his second mandate, there was a certain fatigue in pushing the Middle East Peace Process dossier (Interview 1). In contrast, especially since the end of 2004, Chirac tried to re-establish close ties with Israel, also in an attempt to improve French relations with the United States (Interview 6; Nouzille, 2018). In 2005, during a visit by the Israeli Prime Minister Ariel Sharon, France and Israel agreed to establish a France-Israel Foundation to improve their respective images in the two countries.[11]

Chirac's successors strengthened this rhetoric of friendship and alliance with the State of Israel. Sarkozy (2007–2012) openly expressed his sympathy for Israel even before becoming President in 2007. This is likely to be related to his personal experience (Nouzille, 2018) as well as the influence of the so-called *néocons à la français*, a group of people that considered the alliance with the US, and hence with Israel, a key and strategic priority for France (Interviews 1, 2).[12] Demonstrating profound attention to the French Jewish community, Sarkozy was the first President to go to the annual dinner organized by the *Conseil Représentatif des Institutions Juives de France* (CRIF), which has now become a place-to-be for French politicians. At the political level, an annual strategic dialogue between the Secretary-Generals of the Foreign Ministries of France and Israel started in

2009.[13] Similarly, military cooperation was strengthened, covering both technological and operational aspects (Nouzille, 2018). Since 2000 numerous branches of French firms have been established in Israel, employing more than 6,000 people in sectors such as energy, consumer goods, infrastructure, health, transport, etc.[14] Moreover, French investments have more than tripled since 2006.

Hollande (2012–2017) continued the policy initiated by his predecessor. During a visit to Israel in 2013, he declared his friendship to Israel and that he would always find a "chant d'amour" for Israel and his leaders (Gresh & Aldeguer, 2017).[15] Most importantly, despite France's continued rhetorical support for Palestinian self-determination, Paris fell short of recognizing Palestine as a state. The government did not follow up on a resolution in favour of recognition of the Assemblée Nationale in December 2014 (339 votes in favour, 151 against).[16] The government did not keep the promise made in January 2016 by the then foreign ministry Laurent Fabius, who declared that the French government was ready to recognize the Palestinian state, if diplomacy failed to lead to a solution.[17] France indeed organized two international conferences on the Middle East, in June 2016 and January 2017, with the clear goal of relaunching the peace process. Although the situation between Israel and Palestine did not change, it was an opportunity for the international community to clearly state its position on the conflict (also vis-à-vis the Israeli government), the last time in which it was possible to reach a united stance within the international community on the dossier (Interview 7). Yet, despite the diplomatic failure to advance peace in the region, France did not follow up on Palestinian recognition, mainly due to Hollande's opposition, who considered the decision politically too costly and as hampering any possibility for France to be a mediator (Interviews 2, 7).

Elected in May 2017, Emmanuel Macron has yet to clearly define its policy vis-à-vis the conflict. He has maintained a strong opposition to Israeli settlements, while also stressing the importance of French-Israeli bilateral relations. For example, in a press conference with Israeli Prime Minister Benjamin Netanyahu on 10 December 2017, Macron said that France considers the US's declarations on the recognition of Jerusalem "contrary to international law and dangerous to peace".[18] At the same time, however, he also reaffirmed the "special relationship" between France and Israel, to which France is "strongly attached".[19]

Therefore, while the rhetoric in favour of the two-state solution and against Israeli occupation has remained stable since 1967, the French position vis-à-vis Israel has fluctuated. The tensions at times emerging from these two strands have partially been solved by acting diplomatically at the international and European level when it comes to the Israeli-Palestinian conflict, while working at the bilateral level when it comes to Israel. As the next section will show, however, this has not addressed the mismatch between the rhetoric of resistance to Israeli occupation and the French bilateral policy practice.

France and Israeli settlements in practice

Despite its clear and consistent rhetoric of condemnation of Israel's occupation, France's implementation of such a position has been patchy. While it has supported (and at times been the driver of) EU measures aimed at the non-recognition of Israeli occupation, France's track record at home and in bilateral dealings has been partial at best.

At the EU level, France has backed the so-called "policy of differentiation", i.e. the distinction between Israel within the 1967 border and its settlements in the Palestinian territories when it comes to bilateral dealings between the EU and Israel (Lovatt & Toaldo, 2015). The differentiation policy implies the *"non-applicability* in the occupied territories (i.e. in Israeli settlements) of legal regimes beneficial for Israel that are set up under EU law" (Nikolov, 2014, p. 171). This has been the way embraced by European countries to make sure that they do not grant indirect recognition to occupation (cf. Azarova, 2018). Examples of this policy of differentiation have been the 2013 "Guidelines on the eligibility of Israeli entities and their activities in the territories occupied by Israel since June 1967 for grants, prizes and financial instruments funded by the EU from 2014 onwards" and the 2015 "Interpretive Notice on indication of origin of goods coming from the territories occupied by Israel since June 1967" (cf. Bicchi & Voltolini, 2018). France expressed support for these measures on different occasions, such as by signing a letter to the High Representative Catherine Ashton in 2013, asking for guidelines on the labelling of settlement goods, and by supporting the strong language of the draft Council Conclusions on the Middle East in January 2016, which was however watered down after Israel successfully managed to influence some member states (Lovatt, 2016).

Yet, France's performance at home and in bilateral agreements with Israel has been much more ambiguous. On the one hand, key EU decisions have been transposed at the national level. France published an advice concerning the implications for citizens and businesses in the occupied territories on the website of the Ministère de l'Europe et des Affaires étrangères (MEAE) in 2014.[20] This followed the agreement taken in the Council's Maghreb/Mashreq Working Group in June 2013 concerning the need for a common message that all member states should use to raise awareness among citizens and businesses of the economic, legal and reputational damages and risks they might incur if they engage in activities in or related to Israeli settlements. In its short notice, the Quai d'Orsay also included an invitation to those that intend to conduct economic or financial activities in the settlements to get a juridical opinion before proceeding.

On the other hand, however, the actual implementation and enforcement of the differentiation policy, which pertains to national authorities, has been weak, as the case of labelling shows. According to EU legislation and as reiterated in the Interpretive Notice of November 2015, labels indicating the origin of goods have to be precise and not misleading to the consumer.[21] Hence, settlement goods need to be labelled as "product from the Golan Heights (Israeli settlement)" or "product from the West Bank (Israeli settlement)". France reacted rather slowly to the issue of the Notice and it did so only in response to pressure from civil society organizations and the Parliament. The *Plateforme des ONG françaises pour la Palestine* and the *Association France Palestine Solidarité* sent letters to the *Direction Générale de la Concurrence, de la Consommation e de la Répression des Fraudes* (DGCCRF) – which is a department of the Ministry of Economics and Finance in charge of issues related to consumer protection, including the labelling of products – to inquire how the DGCCRF envisaged ensuring the implementation and enforcement of EU legislation.[22] Numerous parliamentary questions on the subject were also tabled, inquiring how the government intended to correctly implement the EU's notice.[23] As a result of these different pressures, in September 2016 the government confirmed that the Ministry of Economics would be in charge of this.[24] Shortly afterwards, on 24 November 2016 a notice to business actors was published in the *Journal Officiel de la République*

Française.[25] The DGCCRF recalled that the West Bank, East Jerusalem and the Golan Heights are not part of Israel according to international law. Therefore, the labelling of food products needs to precisely indicate the origin of the goods to properly inform consumers, meaning that labels for products coming from Israeli settlements have to include the mention "Israeli settlements". Although the notice is partial, as it only refers to food products and does not specify which types of sanctions are imposed in case of violations of the labelling regulations, it is obviously the first step in the implementation of the declaratory stance against Israeli occupation.

However, the trickiest part remains its enforcement. On the one hand, evidence collected by civil society organizations has shown that a majority of products continue to be labelled as "Made in Israel", even when goods come from the settlements. For example, the wine bottles produced by Golan Heights Winey (GWH) and sold by the French importer *Casimex* did not make any reference to the fact that the wine is produced in an Israeli settlement.[26] Similarly, civil society actors have collected evidence in supermarkets, demonstrating how the regulation on labelling is not properly implemented and not enforced (Interview 3), and encouraging activists to send letters to the retailers and the DGCCRF when they encounter cases of non-compliance.[27] Three factors are likely to contribute to this. First, it is very difficult for retailers as well as French authorities to clearly distinguish between products from Israel and from its settlements. One of the main sources of information should be the EUR.1 certificate of origin which is produced when a product is imported into the EU under preferential treatment. Yet, distinguishing between Israeli and settlement goods is rather difficult, if not impossible, due to the Israel's postal code system of 2013, for customs authorities (Interviews 3, 4).[28] Second, the DGCCRF has limited resources to ensure full enforcement of this legislation. Given the relatively small impact in economic terms, this is not the main priority of the Department. A similar difficulty is also voiced by retailers, which do not necessarily know how to ensure the correct implementation of the labelling regulation (Interviews 2, 3, 4). Finally, political will is absent. The higher (and political) levels in the hierarchy are not prepared to take further steps in this direction, hence not encouraging moves that would go for a stricter enforcement (Interview 3).

More recently, the notice was challenged in front of the *Conseil d' Etat*, the highest administrative jurisdiction in France, in 2017. The *Organisation juive européenne* and the winery society Psagot Ltd asked the *Conseil* to annul the notice published in 2016, arguing that the use of the word "settlement" is political and goes beyond the purpose of EU legislation on the labelling of products, and that it imposes double standards on Israeli business actors, given that other cases of occupation are not treated in the same way.[29] On 30 May 2018, the French court referred the case to the European Court of Justice (ECJ), asking whether the mention of "settlement" is permitted and/or imposed by EU law.[30] While the referral delays the decision on the specific case, the implications will have EU-wide repercussions, as the ECJ's interpretation will apply to all member states and will define whether the interpretation of EU law provided by the Commission in 2015 and then transposed into national notices by member states is in line with EU legislation.

France's differentiation policy is further deficient when bilateral agreements are scrutinized. Cooperation has developed across a wide range of issues, such as tourism, cinema, environment and R&D, with the prospect of further strengthening relations.[31] So far, however, none of the existing bilateral agreements between France and Israel contains a clause limiting their territorial applicability to the territory of Israel within the 1967 border. This lack of a formal exclusion of settlements from bilateral treaties is not supplemented by informal measures that would limit the scope of application in practice. Because settlements are not left out, either formally or informally, Israel is hence in the position to implement these bilateral agreements in accordance with treaty law and Israeli law. This means that settlements as well as the occupied areas of East Jerusalem and the Golan Heights, which have been annexed in 1980 and 1981, are included by Israel.

Therefore, rhetorical commitment against the occupation is often not accompanied by non-recognition in practice. On the one hand, France condemns Israeli settlements, in accordance with international law and the consensus of the international community. It has often promoted tougher action at the international and EU level, supporting UN resolutions critical of settlements as well as the EU's policy of differentiation. On the other, Paris tends to become much more accommodating of Israel's occupation in practice, either via the lack of territorial clauses in its bilateral treaties with Israel or when it comes to the implementation and enforcement of concrete measures that would differentiate between Israel and its settlements.

Conclusions

Interwoven strands in French foreign policy vis-à-vis the Israeli-Palestinian conflict have led to a mismatch between French rhetoric on Israel's occupation and French policy practice vis-à-vis Israel. On the one hand, France's rhetorical position has remained consistent since 1967. It has always condemned Israeli occupation, while supporting the cause of a Palestinian state. Paris has acted rather consistently at both the UN and EU levels, supporting resolutions against the settlements and measures to differentiate between Israel and its settlements in EU-Israel dealings. While recent years have shown an increasing rapprochement towards Israel, the condemnation of the settlement enterprise and the support for the two-state solution continue to be the cornerstone of French policy. Yet, France's performance in the implementation and enforcement stages still leaves margin for improvement. Not only has implementation of EU measures aimed at the non-recognition of Israeli settlements been sketchy, but there has been no substantial move in differentiating between Israel and its settlements at the level of France-Israel bilateral treaties.

Rhetoric-practice gaps are normal features in politics, so this is not at all surprising. While a similar gap at the EU level has been progressively closing (Bicchi & Voltolini, 2018), the tensions between different types of practices has not lead to a similar pattern in the case of French foreign policy. While more research is necessary, potential explanations for this persisting mismatch are to be found in French societal dynamics and how the actions, practices and narratives proposed by different domestic actors shape the formulation of French foreign policy. The lack of political willingness, which is often mentioned as the reason for the failure to recognize Palestine or to enforce the labelling regulation, emerges from deeper trends in French society. Despite attempts at avoiding that the conflict becomes a domestic issue, it is undeniable that it has a strong resonance and is very politicized in the French domestic debate.

First of all, the pillars of French policy are contested by several societal groups that aim to influence the debate. Challenges range from the role and implications of international law and human rights law to anti-Semitism. Lobbying on the French government and Member of Parliaments come from opposite fronts, which try to shift French foreign policy in their preferred direction. For example, the CRIF has been particularly vocal in recent years on issues of French foreign policy towards Israel and of anti-Semitism (Ghiles Meilhac, 2011). It is considered as strongly influential, with a relatively easy access to the President and the Foreign Minister (Interview 7). Similarly, the Plateforme des ONG françaises pour la Palestine and the Association France Palestine Solidarité also aim to influence French policy in favour of Palestinian rights and lobby for an effective implementation of measures against Israeli settlements.[32]

Second, the debate about French foreign policy vis-à-vis Israel and Palestine has become entangled with the domestic discussion about anti-Semitism, which remains a challenge in French society (see Mayer, 2018). There is a trend, supported by some groups such as CRIF, to scrutinize all criticisms of the government of Israel as a form of anti-Semitism.[33] According to the 2017 report on racism, anti-Semitism and discrimination by the Commission Nationale Consultative des Droits de l'Homme, anti-Semitism in France continues to be linked to the old stereotypes linking the Jews to money and power. The so-called *nouvelle judéophobie* revolving around a negative image of Israel and Zionism remains in the minority. The report also warns against mixing racism and anti-Semitism with the criticism of the government of Israel and its policies.[34]

Despite this warning, the public debate in France can at times use anti-Semitism, anti-Zionism and criticism of the government of Israel interchangeably. Macron too stated that anti-Zionism is "the mere reinvention of anti-Semitism" in his discourse on the occasion of the remembrance of the raid of Vel d'Hiv in July 2017.[35] Similarly, the case of the Boycott Divestment and Sanction (BDS) movement seems to point towards the criminalization of the criticism of Israeli policies.[36] Already in 2010 and 2012 the Minister of Justice issued two *circulaires*, i.e. two administrative documents, to public prosecutors asking to report and prosecute those individuals calling for the boycott of Israeli products.[37] Since 2010 there have been trials against BDS activists, without a common line of judgement across cases (Interview 3). In October 2015 the Cour de Cassation confirmed the accusations against some BDS activists on the basis of articles 225-2 of the criminal code (obstacle to the normal exercise of economic activity) and art. 24.8 of the law 1881 on freedom of press, which includes the crime of provocation to discrimination, to hatred or to violence against a person or a group of people due to their origin, their belonging (or not) to an ethnic group, a nation, a race or a specific religion.[38] Moreover, President Hollande proudly declared, at the annual dinner of the CRIF on 22 February 2017, that "France is the only country to have a law that forbids the appeal to boycott and I will assure you that we will enforce it".[39]

It is quite unlikely that the gap between French rhetoric about the occupation and its policy practice vis-à-vis Israel will be closed in the short term. Politicians are caught between their rhetorical and principled position vis-à-vis the two-state solution and the illegality of Israeli settlements in the occupied Palestinian territories on the one hand, and the existing practice towards Israel, on the other. While the tension has been partially solved by discussing the issue of Palestinians and occupation within the EU and the UN, domestic pressures are challenging French foreign policy and the sustainability of this mismatch in the long run. Foreign policy practices are increasingly entangled with domestic policies and politics. "Contestation from below", i.e. the actions and narratives of domestic societal actors, tends to increasingly shape the contour of foreign policy and transforming it into a domestic issue.

List of interviews

(1) Former diplomat, 24/10/2017
(2) Diplomat, 13/10/2017
(3) NGO representative, 18/10/2017
(4) NGO representative, 05/10/2017
(5) Expert, 06/09/2016
(6) Historian, 19/02/2018
(7) Diplomat, 16/05/2018

Funding

This work was supported by the European Union's Horizon 2020 research and innovation programme under the Marie Skłodowska-Curie grant agreement No. 657949.

Notes

1. Quoted in Vaïsse, 2009, p. 364.
2. Lots of ink has been spelt on the difference between the French and the English version of the resolution. According to Vaïsse (2009), de Gaulle was ready to accept adjustments to the 1967 border, while the Quai d'Orsay had a stricter interpretation, implying the need for a full withdrawal of Israel from all occupied areas.
3. France opened the liaison office of the PLO in France in 1975.
4. For the full text of the Venice declaration, see: http://eeas.europa.eu/archives/docs/mepp/docs/venice_declaration_1980_en.pdf.
5. http://discours.vie-publique.fr/notices/827006800.html.
6. http://www.reuters.com/article/us-palestinians-unesco-idUSTRE79U1ZY20111101.
7. https://www.un.org/press/en/2012/ga11317.doc.htm.
8. https://www.un.org/press/en/2015/ga11676.doc.htm.
9. https://www.diplomatie.gouv.fr/fr/dossiers-pays/israel-territoires-palestiniens/processus-de-paix/evenements/article/proche-orient-explication-de-vote-de-francois-delattre-representant-permanent#.
10. http://discours.vie-publique.fr/notices/967015700.html.
11. "PM Sharon visit herald symbolic upturn in French-Israeli relations", telegram of the US Embassy in Paris, 01/08/2005, available at: https://wikileaks.org/plusd/cables/05PARIS5263_a.html; cf. http://www.fondationfranceisrael.org/qui-sommes-nous/missions.
12. The influence of this group of people is particularly evident on the Iranian nuclear proliferation dossier (cf. Pouponneau, 2015). According to one diplomat, the sway exerted by the *neocons* is less significant in the case of Israel-Palestine (Interview 7; but see Nouzille, 2018 for a different account).
13. https://www.diplomatie.gouv.fr/en/country-files/israel-palestinian-territories/israel/france-and-israel/presentation/.
14. As documented by numerous NGOs, numerous French companies are involved in the settlement industry (cf. www.whoprofits.org). For example, Alstom, Systra and Egis Rail are involved in the construction of the Jerusalem Light Rail (Veolia was involved, but then withdrew from it) (http://www.france-palestine.org/IMG/pdf/20180524_tramwaypalestine_livret_final_b.pdf). Similarly, French banks finance Israeli banks or settlement activities (http://www.france-palestine.org/Les-liaisons-dangereuses-des-banques-et-assurances-francaises-avec-la). See also Martins (2018) in this special issue.
15. http://www.lepoint.fr/monde/pourquoi-hollande-defend-corps-et-ame-israel-18-11-2013-1758330_24.php; http://www.bfmtv.com/politique/francois-hollande-chant-damour-israel-654824.html.

16. http://www.assemblee-nationale.fr/14/ta/ta0439.asp.
17. https://www.francetvinfo.fr/monde/proche-orient/israel-palestine/video-laurent-fabius-la-reconnaissance-de-la-palestine-c-est-un-droit-pas-un-passe-droit_763967.html.
18. http://www.elysee.fr/declarations/article/transcription-de-la-conference-de-presse-du-president-de-la-republique-emmanuel-macron-et-du-premier-ministre-israelien-benyamin-netanyahou/.
19. Ibid.
20. http://www.diplomatie.gouv.fr/fr/conseils-aux-voyageurs/conseils-par-pays/israel-territoires-palestiniens/#complements.
21. The Notice refers to the specific pieces of legislation for separate sets of products such as fresh vegetables and fruit, cosmetics, wine, oil, etc.
22. https://plateforme-palestine.org/La-mise-en-oeuvre-de-l-etiquetage-des-produits-des-colonies; https://plateforme-palestine.org/La-mise-en-oeuvre-de-l-etiquetage-differencie-des-produits-en-provenance-des.
23. http://palestine-nos-elus.org/spip.php?page=liste_nuage&id_mot=61.
24. http://questions.assemblee-nationale.fr/q14/14-96124QE.htm.
25. https://www.legifrance.gouv.fr/affichTexte.do;jsessionid=AE9D6C55B501756D63EBDF11A39F4D43.tpdila09v_2?cidTexte=JORFTEXT000033464109&dateTexte=&oldAction=rechJO&categorieLien=id&idJO=JORFCONT000033463474.
26. http://www.france-palestine.org/De-Vinisud-a-Casimex-les-colons-debusques.
27. http://www.france-palestine.org/Lettre-type-a-la-Direction-de-la-Protection-des-Populations-DDPP; http://www.france-palestine.org/Lettre-au-magasin-carrefour.
28. Cf. https://electronicintifada.net/blogs/david-cronin/checking-settlement-exports-impossible-eu-admits.
29. https://www.opinion-internationale.com/2018/05/29/etiquetage-des-produits-israeliens-et-droit-de-lunion-europeenne-la-parole-est-au-conseil-detat-lanalyse-de-maitre-francois-henri-briard_53774.html.
30. Conseil d'Etat, Lecture du mercredi 30 mai 2018, No. 407147, ECLI:FR:CECHR:2018:407147.20180530.
31. E.g. http://www.elysee.fr/declarations/article/transcription-de-la-conference-de-presse-du-president-de-la-republique-emmanuel-macron-et-du-premier-ministre-israelien-benyamin-netanyahou/.
32. Cf. some of the campaigns that have been launched over time: https://plateforme-palestine.org/Campagnes-706 and http://www.france-palestine.org/+-Campagnes-Actions-+.
33. E.g. http://www.crif.org/fr/prisesdeparole/discours-de-cloture-7eme-convention-nationale-du-crif-francis-kalifat.
34. In particular, pp. 15-16 and section 2.4. The full report is available at: http://www.cncdh.fr/sites/default/files/cncdh_rapport_2017_bat_basse_definition.pdf.
35. http://www.elysee.fr/declarations/article/discours-du-president-de-la-republique/.
36. Cf. Bicchi, 2018 in this special issue for similar trends in the British context.
37. CRIM-AP n°09-900-A4 (12/02/2010) and CRIM-AP n° 2012-0034-A4 (15/05/2012).
38. See also Médiapart : enquête sur BDS, available at: http://ujfp.org/spip.php?article4802.
39. https://jssnews.com/2017/03/01/discours-integral-de-francois-hollande-au-diner-du-crif-22022017/.

Funding

This work was supported by the European Union's Horizon 2020 research and innovation programme under the Marie Skłodowska-Curie grant agreement No. 657949.

Disclosure statement

No potential conflict of interest was reported by the author.

ORCID

Benedetta Voltolini http://orcid.org/0000-0002-4212-5528

References

Allen, D., & Pijpers, A. (1984). *European foreign policy-making and the Arab-Israeli conflict.* The Hague: Martinus Nijhoff Publishers.
Azarova, V. (2018). The secret life of non-recognition: EU-Israel Relations and the obligation of non-recognition in international law. *Global affairs 4*(1), 1–15.
Benraad, M. (2014). *France's fascination with Israel and Palestine.* European Council on Foreign Relations. Retrieved from http://www.ecfr.eu/article/commentary_frances_fascination_with_israel_and_palestine290
Bicchi, F. (2018). The debate about the occupation of Palestinian territories on UK campuses, from politicisation to re-writing the rules. *Global Affairs, 4*(1). doi:10.1080/23340460.2018.1507282
Bicchi, F., & Voltolini, B. (2018). Europe, the Green Line and the issue of the Israeli-Palestinian border: Closing the gap between discourse and practice? *Geopolitics, 23*(1), 124–146.
Bozo, F. (2012). *La Politique étrangère de la France depuis 1945.* Editions Flammarion.
Filiu, J.-P. (2009). François Mitterrand and the Palestinians: 1956–95. *Journal of Palestine Studies, 38*(2), 24–41.
Ghiles Meilhac, S. (2011). *Le CRIF. de la résistance juive à la tentation du lobby, de 1943 à nos jours.* Paris: Robert Laffont.
Gresh, A., & Aldeguer, H. (2017). *Un chant d'amour.* Paris: La Découverte.
Leveau, R. (2003). France's Arab policy. In C. L. Brown (Ed.), *Diplomacy in the Middle East: The international relations of regional and outside powers* (pp. 3–20). London/New York: I. B. Tauris.
Lovatt, H. (2016). *EU differentiation and the push for peace in Israel-Palestine.* London: ECFR. Retrieved from http://www.ecfr.eu/publications/summary/eu_differentiation_and_the_push_for_peace_in_israel_palestine7163
Lovatt, H., & Toaldo, M. (2015). *EU differentiation and Israeli settlements.* London: ECFR. Retrieved from http://www.ecfr.eu/publications/summary/eu_differentiation_and_israeli_settlements3076
Martins, M. (2018). Missing the train. International governance gaps and the Jerusalem Light Railway. *Global affairs 4*(1), 1–14.
Mayer, N. (2018, May 16). Antisémitisme, un état des lieux. *AOC - Analyse Opinion Critique.* Retrieved from https://aoc.media/analyse/2018/05/16/antisemitisme-etat-lieux
Miller, R. (2011). *Inglorious disarray: Europe, Israel and the Palestinians since 1967.* London: C Hurst & Co Publishers Ltd.
Müller, P. (2012). *EU foreign policymaking and the Middle East conflict: The Europeanization of national foreign policy.* London: Routledge.
Nikolov, K. Y. (2014). ASHTON's SECOND HAT: The EU funding guidelines on Israel as a post-Lisbon instrument of European foreign policy making. *Diplomacy, 11,* 168–188.
Nouzille, V. (2018). *Histoires secrètes. France-Israel, 1948–2018.* France: éditions Les Liens qui Libèrent.
Pouponneau, F. (2015). *La politique française de non-prolifération nucléaire. De la division du travail diplomatique.* Brussels: Peter Lang.

Schillo, F. (2008). *La politique française à l'égard d'israël, 1946–1959*. Paris: Institut d'études politiques, Paris.
Sieffert, D. (2004). *Israël-Palestine, une passion française*. Paris: La Découverte.
Vaïsse, M. (2009). La politique arabe. In Fayard (Ed.), *La puissance ou l'influence ?: La France dans le monde depuis 1958* (pp. 351–416). Paris: Fayard.

Germany and the Israeli Occupation: Torn Between Special Relationship and Two-State-Commitment

Jan Busse

ABSTRACT

Over time, Germany's stance towards the Israeli occupation settlement construction has become more critical. This article will show that one reason for this shift lies in a widening gap between German public opinion and government policies. Accordingly, while the German population has become more critical towards the occupation over time, the German government has only responded to this trend with certain delay. At the same time, however, as a crucial historical context, Germany's stance towards the occupation can only be understood if contextualized with the German special relationship with Israel. As this contribution will point out, the German government follows an interrelated strategy of Europeanization and legalization, which enables Germany to follow a critical stance towards Israel without questioning this special relationship. In this context, the article will not only deal with the German position on Israeli settlements and labelling but also with the different positions on a boycott of settlement products, also pointing to the shrinking spaces for an endorsement of a boycott.

Introduction

This article will show that, despite close ties towards the Israeli government, Germany's stance towards the occupation has become more critical over time. It will be demonstrated that one important reason for that lies in a widening gap between public opinion and government policies. Accordingly, while the German population has become more critical towards the occupation over time, the German government has only responded to this trend with certain delay. Crucially, however, there is growing awareness also among government officials that government policies need to become more responsive towards the German public. At the same time, however, it should not be underestimated that the spaces criticizing the Israeli occupation and asking for a boycott of settlement products or endorsing the Boycott – Divestment and Sanctions Movement are decreasing in Germany. Accordingly, as a crucial historical context, Germany's stance towards the occupation can only be understood if contextualized with the German special relationship with Israel (for a detailed analysis see Busse, 2012 and Asseburg & Busse, 2011). So, before turning to Germany's stance towards Israel's occupation of the Palestinian territories, some elaboration on this special relationship is appropriate. The German-Israeli special relationship is premised on the historic responsibility of Germany not only towards the Jewish people due atrocities perpetrated by Nazi Germany, but it is also extended to a responsibility to the State of Israel as the home of the Jewish people (see Gardner Feldman, 2012; Weingardt, 2002). In practice, this special relationship is translated into a German commitment for Israel's security, which can be witnessed, most prominently in the delivery of several German submarines to Israel, subsidized by the German government with hundreds of millions of Euros (Bergman et al., 2012; Nassauer, 2016). As these submarines are capable of launching Israeli nuclear missiles they are of utmost strategic importance for Israel as they guarantee a second-strike capability with considerable deterrent potential.

When, however, in 2011 Israel requested another submarine from Germany, the German government originally tried to condition the deal to Israeli concessions in the peace process with the Palestinians. For the German daily newspaper *Die Welt* this was a "radical change of course in German foreign policy" (Alexander & Wergin, 2011) as it was the first time that security-related issues were tied to political demands. After, however, the Israeli government was unwilling to compromise in this regard, in March 2012 Germany agreed to sign the official contract for the sixth submarine, incl'uding the willingness to again cover two thirds of the costs (Nassauer, 2016).

While this represents only an episode without tangible consequences, the incident should not be underestimated. On the one hand, it can be seen as a warning towards the Israeli government that, while not questioning the overall commitment to Israel's security, the German government ascribes great importance to the two-state solution. On the other hand, even though the German government eventually did not penalize Israel for settlement construction and a lack of progress in the peace process, these two cases show that Germany has gradually started to connect the previously separate dimensions of a commitment to Israel's security to the Israel-Palestine conflict.

Hence, this example illustrates the paper's argument that over time, it is possible to observe the emergence of a more critical German approach towards Israel concerning the occupation and settlement construction. At the same time, though, there is a trend of German policy-makers increasingly condemning or marginalizing positions being particularly critical of Israeli government policies, as exemplified by the Boycott – Divestment and Sanctions Movement. As a result, and combined with results of public opinion polls, it can be argued that there is a striking decoupling between the German government's and the German public's position towards the occupation. Accordingly, the observed increased criticism can, at least to a certain extent, be related to the growing gap between government policies and public opinion concerning the occupation.

While this article takes into account historically important instances of Germany's policies towards the occupation, it primarily focuses on the period since German re-unification when Germany has started to pursue a more active foreign policy (see e.g. Rittberger, 2001). It should be noted that overall, there is a great deal of continuity between the different government coalitions, regardless of the party affiliation. To some extent, however there are parallels between the approaches of the two last social-democratic Chancellors Schmidt and Schröder on the one hand and the last two Christian democratic ones Kohl and Merkel. In the case of Schmidt and Schröder, there was a certain individual detachment observable which was exemplified by the fact Chancellor Schmidt never visited Israel in office, while Schröder came to Israel only once. At the same time, both Schmidt and Schröder were primarily focused on fostering economic ties towards Arab countries. In the case of Schmidt, this was mainly due to the experiences of the energy crisis of the 1970s. It can be added that in Schröder's government, there was a division of labour between him and his foreign minister Joschka Fischer. While Schröder was mainly engaged in economic cooperation with Arab Gulf countries, Fischer was in charge of the Israel/Palestine portfolio. By contrast, Chancellors Kohl and Merkel rather highlighted the dimension of the special relationship towards Israel, and it was Merkel herself who has been in charge of shaping the policies towards the Israel-Palestine conflict (Asseburg & Busse, 2011; Busse, 2012; Gardner Feldman, 2012).

As this contribution will point out, the German government follows an interrelated strategy of Europeanization and legalization towards the Israel-Palestine conflict which enables Germany to follow a critical stance towards Israel without questioning the special relationship.[1] In other words, Europeanization and legalization serve as strategic foreign policy instruments that provide Germany with a justification for a harder stance towards Israel but at the same time upholding its commitment towards Israel. Strategic Europeanization means that Germany deliberately addresses criticism towards the occupation and settlement building via the European Union. In this sense, the Europeanization of national foreign policies as the result of European integration has equipped the German government with a means to address contentious issues in a way it rather refrains from in bilateral relations with Israel (see Müller, 2011).

At the same time, the strategy of Europeanization is accompanied by a strategy of legalization (Müller & Slominski, 2017). Accordingly, Germany attempts to address controversial points with reference to international or European law. Thereby, German foreign policy is rooted in a broader trend of the legalization of world politics (see e.g. Goldstein, Kahler, Keohane, & Slaughter, 2000) that also affects the way the international community deals with the Israel-Palestine conflict.

In order to develop the suggested line of argument, this article will proceed as follows. The next section will give an overview over Germany's position on Palestinian self-determination and the recognition of Palestine as a state. Subsequently, the article will deal with the German position on Israeli settlements, while the section that follows focuses on the government's stance on the issue of the labelling of products originating in Israeli settlements. This section is followed by a presentation of the different positions on a boycott of settlement products, also pointing to the shrinking spaces for an endorsement of a boycott. Thereafter, the paper will address the considerable gap between the German government's approach towards Israel and the occupation and public opinion. The conclusion will reflect on whether the observed change in rhetoric will also be followed by more tangible steps by the German government in order to condemn the occupation.

Germany, Palestinian self-determination, and the international recognition of Palestine

In accordance with the EU's position, the German approach towards the peace process rests on the insight that enduring peace in the region can best be achieved by a two-state settlement of the Israel-Palestine conflict. Germany's policies towards the Palestinian

Authority need not only to be contextualized with the Israel-Palestine conflict but also with the German-Israeli special relationship. While this special relationship can often be interpreted as an obstacle for a more critical approach towards Israel, it also leads to Germany initiating certain balancing measures towards the Palestinians. Namely, when Germany and Israel decided to hold joint cabinet meetings on a regular basis to deepen the bilateral relations on multiple levels, subsequently the German government established a similar format with the Palestinian Authority. Initiated in 2010, and meant to acknowledge Palestinian progress in state- and institution building, the German-Palestinian Steering Committee is dedicated to coordinating the German support for the PA in different fields. Since its inception this format has meet on a bi-annual basis, the last time in October 2016. Moreover, Germany is one of the greatest international donors to Palestine. In 2016, German bi-lateral aid amounted to a total of about € 154 million (Auswärtiges Amt, 2016, 2017).[2]

In accordance with other EU countries, the German government is especially concerned about the dire humanitarian situation for the Palestinian population in "Area C" of the West Bank where the Israeli army maintains full administrative and security control and where the Israeli settlements are located. As a response to the humanitarian misery, Germany and other European states have started supporting projects despite Israeli legal restrictions on building in Area C, leading to demolition orders issued by the Israeli Army and possible destruction (Bundestag, 2012a).

The German positions concerning Palestinian self-determination and the international recognition of Palestine developed in close interaction with the European level.[3] In 1980, West Germany supported the European Community's Venice Declaration which recognized the Palestinian right to self-determination (European Community, 1980). As government archives show, on the one hand, Germany was responsible for including a clear condemnation of the Israeli settlement policy that had been intensified ever since Likud Prime Minister Menachem Begin assumed office in 1977 (Leber, 2015: fn. 75). On the other hand, Germany prevented both the European Community endorsing the creation of an independent Palestinian state and a European call for an explicit "participation" of the Palestine Liberation Organization (PLO) in peace negotiations instead of a mere "association" of the PLO as stipulated in the final document (Leber, 2015: fn. 72). At the same time, however, as Hubert Leber (2015) shows, the German government possessed a leading role regarding the promotion of the Palestinian right to self-determination. Accordingly, already in 1974, despite an eventual abstention in the vote, the German government supported Palestinian self-determination in the context of the United Nations General Assembly which included this principle in resolution 3236 (Leber, 2015: fn. 77). Moreover, Leber stresses that already since 1978, German Chancellor Schmidt publicly not only supported the Palestinian right to self-determination but also the Palestinians' "right to organize in a state-like manner" (quoted from Leber, 2015). Thus, Schmidt represented a position that only emerged as common position of European and German policy about twenty years later.

As part of the European position, Germany supported the Oslo peace process. In this context, in 1994, Germany was the first western country to establish a diplomatic representative office in the Palestinian territories. The interconnectedness of German and EU policies can be witnessed in the Berlin Declaration of 1999 adopted during the German presidency of the European Council, which for the first time in a formal EU document explicitly acknowledged the "Palestinian right to self-determination including the option of a state (…)". The EU further declared "its readiness to consider the recognition of a Palestinian State in due course" (European Council, 1999, p. 24).

The Council Conclusions of December 2009 picked up the Berlin Declaration's qualified commitment to Palestinian independence by stating that the EU "Council also reiterates its support for negotiations leading to Palestinian statehood, all efforts and steps to that end and its readiness, when appropriate, to recognise a Palestinian state" (Council of the European Union, 2009, p. 2).

Chancellor Merkel rejected the Palestinian initiative for full UN membership in September 2011 and described it as a unilateral step that is unhelpful for advancing the peace process. Accordingly, the German government supported Israel in averting a Security Council vote supportive of Palestinian UN membership. The Israeli decision to approve 1,000 housing units in East Jerusalem right in the aftermath of the averted vote caused an "unprecedented diplomatic crisis" (Ravid, 2011) between Israel and Germany. According to Haaretz, Merkel was furious, in particular because she expected Israel after the averted vote to take trust-building measures towards the Palestinians instead of settlement expansion.

When in November 2012 the UN General Assembly granted Palestine the status of "non-member observer state", the German abstention took Israel's government by surprise, as it was expected that Germany voted against it as it has done in previous cases. In the aftermath of the UN vote, Foreign Minister Westerwelle described the German abstention as a carefully considered and balanced decision that takes into account both the legitimate Palestinian demands for independent statehood as well as Germany's special responsible towards Israel (Brössler, 2012).

The German position on settlements

The EU's policy of differentiation between the internationally recognized territory of Israel and the territories occupied in the June war of 1967 has become a central element of the EU's approach towards Israel related to the non-recognition of Israeli settlements (Lovatt, 2016; Lovatt & Toaldo, 2015; Müller & Slominski, 2017). Germany's position towards Israeli settlements clearly corresponds to the EU's approach, which emphasizes the illegality of the settlements according to international law. This can already be seen at a time when the principle of differentiation has not been spelled out as such, as for instance in the context of the German-Israeli cooperation in the field of science. Already in 1986, the founding agreement for the establishment of the German-Israeli Foundation for Scientific Research and Development (GIF) stipulates that "[p]rojects sponsored by the Foundation in Israel shall be conducted only within the geographic areas which were under the jurisdiction of the State of Israel prior to June 5, 1967" (GIF, 1986). The German government again raised the topic of science cooperation in the context of the EU's negotiations to allow Israel access to Horizon 2020 grants for research projects. In this regard, following the EU's stance, in January 2014, Germany expressed the intention to condition similar bilateral grants to a territorial clause which exclude funding for institutions located in Israeli settlements. This move can also be seen as a response to the upgrading of a college in the settlement of Ariel to the status of university (Ravid, 2014).

Especially since Prime Minister Netanyahu has assumed office in 2009, Israel's ongoing settlement activities negatively impacted the bilateral relations with Germany. After Netanyahu took office, Germany postponed the second round of German-Israeli intergovernmental consultations, originally scheduled for 2009 (Der Spiegel, 2009). In addition, on the occasion of the second and third German-Israeli joint cabinet meetings in March 2010 and January 2011 respectively, Merkel criticized – with unusual explicitness – Israeli settlement activities in the West Bank and East Jerusalem as an obstacle to peace (Federal Government, 2010, 2011). Moreover, in February 2017 the German government cancelled the government consultations as a reaction to Israel's ongoing settlement policy. In particular, the cancellation can be related to Germany's disapproval of the passing of the so-called "Land-Grab-Law" in the Knesset, which retroactively legalizes settlement outposts in the occupied territories built on private Palestinian land. The German Foreign Ministry's spokesperson condemned this move in explicit terms, stating that Germany's "trust in the Israeli government's commitment to the two-state solution has been fundamentally shaken" (quoted in Ravid, 2017).

The German government's stance on labelling settlement products

The EU expresses the policy of differentiation most explicitly in two Council conclusions of 2012. In the May 2012 conclusions, the EU states its "commitment to fully and effectively implement existing EU legislation and the bilateral arrangements applicable to settlement products" (Council of the European Union, 2012a, p. 2), while in the December 2012 conclusions the EU highlights that "all agreements between the State of Israel and the European Union must unequivocally and explicitly indicate their inapplicability to the territories occupied by Israel in 1967" (Council of the European Union, 2012b, p. 2). What is remarkable in this regard is that Germany not only accepted these two Council conclusions and shares the policy of differentiation, but, as Foreign Ministry's Minister of State Michael Link publicly declared in the Bundestag, the German government played a leading role in drafting the Council Conclusions of May 2012 (Bundestag, 2012b, p. 9).[4]

In line with the policy of differentiation, in May 2013, the German government clarified its position regarding the labelling of settlement products from the occupied West Bank in an official answer to a parliamentary interpellation from the Green party. The government stated that it considers the label "Made in Israel" only admissible for products originating in Israel within the borders before 1967. In addition, the government clarifies that "Germany implements stipulations of EU legislation" (Bundestag, 2013, p. 3, own translation).

In November 2015, the European Commission issued guidelines for the labelling of products from Israeli settlements. This interpretative notice clearly states that settlement products need to be unequivocally identifiable as originating in an Israeli settlement. Hence, "[e]ven if [products from the West Bank or Golan Heights] would designate the wider area or territory from which the product originates, the omission of the additional geographical information that the product comes from Israeli settlements would mislead the consumer as to the true origin of the product. In such cases the expression 'Israeli settlement' or equivalent needs to be added (…)" (European Commission, 2015, p. 4). According to the Jerusalem Post, both the Federal Foreign Office as well as the Chancellery expressed their support concerning the EU's decision towards the newspaper (Weinthal et al., 2015).

Related to the issue of labelling of settlement products, three aspects of the German government's position are worth highlighting. First, besides repeating that the settlements violate against international law, the German government framed its position regarding settlement products with explicit reference to existing EU legislation. Second, the German position expresses the policy of differentiation between Israel and the illegal settlements, which has been made explicit in particular in the Council Conclusions of May 2012. At the same time, in the German government's position another important element of the policy of differentiation comes up. Accordingly, the German government emphasizes that it rejects boycotts, and that the debate about labelling settlement products does not equal a debate about boycotting Israel. In a similar language, the EU Foreign Affairs Council of January 2016 makes this distinction and clarifies that the differentiation between the State of Israel in the borders before 1967 and the occupied territories "does not constitute a boycott of Israel which the EU strongly opposes" (Council of the European Union, 2016). Third, and remarkably, in line with the EU's approach, the German government frames the potentially contentious issue of labelling settlement products with reference to consumer protection, thereby attempting to depoliticise it.

The debate about boycotting settlement products in Germany

While among the German political establishment already the labelling of settlement products is a controversial issue, numerous politicians explicitly reject both a differentiated boycott of settlement products and the Boycott, Divestment and Sanctions (BDS) movement. Moreover, contrary to the situation in other countries such as the UK (Bicchi, 2018), initiatives attempting to put forward these issues are often confronted with considerable public opposition. In several cases, events critical of the Israeli occupation or including BDS-supporters as participants had to be cancelled after criticism from civil society organizations and politicians who oppose BDS (Frank, 2016; Weinthal, 2017). In one case, a bank temporarily closed the account of an NGO which supports a boycott (Bax, 2016).

At the same time, however, and in line with the policy of legalization, the German Foreign Office informs potential German companies interested in investing in Israel about "considerable risks associated with economic and financial activities in and for the benefit of settlements" (Federal Foreign Office, 2017). In addition, the Foreign Office also highlights that "German companies and private individuals should also be aware of the reputational risks associated with economic and financial activities in and for the benefit of settlements. The Federal Government further points to potential violations of international humanitarian law and human rights conventions in connection with settlements in the occupied territories" (Federal Foreign Office, 2017).

German government vs. public opinion?

It is striking that the German population does not share the government's commitment and the special responsibility towards Israel in the same way. Opinion polls clearly show that the majority of the population considers the German government displays a bias in favour of Israel (ADL Survey, 2007). The German attitude towards Israel has continuously worsened in recent years (Stern, 2009, 2012, 2014). For instance, in contrast to the German government, only one third of the population acknowledged a special responsibility of Germany towards Israel in 2012, whereas 60 percent do not see such a responsibility any longer. Related, in April 2017, only 21 percent of the German citizenry believed that Germany should show restraint regarding the condemnation of Israel's settlement policy because of the special relationship towards Israel. Both in 2012 and in 2017 a majority of about 65 percent favoured a German recognition of Palestine as an independent state (Stern, 2012, 2017).

The above mentioned polls point to a striking discrepancy between the German government's approach towards the Israel-Palestine conflict and the German public opinion. While this decoupling has been existent for years, Germany's foreign policy could become more responsive to the views of the population. In this regard, in an interview with the German weekly magazine Der Spiegel, Avi Dichter, chairman of the Knesset's foreign affairs committee reported about a meeting with Foreign Minister Gabriel in March 2017. According to Dichter, the Foreign Minister explained "that it was growing increasingly difficult for the political elite to defend justified Israeli interests because the German population was growing increasingly critical of Israel" (Schult, 2017).

At the same time, also on the government level, one can identify certain changes in the direction of a harder line towards Israel. In April 2016, Rolf Mützenich, deputy chairman of the social-democratic parliamentary group in the Bundestag, emphasized the growing concern towards Israel: "The perception has been growing in the German government that Netanyahu is instrumentalizing our friendship" (quoted in Neukirch & Schult, 2016). According to Mützenich "it would be a welcome change if the Foreign Ministry and the Chancellery were to rethink the relationship with Israel" (Neukirch & Schult, 2016).

The growing tensions erupted publicly during a visit of German foreign minister Sigmar Gabriel to Israel in April 2017. Besides planned meetings with Israeli officials, Gabriel intended to meet the human rights NGOs "Breaking the Silence" and "B'Tselem" which are both critical of Israeli policies in the occupied territories. Netanyahu, who also serves as acting foreign minister and thus as Gabriel's Israeli counterpart, disapproved Gabriel's plans to meet these two NGOs and made a meeting with the German minister conditional on their cancelation. After Netanyahu's ultimatum, the German foreign minister made publicly clear that he considers it a normal procedure during foreign diplomatic visits to also meet civil society representatives. To de-escalate the situation, Gabriel suggested that there would be neither photos nor public statements from the meeting. The public controversy increased when Netanyahu claimed that Gabriel was unwilling to hold a telephone conversation with him on this issue. According to the German side, however, Netanyahu only wanted to speak to him if Gabriel also accepted to meet pro-government groups which he rejected. In the end, Gabriel did not succumb to the pressure and met the NGOs, to which Netanyahu reacted with the cancellation of the scheduled meeting as threatened (Braun & Roßmann, 2017; Fras, 2017). Remarkably, in the aftermath of this diplomatic stir, Chancellor Merkel publicly endorsed Gabriel's stance. Her spokesperson stated that the German government "is of the opinion that is has to be possible in a democratic country to also meet critical NGOs without leading to such consequences" (quoted in Braun & Roßmann, 2017).

Conclusion: towards a harder approach?

Referring to the issues of Palestinian recognition, Israeli settlements, labelling of settlement products and the debate about boycotting them, this article has tried to show a growing trend towards a more critical approach of the German government's policies towards Israel's occupation. It has been argued that the reason for this can be related to the German government becoming more responsive to public opinion where a more critical stance has been increasing for years. At the same time, this article has highlighted that the above mentioned developments need to be contextualized with the historical background of Germany's special relationship towards Israel as it represents an important pillar of the overall German approach towards the Israel-Palestine conflict. The article pointed out that the strategies of Europeanization and legalization have been important means for Germany to formulate more critical positions towards the Israeli occupation without questioning its overall commitment which is rooted in the historic responsibility towards the state of Israel.

Taken together, there are certain indications that Israeli Prime Minister Netanyahu's intransigence related to the ongoing settlement expansion that make a two-state solution increasingly unlikely, also contribute to a decreasing reluctance to formulate more critical positions in relation to the occupation on the German side. The recent change in the Federal Foreign Office, however, points to a softening tone towards the Israeli government, at least on a declaratory level. While Foreign Minister Gabriel did not shy away from criticizing Israeli settlement policies and the occupation, his successor Heiko Maas, also a social democrat, seems to be eager to maintain positive relations in the light of Germany's historic responsibility towards Israel. Thus far, he has also been less critical towards the Netanyahu's right-wing government, illustrated, for instance, by what he describes as personal friendship with Israeli Minister of Justice Ayelet Shaket, who is an advocate of settlement expansion and who repeatedly expressed racist views towards Arabs. Moreover, during his first visit to Israel as Foreign Minister, his assessment of the Israel-Palestine conflict remained very close to the position of the Israeli government (Frehse, 2018). Regardless of this apparent change of tone, however, Germany continues to adhere to a legalistic and Europeanized strategy, which makes it unlikely that the German government will withdraw from its previously stated positions. Rather, the crucial question will be to what extent the observable overall shift in rhetoric will also translate into more critical tangible political decisions. In this context, though, the European level shows that Germany, for instance as a firm supporter of the policy of differentiation, is willing to undertake such stakes steps, however certainly not in a leading position.

Notes

1. Azarova (2018) and Lynk (2018) provide detailed engagements with the overall importance of international law concerning the occupation.
2. For an overview over EU development aid to the OPT see Wildeman (2018).
3. Eriksson (2018) discusses the Swedish recognition of Palestine.
4. Voltolini (2018) addresses the differentiation debate in France.

Disclosure statement

No potential conflict of interest was reported by the author.

References

ADL Survey. (2007, May). *Attitudes toward jews and the Middle East in five European countries.* Retrieved from www.adl.org/anti_semitism/European_Attitudes_Survey_May_2007.pdf

Alexander, R., & Wergin, C. (2011, April 12). So lief Kanzlerin Merkels U-boot-deal mit Israel. *Welt Online.* Retrieved from http://www.welt.de/politik/ausland/article13749068/So-lief-Kanzlerin-Merkels-U-Boot-Deal-mit-Israel.html

Asseburg, M., & Busse, J. (2011). Deutschlands Politik gegenüber Israel. In T. Jäger, A. Höse, & K. Oppermann (Eds.), *Deutsche Außenpolitik* (pp. 693–716). Second revised and extended edition. Wiesbaden: VS Verlag für Sozialwissenschaften.

Auswärtiges Amt. (2016, October 26). *Vierte Sitzung des Deutsch-Palästinensischen Lenkungsausschusses.* Press Release. Retrieved from https://www.auswaertiges-amt.de/DE/Aussenpolitik/Laender/Aktuelle_Artikel/PalaestinensischeGebiete/161026-D-PAL_Lenkungsausschuss.html

Auswärtiges Amt. (2017). *Hilfe für Palästina.* Retrieved from https://www.auswaertiges-amt.de/DE/Aussenpolitik/RegionaleSchwerpunkte/NaherMittlererOsten/01_KonfliktNahost/ZukunftPalaestina/Uebersicht_node.html

Azarova, V. (2018). The secret life of non-recognition: EU-Israel relations and the obligation of non-recognition in international law. *Global Affairs.* doi:10.1080/23340460.2018.1507278

Bax, D. (2016, December 23). BDS-Unterstützer ohne Bankkonto: Wegen Boykottaufruf gekündigt. *die tageszeitung.* Retrieved from https://www.taz.de/!5366334/

Bergman, R., Follath, E., Keinan, E., Nassauer, O., Schmitt, J., Stark, H., ... Wiegrefe, K. (2012). Made in Germany: Wie Deutschland die Atommacht Israel aufrüstet. *Der Spiegel* (23/2012), pp. 20–33.

Bicchi, F. (2018). The debate about the occupation of Palestinian territories on UK campuses, from politicization to re-writing the rules. *Global Affairs.* doi:10.1080/23340460.2018.1507282

Braun, S., & Roßmann, R. (2017, April 26). Wie es zum Eklat mit Israel kommen konnte. *sueddeutsche.de.* Retrieved from http://www.sueddeutsche.de/politik/abgesagtes-treffen-wie-es-zum-eklat-mit-israel-kommen-konnte-1.3479399

Brössler, D. (2012, November 30). Die Haltung hinter der Enthaltung; Westerwelle erklärt die deutsche Antwort auf den UN-Antrag der Palästinenser. *Süddeutsche Zeitung,* p. 9.

Bundestag. (2012a, April 5). *Antwort der Bundesregierung auf die Kleine Anfrage der Bundestagsfraktion Die Linke.* (Drucksache 17/9289). Retrieved from http://dipbt.bundestag.de/dip21/btd/17/092/1709289.pdf

Bundestag. (2012b, July 13). *Schriftliche Fragen mit den in der Woche vom 9. Juli 2012 eingegangenen Antworten der Bundesregierung.* (Drucksache 17/10305). Retrieved from http://dipbt.bundestag.de/doc/btd/17/103/1710305.pdf

Bundestag. (2013, May 15). *Importe von Produkten aus israelischen Siedlungen in der Westbank in die Europäische Union und nach Deutschland.* (Antwort der Bundesregierung auf die Kleine Anfrage der Grünen Brundestagsfraktion (Drucksache 17/13511). Retrieved from http://dipbt.bundestag.de/dip21/btd/17/135/1713511.pdf

Busse, J. (2012). Continuity and change: Deconstructing German foreign policy toward the Middle East conflict. In E. Ratka & O. Spaiser (Eds.), *Understanding European neighbourhood policies: Concepts, actors, perceptions* (pp. 141–155). Baden-Baden: Nomos.

Council of the European Union. (2009, December 8). *Council conclusions on the Middle East peace process* (2985th Foreign Affairs Council meeting) Brussels. Retrieved from http://www.europarl.europa.eu/meetdocs/2009_2014/documents/wgme/dv/200/200912/20091216councilcon081209_en.pdf

Council of the European Union. (2012a, May 14). *Council conclusions on the Middle East peace process* (3166th Foreign Affairs Council meeting) Brussels. Retrieved from http://www.consilium.europa.eu/uedocs/cms_Data/docs/pressdata/EN/foraff/130195.pdf

Council of the European Union. (2012b, December 10). *Council conclusions on the Middle East peace process* (3209th Foreign Affairs Council meeting) Brussels. Retrieved from http://www.consilium.europa.eu/uedocs/cms_Data/docs/pressdata/EN/foraff/134140.pdf

Council of the European Union. (2016, January 18). *Council conclusions on the Middle East peace process* (3443th Foreign Affairs Council meeting) Brussels. Retrieved from http://www.consilium.europa.eu/en/press/press-releases/2016/01/18-fac-conclusions-mepp/

Der Spiegel. (2009, April 6). *Diplomatische Kritik.* p. 22.

Eriksson, J. (2018). Swedish recognition of Palestine: Politics, law, and prospects for peace. *Global Affairs*. doi:10.1080/23340460.2018.1507279

European Commission. (2015, November 11). *Interpretative notice on indication of origin of goods from the territories occupied by Israel since June 1967.* Brussels. Retrieved from http://www.eeas.europa.eu/delegations/israel/documents/news/20151111_interpretative_notice_indication_of_origin_of_goods_en.pdf

European Community. (1980, June 13). *Venice declaration.* Venice. Retrieved from http://eeas.europa.eu/mepp/docs/venice_declaration_1980_en.pdf

European Council. (1999). *Presidency Conclusions: Berlin European Council.* D/99/1. Berlin. Retrieved from http://ec.europa.eu/regional_policy/sources/docoffic/official/regulation/pdf/berlin_en.pdf

Federal Foreign Office. (2017). *Israel: Economic relations.* Retrieved from https://www.auswaertiges-amt.de/EN/Aussenpolitik/Laender/Laenderinfos/01-Laender/Israel.html?nnm=479780#doc472758bodyText2

Federal Government. (2010, March 15). *Middle East peace process in jeopardy.* Press Release. Retrieved from www.bundeskanzlerin.de/nn_704412/Content/EN/Artikel/2010/03/2010-03-15-hariri-bkin-libanon__en.html

Federal Government. (2011, March 31). *Pressekonferenz Bundeskanzlerin Merkel und Ministerpräsident Netanyahu.* Jerusalem. Retrieved from www.bundeskanzlerin.de/Content/DE/Mitschrift/Pressekonferenzen/2011/01/2011-01-31-deutsch-israelische-regkonsultationen.html.

Frank, J. (2016, December 9). Jüdischer Kongress: Israel-Botschafter kritisiert "breaking the silence". *Kölner Stadt-Anzeiger.* Retrieved from http://www.ksta.de/politik/juedischer-kongress--israel-botschafter-kritisiert--breaking--the-silence--24718574

Fras, D. (2017, April 25). Israel-Besuch: Netanjahu sagt Treffen mit Gabriel ab. *Frankfurter Rundschau.* Retrieved from http://www.fr.de/politik/israel-besuch-netanjahu-sagt-treffen-mit-gabriel-ab-a-1266775

Frehse, L. (2018, March 27). Heiko Maas: Eine Reise mit vielen Botschaftern. *Die Zeit.* Retrieved from https://www.zeit.de/politik/ausland/2018-03/heiko-maas-israel-analyse-botschaften

Gardner Feldman, L. (2012). *Germany's foreign policy of reconciliation.* Lanham, MD: Rowman & Littlefield.

GIF. (1986). *Agreement between the Federal Minister for Research and Technology of the Federal Republic of Germany and the Minister of Science and Development of the State of Israel on the Establishment of a Foundation for Scientific Research and Development.* Retrieved from http://www.gif.org.il/SiteAssets/Agreement%20on%20the%20Establishment%20of%20GIF.pdf

Goldstein, J., Kahler, M., Keohane, R. O., & Slaughter, A-M. (2000). Introduction: Legalization and world politics. *International Organization*, 54(3), 385–399.

Leber, H. (2015). Chancellor Helmut Schmidt, his policy toward Israel, and the German responsibility for the jewish people. *American Institute for Contemporary German Studies.* Retrieved from http://www.aicgs.org/publication/chancellor-helmut-schmidt-his-policy-toward-israel-and-the-german-responsibility-for-the-jewish-people

Lovatt, H. (2016). EU differentiation and the push for peace in Israel-Palestine. *ECRF Policy Brief*. Retrieved from http://ecfr.eu/page/-/ECFR_194_-_EU_DIFFERENTIATION_AND_THE_PUSH_FOR_PEACE_IN_ISRAEL-PALESTINE_%281%29.pdf

Lovatt, H., & Toaldo, M. (2015). EU differentiation and Israeli settlements. *ECRF Policy Brief*. Retrieved from http://ecfr.eu/page/-/EuDifferentiation-final3.pdf

Lynk, M. (2018). The challenge for Europe: Making international law work for Middle East peace. *Global Affairs*. doi:10.1080/23340460.2018.1507275

Müller, P. (2011). The Europeanization of Germany's foreign policy toward the Israeli–Palestinian conflict: Between adaptation to the EU and national projection. *Mediterranean Politics* 16 (3), 385–403.

Müller, P. & Slominski, P. (2017). The role of Law in EU foreign policy-making: Legal integrity, legal spillover, and the EU policy of differentiation towards Israel. *JCMS: Journal of Common Market Studies* 55 (4), 871–888.

Nassauer, O. (2016, October 21). *Weitere U-Boote für Israel?* Berlin Information Center for Transatlantic Security. Retrieved from http://www.bits.de/public/unv_a/orginal-211016.htm

Neukirch, R., & Schult, C. (2016, April 29). Foreign policy shift: Skepticism of German-Israeli friendship growing in Berlin. *SPIEGEL ONLINE*. Retrieved from http://www.spiegel.de/international/world/germany-begins-to-look-critically-at-support-for-israel-a-1090044.html

Ravid, B. (2011, February 2). Israel and Germany in unprecedented diplomatic crisis over Jerusalem construction. *Haaretz*. Retrieved from http://www.haaretz.com/print-edition/news/israel-and-germany-in-unprecedented-diplomatic-crisis-over-jerusalem-construction-1.387572

Ravid, B. (2014, January 23). Germany conditions high-tech, science grants on settlement funding ban. *Haaretz*. Retrieved from http://www.haaretz.com/news/diplomacy-defense/.premium-1.570071

Ravid, B. (2017, February 13). Germany's Merkel Cancels summit with Israel in wake of Palestinian land-grab law. *Haaretz*. Retrieved from http://www.haaretz.com/israel-news/1.771426

Rittberger, V. (Ed.) (2001). *German foreign policy since unification: Theories and case studies*. Manchester: Manchester University Press.

Schult, C. (2017, April 28). Eroding friendship: German-Israeli relations take a turn for the worse. *SPIEGEL ONLINE*. Retrieved from http://www.spiegel.de/international/germany/german-israeli-relations-take-turn-for-the-worse-a-1145297.html

Stern. (2009, January 14). Umfrage: Jeder Zweite nennt Israel 'aggressiv'. *Stern*. Retrieved from www.stern.de/politik/deutschland/stern-umfrage-jeder-zweite-nennt-israel-aggressiv-651466.html

Stern. (2012, May 23). Israel verliert bei den Deutschen an Ansehen. *Stern*. Retrieved from http://www.stern.de/politik/deutschland/stern-umfrage-israel-verliert-bei-den-deutschen-an-ansehen-1830648.html

Stern. (2014, July 16). Deutsche geben Israel eine Mitschuld am Nahost-Konflikt. *stern.de*. Retrieved from: http://www.stern.de/politik/ausland/stern-umfrage-deutsche-geben-israel-eine-mitschuld-am-nahost-konflikt-2124202.html

Stern. (2017, May 3). Kritik an Israel darf sein. *stern.de*. Retrieved from http://www.stern.de/7435842.html

Voltolini, B. (2018). France and the Israeli occupation: Talking the talk, but not walking the walk? *Global Affairs*. doi:10.1080/23340460.2018.1507286

Weingardt, M. A. (2002). *Deutsche Israel- und Nahostpolitik: Die Geschichte einer Gratwanderung seit 1949*. Frankfurt: Campus.

Weinthal, B., et al. (2015, July 12). Merkel's government announces support for EU labeling of settlement products. *The Jerusalem Post*. Retrieved from: http://www.jpost.com/Israel-News/Politics-And-Diplomacy/Merkels-government-announces-support-for-EU-labeling-of-settlement-products-436579

Weinthal, B. (2017, March 21). German BDS events canceled in Frankfurt and Bonn. *The Jerusalem Post*. Retrieved from http://www.jpost.com/Diaspora/German-BDS-events-canceled-in-Frankfurt-and-Bonn-484735

Wilderman, J. (2018). EU Development aid in the occupied Palestinian territory, between aid effectiveness and World Bank guidance. *Global Affairs*. doi:10.1080/23340460.2018.1507285

The debate about the occupation of Palestinian territories on UK campuses: from politicisation to re-writing the rules

Federica Bicchi

ABSTRACT
This paper traces the evolution of the debate on UK campuses since 2001 and shows how in the UK the occupation of Palestinian territories has become more a matter of domestic politics than an issue of foreign policy. It argues that the collapse of diplomatic processes in 2001 and 9/11 contributed to spark a (re)politicization of debates about the occupation on UK campuses, ignited predominantly by the Boycott Divestment and Sanction (BDS) movement and centred on what citizens in the UK should do. The process then evolved into a partial securitization of the discussion, entailing emergency and law-based measures, as groups countering BDS made use of new (and unrelated) rules introduced by the British government in 2011 to fight radicalization. As a consequence, not only the conflict has been transposed into UK domestic politics, but also the debate on UK campuses contributes to define who has the right to say what in the UK in relation to the occupation.

Introduction

The unifying characteristic of contemporary discourses in the UK about the Israeli occupation of the Palestinian territory is that they tend to have a largely domestic focus, rather than centre on British foreign policy. This is particularly visible in the evolution of debates on UK campuses, which will be examined here. From a call in 2002 for an academic boycott of Israeli universities to the later emergence of the international BDS movement, actions on campuses contributed to the politicization of the discussion in the UK with an emphasis on how domestic non-governmental actors should relate to the occupation. When new (and unrelated) rules against radicalization on campus were introduced in 2011, the discussion turned towards becoming a security matter, involving emergency measures and domestic security providers. Therefore, as diplomatic processes grounded to a halt in 2001 on the back of the Second Intifada and 9/11, part of the conflict moved to debates on UK campuses.

The UK's history of involvement with the conflict is long, but the strength, focus and influence of its foreign policy have diminished with time. The British Mandate over Palestine occurred during Britain's "moment" in the Middle East (Monroe, 1981, p. 342), when it was able to frame in legal terms the content of the Balfour Declaration of 1917 (Shlaim, 2005). However, the disorderly withdrawal from Palestine in 1947–48 and the retreat from East of Suez busted the "interwar illusion of hegemony" (Brown, 1984, p. 122; McCourt, 2009), while more generally the post-imperial legacy pointed to a diminished "junior" role for the UK in the area (Levey & Podeh, 2008), suiting "just a trading nation" (Mangold, 2016).

Therefore, especially since the Suez crisis in 1956, British foreign policy on the conflict has been mostly confined to an indirect role, supporting the US as well as European unity in the search for the elusive peace (Edwards, 1984). As time passed, the emphasis shifted from the latter to the former. While during the 1980s and 1990s "Britain was considered a bridge-builder *within* Europe" on the issue, from 2001 it "was more likely to be found trying to straddle the divide between Washington" and continental Europe (Hollis, 2010, pp. 135–36). While Prime Minister, Tony Blair was active, particularly in parallel to the invasion of Iraq, no real initiative has been launched by the UK after the London conference organized in March 2005, apart from regular gatherings aimed at aid coordination.

Debates inside the UK about the occupation have not abated, though. On the contrary, it is the main contention here that since the collapse of diplomatic talks in 2001 and in concomitance with discussions about 9/11, debates in the UK have become a key venue for the conflict, calling into question the attitude not only of the British government, but also and especially of non-governmental actors and private citizens in relation to the occupation. Rather than a discussion to keep the government accountable for its foreign policy, debates have become more personal and passionate, but equally political and public. While discussions about the conflict within the UK are nothing new, what is new is the characterization of the conflict and of the occupation as something that directly and personally interrogates actors in British society. This characterization was particularly visible in the run-up to the centenary of the Balfour Declaration and it was captured in the commonalities between 1) the proudness with which the anniversary should be celebrated according to the Prime Minister Theresa May,[1] 2) the "neither celebrate nor condemn" position of her Under-Secretary of State for the Middle East, Tobias Ellwood, and 3) the request by the Palestinian Authority echoed by activists in the UK to issue an apology for the unfinished business. In all cases, the debate's focus was on the attitude of British citizens in relation to the anniversary, rather than the UK's international responsibility for it and its future foreign policy actions.

The transposition of the conflict lines onto debates in UK campuses occurred in two steps: the BDS campaign contributed to the (re)politicization of debates about the occupation with an emphasis on domestic action, while groups countering BDS contributed to the partial securitization of debates and the questioning of rules for academic debates. I am embracing a definition of politicization as "making a matter a subject of public discussion" (Zürn, 2014, p. 48), thus bringing an issue into the public sphere and making it something that is decided upon, that entails choice and responsibility. The Israeli-Palestinian conflict has gone through a number of stages in the British public sphere, with attention at times wavering, but 2001 marked a re-politicization of the debate. Securitization, for its part, means that an issue is presented as a threat, requiring emergency measures and justifying actions outside the normal bounds of procedure (cf. Buzan, 1991; Buzan, Wæver, & de Wilde, 1998). The use of emergency rules has become a feature of how debates have been handled on UK campuses, especially since 2011 when the government introduced new and largely unrelated legislation targeting radicalization in universities. Therefore, the emphasis on UK campuses has shifted from using existing rules to debate action related to the occupation (politicization), to questioning existing rules through the use of judicial processes and investigations (securitization).

It would be tempting to suggest that this trajectory is a case of "lawfare," defined as the strategy of using law as a weapon of war (Cohen & Freilich, 2018; Kittrie, 2016). However, specific instances of lawfare in this story have been part of a broader evolution and have occurred only following the UK government's reform of rules for academic debates, which provided an opportunity to shift the focus of the discussion to the rules of the debate itself. Moreover, this is not a case of "purely domestic" influence over an international issue. The re-politicization of the debate occurred also because of the international BDS movement, while Israel has become increasingly involved in helping the organization of anti-BDS activities in the UK.[2] In a dynamic that also marks other European countries (see Busse, Pace and Voltolini in this special issue), this evolution shows the tension between domestic actors within the UK, with civil society being particularly pro-active.

The Arab-Israeli conflict has always been present to a degree in students' politics and campuses are indeed "ideological breeding grounds for political experiments" (Schleifer, 2016, p. 212), on this topic and in general. The key point here is that with the collapse of diplomatic processes in 2002 the debate on this topic on UK campuses was revived as a way to address the *domestic* issue of what should people and institutions (and academia in particular) do in relation to the Israeli-Palestinian conflict. This occurred at first through political means (2002–2011), and then through more security and law-related measures (after 2011). The article analyses these two stages in turn.

The (re-)politicization of the debate on campus

The first sign that the debate on the Israeli-Palestinian conflict was changing came in 2002 when a number of UK-based academics called for a boycott of Israeli universities.[3] The call asked for a moratorium on grants allocated to Israeli universities by the EU[4] and by the European Science Foundation until Israel were to comply with the relevant UN resolutions.[5] This call was followed by an open letter in which academic signatories announced their refusal to cooperate *tout court* with Israeli institutions, and with Israeli universities in particular (but excluded Israeli individuals).[6] However, the outcome of the 2002 call was mixed.[7]

The campaign for an academic boycott gathered new steam as the international BDS movement, which emerged in 2005, made it into one of its main initiatives,[8] and reached out to non-governmental actors across the globe. The BDS movement,[9] which advocates a number of general goals,[10] justified the academic boycott as a way to protest against the complicity of Israeli academic institutions in supporting the occupation,[11] thus embracing the academic boycott sponsored by the Palestinian Campaign for the Academic and Cultural Boycott of Israel (PACBI, one of the founding members of BDS).[12] It quickly became "the most contentious of the BDS mechanisms" (McMahon, 2014, p., 71).

As the BDS movement spread across UK academia, groups were formed with the explicit goal to promote or resist it. Countless pro-Palestinian and pro-Israeli entities also took a (more or less explicit) stance. For instance, the British Committee for the Universities in Palestine (BRICUP)[13] and the Boycott Israel Network (BIN)[14] were created, among their aims the boycott of Israeli universities. Several groups organized their responses against the spread of BDS, including Engage[15] and Academic Friends of Israel.[16] The discussion of the academic boycott reverberated onto Israel, where it was often considered as posing a de-legitimation risk to the state of Israel and action was taken accordingly, both in law and available resources. Israel's President Rivlin, for instance, described the academic boycott as a "strategic threat of the first order."[17] The Israeli Ministry of Strategic Affairs has also made it part of its mission to address the challenges posed by the BDS movement.

The issue remained unsettled on UK campuses and was played out in a ritualized way, generally within a well-established repertoire of campus politics' instruments. Based on existing rules, resolutions were passed, actions agreed and then both would be challenged again. Dynamics in the association of UK university staff members, the University and College Union (UCU), were paradigmatic in this sense. In June 2007, it voted to support the boycott campaign, but after taking legal advice, it backtracked in September of the same year. The issue would not lie, though. Motions related to the academic boycott and BDS were tabled, discussed, passed or opposed at UCU annual Congress meetings in 2008–2011, before the issue landed in court, as next section analyses. Conflict in Gaza in 2009 provided new (and, according to some, decisive)[18] impetus to BDS, and thus to the debate. For instance, in January 2009 a group of British academics called for the British government and the British people to take all feasible steps "starting with a programme of boycott, divestment and sanctions."[19] The 2009 Gaza war sparked a wave of students' activism, including occupations,[20] on the backdrop of an endorsement of BDS by the Scottish Trade Union and then the British Trades Union.

The main innovation on traditional campus dynamics was probably represented by "Israel Apartheid Week," which was launched in Toronto in 2005[21] and spread to several UK campuses, where it became a major point not only for discussion about the Arab-Israeli conflict but increasingly of friction and confrontation.

The situation in the UK did not become as polarized as in the United States, where several academics were involved in e.g. voting in favour or against boycotts[22] and groups emerged, targeting university administrations (e.g. Abowd, 2014) or BDS narratives, such as AMCHA.[23] But discussions in the US tended to centre more on the issue of universities' assets, as in the case of UC Berkeley's Student Government Divestment Bill in September 2010, which escalated to national attention (Hallward, 2013), while in the UK there were fewer financial issues at stake, as in the case of Eden Springs' contract with a number of British universities or of Sheffield University not renewing its waste collection contract with Veolia in 2013.[24] However, the UK stands out in relation to academic contexts in continental Europe, where there has been less or no *re*-politicization on campus. Part of this is probably linked to the long-standing tradition of freedom of expression in the UK, but part is also due to other reasons, such as some governments moving very quickly to limit the range of BDS activities (as in France, cf. Voltolini in this collection) or public opinion being historically reluctant to embrace such a path (as in Germany, cf. Busse in this collection).

In the UK, the first stage of the process was the re-politicization of the debate on the Israeli-Palestinian conflict on UK campuses, with actions in favour or against centred on domestic actors and institutions. This phase entailed at times attempts at forcing the rules for debates, but not it did not question the rules. However, this was soon to change.

From emergency measures to re-writing the rules for debates on campus

Debates about the Israeli-Palestinian conflict were partially securitized through the use of emergency measures when, in an unrelated development, the UK Government begun to change the rules for academic debates in general. Still trying to respond to 7/7 and following terrorist attacks, the government intended to shift the focus of the fight against terrorism from violent to non-violent extremism and, more specifically, to prevent the radicalization of possible terrorists. First developed by the Labour government in 2005, the "Prevent" strategy (as it has come to be known) was reviewed by the Coalition government in 2011, which prioritized the role of the education sector. The aim of the new 2011 "Prevent" strategy was (and is) to intervene "to stop people moving from extremist (albeit legal) groups into terrorist-related activity,"[25] in a significant up-stream shift in government's policy against terrorism. Universities in the UK thus came to be tasked not just with the fight against radicalization but also with the attempt to prevent it, bringing the academic arena under increased scrutiny and under new security rules. The government came also to adopt a controversial definition of anti-Semitism in 2016[26] and the implementation of the new rules changed the dynamics of debates about the occupation on UK campuses, with an increased emphasis on re-writing of rules and judicial litigation.

The background for this development is freedom of expression, which in UK universities (or, more specifically, institutions of further and higher education) is guaranteed by the Education (No. 2) Act 1986 *as long as it is within the law*. Limitations to freedom of expression as specified by the law are well established. They include threatening, abusive or insulting words, or words/behaviour aimed at causing distress or anxiety, a point used to prohibit speech of racist or anti-religious nature.[27] Implementing acts of the "Prevent" strategy suggested a specific set of provisions for higher education bodies, in the attempt reconcile freedom of expression with the new set of duties. The Counter-Terrorism Security Act adopted in February 2015 included a duty to prevent people from being drawn into terrorism and the guidelines issued in 2015 to guarantee correct implementation singled out higher education bodies as "one of our most important arenas for challenging extremist views and ideologies."

The key issue in the implementation of these new rules is the definition of new procedures about risk assessment, on which the duty to prevent radicalization rests in academia. These new procedures, which affect issues from IT policies to welfare support systems, aim at assessing the potential for radicalization, for instance in the organization of events, especially when involving external speakers. According to "Prevent" Guidelines published in 2015,[28] universities must have in place procedures to assess the risk of events drawing people into terrorism and if this is the case, then the institution should cancel the event or take measures to offset the risk, e.g. by including speakers that would challenge such a view.[29]

The new procedures connected to the Prevent strategy introduced a security dimension and indirectly led to the partial securitization of debates on campuses about the Israeli-

Palestinian conflict. The guidelines on Prevent do not automatically trigger police involvement or court cases. However, they imposed a "security lens" through which to scrutinize debates on campus more generally. This provided the opportunity for groups countering BDS to increase pressure on universities, by scrutinizing the formulation and implementation of rules related to Prevent, while the increased polarization of debates on campus seemed to justify the introduction of emergency measures.

For instance, "Student Rights," which is a project of the Henry Jackson Society, developed its own "model external speaker policy" and – via Freedom of Information requests to all English universities – compared it to the speakers' policy of 76 universities in England. Their "model policy" included aspects that are not required by Prevent, such as explicit mention of the Counter-Terrorism and Security Act 2015, the creation of an External Speaker Assessment Panel and the balancing of platforms via strategies such as "giving opponents of the speaker priority during the Q&A."[30] Unsurprisingly, a number of institutions did not meet the extra criteria. By raising the issue of existing policies' adequacy, this type of initiatives challenges and ultimately aims to change existing rules.

It was indicative of this phase that in 2011 a UCU member sued the UCU for a number of complaints amounting to "institutional anti-Semitism"[31] and related to the debates about BDS hosted by the organization in the previous years. The case was paradigmatic in the way it represented an attempt to "legally challenge the ability to discuss or engage in activities surrounding boycotts of Israel" (Morrison, 2015a, p. 116). This was, in the words of the Employment Tribunal adjudicating the case, an "enormous piece of litigation," "with a trial bundle of 23 volumes."[32] In 2013, the Tribunal ruled in favour of the UCU, arguing that the case represented "an impermissible attempt to achieve a political end by litigious means"[33] – an expression that summarizes the state of the art at that point in time.

Groups countering BDS started to make routine reference to Prevent and submit Freedom of Information (FOI) requests aimed at ascertaining whether procedures and policies have been respected in holding events considered biased in their vision of Israel and its policies. For their part, groups supporting BDS continued to promote political activism on UK campuses and kept high the political salience of debates, ranging from the high profile withdrawal of Stephen Hawking from a conference in Israel in 2013, to the letter re-stating the academic boycott signed by 343 academics,[34] to "Israel Apartheid Week," to which with "more than twenty UK campus groups" allegedly participated in 2013 and "more than thirty" in 2017.[35]

Discussions about the occupation and boycott have become prone to emergency measures. An emblematic case occurred in relation to a conference organized by the University of Southampton in February 2015 on "International law and the state of Israel," which was cancelled by the university administration quoting health and safety reasons. The decision was challenged in front of the High Court, but the final judicial review in 2016 upheld the decision. The conference eventually took place at University College Cork in March 2017.[36]

Other events have been more dramatic and required the direct intervention of the police. In the London area, Kings' College first witnessed disruptions to an event with an external speaker in 2014. Marking a deterioration of the context, a similar event at Kings' in January 2016 was disrupted to the point that the police intervened.[37]

The same happened at UCL in October 2016.[38] Events at LSE in March 2017 and at SOAS in November 2017 also were severely disrupted, prompting cancellations.[39] In the ensuing thorough investigation, UCL identified the need to update and tighten existing rules, whereas the conclusions of Kings' investigation also urged policies' reassessment.[40]

The emphasis then shifted to the issue of chairs for events. In November 2017, a public event organized by the Government Department at the LSE on "Palestinian Rights, the BDS Movement and Transnational Solidarity" was to be chaired by a member of staff, who was however replaced at the last minute by a professor member of the directorate, after the previous chair was found to have signed a petition related to the topic of discussion.[41] In the same month, the organization of a very similar event at the University of Cambridge saw the replacement of the chair in favour of the university's Director of Communications. Several more examples exist across the UK. What is noticeable is the attempt to manufacture a balanced expression of views *within the same event*, as opposed to guaranteeing an open floor to different events that would balance each other *across time*.

These illustrative examples do not directly represent a re-writing of the rules for academic debates, but they can be considered influential in two ways. First, they reflected a degree of contestation of existing rules and urged rules' re-assessment, supporting an argument expressed by the UK government that universities had maintained a lax approach to extremism. Second, they put the spotlight on universities, as policies have been reviewed, FOI requests have been filed and fulfilled, emails responded, the reputation of universities attacked and defended. As universities compete to attract students (and even more so in a Brexit context), they must be seen as playing by the rules, even when rules are changing.

The definition of anti-Semitism adopted by the UK Government in December 2016 further contributed to increase the pressure on academic institutions for the provision of new rules. The definition, generally referred to as the IHRA definition,[42] has been contested also because it seems to include examples, among which manifestations targeting the state of Israel, "conceived as a Jewish collectivity."[43] In a legal opinion, the decision of the UK government has been found not to have any direct "binding effect on any public body and no public body is under a resulting obligation to adopt or use this definition" as it is "simply a suggestion" by the Government as to a definition which public bodies might wish to use.[44]

However, this has not stopped the UK Government and supportive groups from asking universities to embrace it, or from acting on it. For instance, in the run up to Israel Apartheid Week in 2017, Israel Britain Alliance and Christians United for Israel launched a campaign based on an automatic link,[45] which created a personalized letter referring to the said definition of anti-Semitism alongside the Equality Act of 2010 and addressed to the President of Universities UK[46] and to the Member of Parliament for the indicated constituency. At the time, both the UK minister for Universities Jo Johnson and Universities UK contacted universities with suggestions about how to run events in connection with Israel Apartheid Week in a way that would be consistent with the law. Pointedly, Johnson's concerns were included in the annual higher education funding letter, explicitly asking universities to adopt the IHRA's definition, a position re-iterated by the Prime Minister Theresa May a few days later in the House of Commons.[47] Since then, a number of groups countering BDS have followed up on Johnson's letter with further correspondence directed to universities' vice-chancellors asking whether they have adopted the IHRA definition and if not, why not. In the case of the University of Central Lancashire, the definition was mentioned as the reason for cancelling a debate.[48]

The most recent development in this stage marked by questioning and re-writing of rules has been an inquiry on freedom of speech in universities conducted by the Joint Committee on Human Rights of the UK Parliament in November 2017.[49] The evidence gathered shows that the debate on issues related to Israel is one of the most prominent examples. The report published in March 2018 as a conclusion includes guidance for universities and students organizing events. And the debate continues, in academia and beyond, as witnessed for instance by the dispute around the Labour Party's chosen definition of anti-Semitism and the attempt to codify the IHRA definition instead.[50]

Conclusions

This overview of how debates on UK campuses about the Israeli-Palestinian conflict have evolved shows how domestic debates in the UK have become a key venue for discussing the conflict in predominantly domestic terms, rather than as an issue of foreign policy. The evolution occurred in two steps. First, new actions centred on domestic issues (re-)politicized the debate, largely in the name of boycotts. Second, as the UK government introduced new legislation in the form of new Prevent guidelines and then the IHRA definition of anti-Semitism, this provided the backdrop for a re-negotiation of the rules for academic debates in the UK, from which groups countering BDS aimed to profit. It has led to the partial securitization of the debate, due to the use of emergency and law-related measures. Incidents "showcase the presence of the Israeli-Palestinian conflict in the political undercurrents of British society" (Groves, 2017, p. 332).

In this new domestic context, the discussion of the occupation as a topic of foreign policy and international politics has been largely secondary in comparison to appropriate actions by private citizen and non-governmental actors in the UK (rather than by the UK). In other terms, debates on UK campuses have expressed a "radical disagreement" (Ramsbotham, 2010) that did not simply mirror the Israeli-Palestinian conflict, but instead highlighted the gap between citizens in the UK, on one hand, and the UK government, on the other, about what should be done after the collapse of diplomatic peace processes. This discussion (and boycotts more generally) is also part of a trend across social movements during the 2000s to embrace consumer strategies to achieve political goals (Hanssen-Bauer, 2005; Micheletti & Stolle, 2015, p. 483) but, consistently with the findings of the literature, impact is difficult to quantify.

The key issue is that new rules with a strategic relevance for the future of the occupation are currently being defined in the UK at the moment, namely who has the right to say what in relation to the occupation. The terms of the debate and its direction suggest that, fifty years after the 1967 war and one century after the Balfour Declaration, once again part of the conflict's future is being decided in Britain.

Notes

1. See e.g. T. May speech at the CFI Annual Business Lunch on 12 December 2016.
2. See e.g. the reportage by Al Jazeera, https://www.aljazeera.com/investigations/thelobby/

3. This call took the cue from a call in late 2001 by the Palestinian Solidarity Campaign to boycott Israeli agricultural products.
4. Israel was the only non-EU country to receive EU funds for scientific research at the time.
5. The call was launched with a letter published in the Guardian on 6 April 2002 with over 120 names on it. https://www.theguardian.com/world/2002/apr/06/israel.guardianletters. A similar letter was published in France and the debate resonated across Europe. See a summary here: "Israeli boycott divides academics" The Guardian, 8 July 2002, https://www.theguardian.com/uk/2002/jul/08/highereducation.israel.
6. Originally posted on www.pjpo.org but no longer active.
7. https://www.theguardian.com/education/2002/dec/12/highereducation.uk.
8. On the emergence of BDS, see Morrison (2015b).
9. It would be more correct to talk about "a network of local BDS movements" in the plural (Hallward, 2013, p. 2) or at least distinguish between a BDS1 and a BDS2, only the second of which focuses on the occupation (Lerner, 2012, p. 329). On BDS, see also Chaitin, Steinberg, and Steinberg (2017); Culcasi (2016) and Morrison (2015a).
10. Namely an end to the occupation "of all Arab lands," full equality of Arab-Palestinian citizens of Israel and the right of return for Palestinian refugees. See www.bdsmovement.net. The ambiguities surrounding the goals give rise to confusion as their meaning in territorial terms, and whether the pre-1967 borders would apply or instead it entails disappearance of Israel as a state.
11. See https://bdsmovement.net/academic-boycott. Affiliation of individual scholars to an Israeli academic institution does not automatically provide ground for boycott. The EU research fund, Horizon2020, has continued to be considered a major issue, despite the 2013 EU Guidelines that expressly forbid the allocation of funds to institutions and project operating beyond the Green Line. See https://bdsmovement.net/pacbi/academic-boycott-guidelines.
12. See http://www.pacbi.org/, discontinued, and https://bdsmovement.net/pacbi
13. http://www.bricup.org.uk/.
14. www.boycottisraelnetwork.net.
15. https://engageonline.wordpress.com/about-engage/.
16. Established in 2002, https://www.academics-for-israel.org/. Not all actors are the same size. As reported in Fraser vs UCU, case n. 2203290/2011, par.55, this particular actor consisted of an academic, "his wife and a computer." But this does not detract from AFI's media footprint.
17. "Rivlin: Academic Boycotts Against Israel Are First-rate Strategic Threat" Haaretz, 28 May, 2015. http://www.haaretz.com/israel-news/.premium-1.658622.
18. See e.g. Barghouti (2011).
19. See e.g. The Guardian, letter, "Growing outrage at the killings in Gaza", 16 January 2009, https://www.theguardian.com/world/2009/jan/16/gaza-israel-petitions
20. See e.g. Independent, "Students are revolting: the spirit of '68 is reawakening," 8 February 2009, http://www.independent.co.uk/news/education/education-news/students-are-revolting-the-spirit-of-68-is-reawakening-1604043.html
21. For a specific take, see Hamdon and Harris (2011).
22. Most notably in December 2013, with the resolution approved by the American Studies Association in favour of a boycott of Israeli academic institutions and in support of the right of students and scholars to support BDS. An appeal on the decision in front of the District Court of the District of Columbia is pending at the time of writing, but will not centre on the jurisdiction of ASA to take the decision. See http://www.courthousenews.com/suit-academic-boycott-israel-advances/, last access 23 July 2018.
23. Funded by two academics based at the University of California, it was recently responsible for naming US academics that should be banned from entry into Israel because of their BDS support. See http://www.amchainitiative.org/; see Haaretz "Jewish Group Releases Blacklist of US Professors Who Back Academic Boycott of Israel" 30 March 2017, http://www.haaretz.com/us-news/1.780297.
24. On Veolia, see Martin in this collection.

25. Revised Prevent Duty Guidance for England and Wales, 16 July 2015 (point 8).
26. The definition reads: "Anti-Semitism is a certain perception of Jews, which may be expressed as hatred toward Jews. Rhetorical and physical manifestations of anti-Semitism are directed toward Jewish or non-Jewish individuals and/or their property, toward Jewish community institutions and religious facilities." https://www.gov.uk/government/news/government-leads-the-way-in-tackling-anti-semitism. More below on the controversy connected to the examples used to illustrate the definition.
27. E.g. Public Order Act 1986, Part 3, revised in 2006 by the Racial and Religious Hatred Act.
28. Which were published after a heated debate in 2014–15. See summary in House of Commons Library, Counter-extremism policy: an overview, Report n. 7238, 9 June 2017 by Joanna Dawson and Samantha Godec, p. 16–17.
29. This occurs on the basis of annual reports. In 2017, it focused on the setting up of policies. From 2018 onwards HEFCE will focus on actual practices. A detailed report is available here: http://www.hefce.ac.uk/pubs/year/2017/201701/ Similar provisions apply for Northern Ireland, Scotland and Wales.
30. P. 8. Report available here: http://www.studentrights.org.uk/article/2455/mitigating_the_risks_an_assessment_of_university_speaker_policies
31. Case n.2203290/2011, Fraser vs University & College Union, available at www.judiciary.gov.uk.
32. Case n.2203490/2011, par.3 and par. 180.
33. Idem, par.178.
34. https://www.theguardian.com/world/2015/oct/27/uk-academics-boycott-universities-in-israel-to-fight-for-palestinians-rights.
35. According to figures provided by Electronic Intifada, https://electronicintifada.net/blogs/michael-deas/israeli-apartheid-week-held-30-uk-universities-despite-repression and https://electronicintifada.net/blogs/michael-deas/sheffield-university-dumps-veolia-capping-successful-year-uk-student-palestine.
36. https://www.southampton.ac.uk/israelpalestinelaw/index.page, http://trinitynews.ie/israel-conference-to-go-ahead-in-cork/.
37. https://www.kcl.ac.uk/newsevents/news/newsrecords/2016/01%20January/Statement-regarding-the-Security-of-Israel-event-.aspx.
38. http://www.independent.co.uk/student/news/police-called-to-ucl-event-as-pro-israel-and-pro-palestinian-students-violently-clash-a7384486.html
39. https://www.independent.co.uk/news/uk/home-news/israel-apartheid-regime-universities-cancel-talks-un-report-co-author-name-security-concerns-a7647986.html.
40. See www.ucl.ac.uk/news/news-articles/0117/Investigation_report.pdf, par 32, last line.
41. On the aftermath to the LSE event, see Chalcraft (2018).
42. From the body that first adopted it, the International Holocaust Remembrance Alliance.
43. Link to definition available here: https://holocaustremembrance.com/media-room/stories/working-definition-antisemitism
44. Hugh Tomlison, QC "In the matter of the adoption and potential application of the International Holocaust Remembrance Alliance Working Definition of Anti-Semitism". 8 March 2017
45. www.cufi.org.uk/latest-action-alert/act-now-stand-up-to-israel-apartheid-week-contact-the-head-of-uk-universities/. The letter then "mutated" into a call to candidates for the General Elections to pledge support to the state of Israel and the IHRA definition of anti-Semitism. Subsequently, it turned into a general letter to MPs to support Israel and condemn Hamas and Islamic Jihad.
46. A body representing universities across the UK and composed of vice-chancellors or principals of universities in the UK. It has no effective power over universities. http://www.universitiesuk.ac.uk/about/Pages/who-we-are.aspx
47. See exchange with Bob Blackman (Harrow East, Cons) https://hansard.parliament.uk/Commons/2017-03-01/debates/62A8D14B-06F5-461B-B9F9-D20941A86413/Engagements#contribution-366A0E88-F597-4BCE-AD13-B88F691C81AE

48. See, which includes other examples: http://freespeechonisrael.org.uk/category/definitions-accusations-antisemitism/#sthash.eVY3345i.dpbs.
49. https://www.parliament.uk/business/committees/committees-a-z/joint-select/human-rights-committee/inquiries/parliament-2017/inquiry/.
50. https://www.theguardian.com/politics/2018/jul/21/labour-mps-peers-plan-defy-corbyn-antisemitism-definition.

Disclosure statement

The author is based at one of the universities analysed in this article.

References

Abowd, T. (2014). The boycott, divestment, and sanctions movement and violations of academic freedom at Wayne State University. In P. Chatterjee & S. Maira (Eds.), *The imperial university. Academic repression and scholarly dissent* (pp. 169–186). Minnesota: Minnesota University Press.
Barghouti, O. (2011). *Boycott, Divestment, Sanctions: The global struggle for Palestinian rights*. Chicago: Haymarket Books.
Brown, C. L. (1984). *International politics and the Middle East. Old rules, dangerous game*. London: I.B.Tauris.
Buzan, B. (1991). *People, states, and fear* (2nd ed.). Hemel Hempstead/Boulder: Harvester Wheatsheaf/Lynne Rienner.
Buzan, B., Wæver, O., & de Wilde, J. (1998). *Security. A new framework for analysis*. Boulder/London: Lynne Rienner.
Chaitin, J., Steinberg, S., & Steinberg, S. (2017). 'BDS – it's complicated': Israeli, Jewish, and others' views on the boycott of Israel. *The International Journal of Human Rights*, 21(7), 889–907.
Chalcraft, J. (2018, March 12). On 'neutral' chairs. *BRICUP Newsletter 119*.
Cohen, M. S., & Freilich, C. D. (2018). War by other means: The delegitimisation campaign against Israel. *Israel Affairs*, 24(1), 1–25.
Culcasi, K. (2016). Engaging in the boycott, divestment, and sanctions (bds) debate. *Geographical Review*, 106(2), 258–263.
Edwards, G. (1984). Britain. In D. Allen & A. Pijpers (Eds.), *European foreign policy-making and the Arab-Israeli conflict* (pp. 47–59). The Hague/Boston/Lancaster: Martinus Nijhoff Publishers/Kluwer.
Groves, A. (2017). 'From Gaza to the streets of Britain': British social media coverage of the 2014 Israel-Gaza conflict. *Jewish Culture and History*, 18(3), 331–349.
Hallward, M. C. (2013). *Transnational activism and the Israeli-Palestinian conflict*. New York: Palgrave Macmillan.
Hamdon, E., & Harris, S. (2011). Dangerous dissent?: Critical pedagogy and the case of Israeli apartheid week. *Cultural and Pedagogical Inquiry*, 2(2), 62–76.
Hanssen-Bauer, J. (2005). Bustling backwards: Lessons from the Norwegian sponsored Israeli-Palestinian people-to-people program. *Palestine-Israel Journal of Politics, Economics, and Culture*, 12(4/1), 39–51.
Hollis, R. (2010). *Britain and the Middle East in the 9/11 era*. London: John Wiley & Sons.
Kittrie, O. F. (2016). *Lawfare. Law as a weapon of war*. Oxford et al.: Oxford University Press.
Lerner, M. R. (2012). *Embracing Israel/Palestine*. Berkeley: Tikkun Books.
Levey, Z., & Podeh, E. (Eds.). (2008). *Britain and the Middle East. From imperial power to junior partner*. Brighton/Portland: Sussex Academic Press.
Mangold, P. (2016). *What the British did. Two centuries in the Middle East*. London: I.B.Tauris.
McCourt, D. M. (2009). What was Britain's "East of Suez role"? Reassessing the withdrawal 1964–1968. *Diplomacy & Statecraft*, 20(3), 453–472.
McMahon, S. F. (2014). The Boycott, Divestment, and Sanctions campaign: Contradictions and challenges. *Race & Class*, 55(4), 65–81.

Micheletti, M., & Stolle, D. (2015). Consumer strategies in social movements. In D. Della Porta & M. Diani (Eds.), *The Oxford handbook of social movements* (pp. 478–493). Oxford: Oxford University Press.

Monroe, E. (1981). *Britain's moment in the Middle East 1914–1971*. London: Chatto and Windus.

Morrison, S. (2015a). *The Boycott, Divestment, and Sanctions movement: Activism across borders for Palestinian justice* (PhD thesis). London School of Economics, London.

Morrison, S. (2015b). The emergence of the Boycott, Divestment, and Sanctions movement. In F. Gerges (Ed.), *Contentious politics in the Middle East: Popular resistance and marginalized activism beyond the Arab uprisings* (pp. 229–255). New York: Palgrave Macmillan.

Ramsbotham, O. (2010). *Transforming violent conflict: Radical disagreement, dialogue and survival*. Abingdon/New York: Routledge.

Schleifer, R. (2016). The Palestinian/Arab strategy to take over campuses in the West – preliminary findings. *Israel Affairs*, 22(1), 211–235.

Shlaim, A. (2005). The Balfour Declaration and its consequences. In R. W. Louis (Ed.), *Yet more adventures with Britannia: Personalities, politics and culture in Britain* (pp. 251–270). London: I.B.Tauris.

Zürn, M. (2014). The politicization of world politics and its effects: Eight propositions. *European Political Science Review*, 6(1), 47–71.

Swedish recognition of Palestine: politics, law, and prospects for peace

Jacob Eriksson

ABSTRACT
Sweden's decision to recognize Palestine on 30 October 2014, was a controversial one and this article explores two key aspects. First, it contextualizes the decision in relation to doctrines about the recognition of states in the international system. Here, the Swedish decision provides further evidence of the growing trend in the twenty-first century that recognition of new states is primarily determined by politics rather than law. Second, the article examines the decision within the history of Swedish policy towards the conflict. By analyzing the position of Sweden's main political parties and of past governments, it shows that recognition simultaneously represents both continuity and change. While Carl Bildt worked through the EU to achieve progress on the two-state solution, by recognizing Palestine Margot Wallström decided to change Swedish foreign policy and sought to affect the positions of EU member states. The outcome has, however, been limited, and much continuity has ensued. Nonetheless, Swedish officials are confident that history will do them justice, despite the current lack of progress.

Introduction

On 30 October 2014, the Swedish government led by the Social Democratic Prime Minister Stefan Löfven recognized the state of Palestine. Predictably, this caused consternation in Israel, with Foreign Minister Avigdor Lieberman commenting that "the Swedish government must understand that relations in the Middle East are more complex than one of IKEA's flat-pack pieces of furniture" (Davidovich, 2014). Just as predictably, the Palestinian President Mahmoud Abbas heralded it as a "brave and historic" decision (AFP, 2014). The decision to recognize Palestine was politically controversial not just in Israel, but also in Sweden itself. It had been debated for many hours over multiple years in parliament, reflecting disagreement over the basis for recognizing new states and the relationship between international law and politics.

Palestine is, to use the term coined by Geldenhuys (2009), a contested state, in that their purported statehood does not enjoy widespread *de jure* recognition or recognition through institutions like the United Nations. While Palestine enjoys widespread titular recognition in that states accept its right to statehood, it is severely constrained in exercising the responsibilities of states due to the ongoing Israeli occupation (Geldenhuys, 2009, p. 1, 25). This continuing conflict with Israel has had a significant impact on international attitudes towards Palestinian statehood, both positively and negatively.

After outlining a brief theoretical framework relating to the recognition of states in the international system, the article will reflect on the Swedish debate over Palestine, and analyse the reasons that motivated recognition. The decision will be contextualized within the history of Swedish policy towards the conflict in order to demonstrate that recognition simultaneously represents both continuity and change. The article will then evaluate whether or not Swedish recognition has had any impact on wider European stances toward the issue and analyse how recognition fits into an overall strategy to affect the peace process and help achieve peace. It argues that the Swedish decision further evidences the growing trend in the twenty-first century that recognition of new states is primarily determined by politics rather than law.

Recognition in theory

The recognition of new states in the international system sits uncomfortably between the realms of international law and international politics. As Crawford (2007) observes, a tension exists

> between the conviction that recognition is at some level a legal act in the international sphere, and the assumption of political leaders that they are, or should be, free to recognise or not to recognise on grounds of their own choosing. If this is the case, the international status and rights of whole peoples and territories will seem to depend on arbitrary decisions and political contingencies. (pp. 18–19)

From a legal perspective, there is a longstanding debate between the constitutive and declaratory theories of recognition.[1] In the constitutive theory, an entity only becomes a state when it is recognized as such, and is thus a relative concept that only exists in relation to other states (Ryngaert & Sobrie, 2011, p. 469). This is necessary to avoid legitimizing illegal entities created through breaches of laws on the use of force or acquisition of territory by force (Crawford, 2007, p. 21). However, it is unclear whether the decision should be based on facts, norms, geopolitical considerations, or a combination of factors (Ryngaert & Sobrie, 2011, p. 469).

In the declaratory theory, statehood is determined by the existence of a set of observable conditions, listed in Article 1 of the 1933 Montevideo Convention on the Rights and Duties of States: "The state as a person of international law should possess the following qualifications: (a) a permanent population; (b) a defined territory; (c) government; and (d) capacity to enter into relations with the other states." (Montevideo Convention, 1933) In this conception, recognition is merely the acknowledgement of something that already exists, and the use of criteria helps establish legal norms and avoid recognition being wielded arbitrarily for political reasons (Ryngaert & Sobrie, 2011, p. 470). These criteria do, however, remain subjective.

Although the declaratory theory is deemed to be dominant in current doctrine and jurisprudence, Geldenhuys (2009) observes that "the very existence of contested states points to the influence of the constitutive theory in world politics." (p. 20) Crawford (2007) concurs, arguing that recognition "can resolve uncertainties as to status and allow for new situations to be regularized," (p. 27) and acknowledging that individual acts of recognition can contribute towards a consolidation of status. While he sympathizes with the merits of combining both elements into a unified theory, he insists that one must take precedence over the other.

The difficulty of applying the Montevideo criteria consistently was highlighted by the confused European reaction to the dissolution of the Federal Republic of Yugoslavia. The European Community (EC) recognized Bosnia and Croatia in 1992 despite the fact that they manifestly failed to meet the criteria of a stable government able to exercise control of the whole of its territory. Moreover, the EC even added new normative criteria, including commitment to democratic governance, and respect for human rights and minority rights, which the new states also fell short of. Significantly, the EC Declaration also mentions "the political realities in each case" as factors to be taken into account, which casts doubt upon the importance of the criteria (Ryngaert & Sobrie, 2011, pp. 474–476).

This dynamic was further strengthened by international reactions to Kosovo's declaration of independence in 2008, where political expediency trumped international law. States who recognized Kosovo "almost invariably justified their decision to grant recognition ... by referring to political considerations, most notably the need for stability, peace, and security in the region, and the positive effect recognition would have on these parameters," with only vague references to "international law" (Ryngaert & Sobrie, 2011, p. 480). Ryngaert and Sobrie argue that when giving an advisory opinion on Kosovo's independence, the International Court of Justice missed an opportunity to give clear guidance on the content, scope, and status of the norms that govern state recognition. Consequently, "[T]he lack of a clear-cut normative framework gives way to uncertainty and incoherent policies based on 'unique cases'" (Ryngaert & Sobrie, 2011, p. 484). This article will now consider how Sweden justified its decision to recognize Palestine and what the effects have been.

Sweden's rationale for recognition

Sweden has long been an advocate of Palestinian self-determination, and was one of the first European countries to endorse this idea in the early 1970's. A Palestinian state living peacefully alongside the state of Israel was seen as the only possible equitable solution to the conflict, and one that was in the best interest of both sides. The Palestinians would have their national aspirations realized, while Israel would end an occupation that former Prime Minister Olof Palme argued was damaging to its democracy, national character, and international standing. Furthermore, it was also a question of respecting and acting in accordance with international law, which was central to Swedish foreign policy (Eriksson, 2015, p. 57, 69–71). A two-state solution would have to be reached through negotiations between the two sides. While governments and ruling parties have changed over decades, this policy has been a constant. Differences between governments have tended to focus on how best to achieve this goal, with significant differences visible even within the Social Democratic party. Prime Minister Göran Persson, for example, who led the country from 1996 to 2006, adjusted what he saw as a traditional pro-Palestinian bias within the party in line with the Palme tradition, and pursued closer relations with Israel (Eriksson, 2015, pp. 165–171). Although this was a substantive change in Swedish policy, manifested for example by an abstention in a United Nations General Assembly vote on a resolution condemning disproportionate Israeli violence towards Palestinians during the second *intifada*, the goal of a two-state solution remained (Eriksson, 2015, pp. 198–200).

During the leadership of Conservative Prime Minister Fredrik Reinfeldt, Foreign Minister Carl Bildt maintained this traditional line on the conflict, but also worked within the EU to articulate policy on certain key issues, particularly when Sweden held the presidency of the EU in 2009. Bildt spearheaded a joint statement of EU foreign ministers that for the first time articulated the need for Jerusalem to be the shared capital of two states. A leaked draft specifically mentioned East Jerusalem as the capital of the state of Palestine, but this initial Swedish formulation was softened due to a lack of consensus among member states and Israeli diplomatic pressure (McCarthy & Black, 2009; Ravid, 2009). Nonetheless, it remained a significant development and was condemned by Israel as pre-judging the outcome of negotiations between the two parties on the issue (Ravid & Reuters, 2009). From an EU perspective, this was a necessary response to decades of unilateral Israeli action to alter the demography of the city, particularly illegal settlement construction around East Jerusalem seemingly designed to disconnect it from the rest of the occupied Palestinian territories (Dahlberg, 2009; ICG, 2012).

The draft document also states, "The Council [of the European Union] also reiterates its commitment to support further efforts and steps towards Palestinian statehood and to be able, at the appropriate time, to recognize a Palestinian state" (Ravid, 2009). Clearly, Bildt was not averse to Sweden and the EU trying to endorse and enshrine certain elements of a two-state solution, but recognizing statehood was deemed to be premature. In parliamentary foreign policy debates on 25 October 2011 (Riksdagen, 2011) and 15 February 2012 (Riksdagen, 2012), Bildt explained his reasoning. Control of territory was, he argued, a basic criteria which the Palestinians could not fulfil as Israel was the ultimate power in the occupied territories. He warned that one should not ignore the reality of the occupation and think that the Palestinians actually exercised sovereignty. Palestinian officials could be democratically elected one day and arrested by Israel the next. While he hoped that circumstances would change to allow recognition, policy could not ignore this frustrating reality. Sweden would continue to work for a "strong and unified European policy" towards the conflict, building on the example of the 2009 statement (Riksdagen, 2012).

The opposition coalition composed of the Social Democrats, the Greens, and the Leftists argued differently.[2] In an op-ed to the newspaper *Svenska Dagbladet* published that day to coincide with the debate, the opposition leaders argued that to follow the government's logic was to put all the power in the hands of the Israeli occupiers (Löfven et al., 2012). In their view, the three main international legal criteria for statehood (borders, a permanent population, and government) were in fact met. In line with UNSC Resolution 242, the borders of a Palestinian state would be based on the so-called 4 June 1967 borders which demarcate the occupied Palestinian territories. Although these are disputed borders and are subject to negotiation with Israel, this has not prevented in the international community from recognizing the state of Israel. The Palestinian Central Bureau of Statistics estimates that 4.88 million Palestinians live in the West Bank and the Gaza Strip, which constitutes a permanent population, and in the event of a peace treaty they could be joined by roughly 6 million Palestinian refugees who would be allowed to exercise their right of return to the state of Palestine (PCBS, 2016). As Bildt suggested, the question of effective government is more complex and contentious. However, the opposition parties emphasised that UN and World Bank officials had acknowledged that, in a number of areas, Palestinian institutions were "ready to assume the responsibilities of statehood." (UNSCO, 2011) This point was also cited by the Swedish government in a 2015 submission to the Parliamentary Constitutional Committee explaining the reason for the decision and how it was implemented. The document further explains that international law experts within the Ministry of Foreign Affairs were consulted, and that international law informed the decision (Cabinet Office, 2015).

In her explanation of the government's 2014 decision, Foreign Minister Margot Wallström acknowledged that the Palestinians did not exercise full control over the West Bank and the Gaza Strip, but also pointed to the Swedish recognition of Croatia in 1992 and Kosovo in 2008, where those nationalist groups were not in full control of their territory either (Riksdagen, 2014a; Wallström, 2014). Indeed, in his justification of the recognition of Kosovo, Foreign Minister Bildt (2008) stated clearly that the decision was not based on the traditional Montevideo criteria. Instead, he emphasised the broader political and conflict context, and the deadlock between Brussels, Moscow, and Washington which made agreement impossible to reach. Kosovo's political and economic development would be a considerable challenge, but one that the international community would help them face.

In the Palestinian case, political factors and the failure of the peace process were central to the Swedish decision. Wallström (2014) stressed the need to support moderate Palestinian political parties (in other words, the deeply unpopular Mahmoud Abbas and Fatah), and prevent violence and extremism by giving some hope of a better future to the younger generation (Riksdagen, 2014a, 2014b). It was the Palestinian Authority's concerted campaign for international recognition, begun in 2009 and taken to the UN in 2012, which brought the issue to the fore, and the Social Democrats were ready to support this Palestinian initiative. As with Kosovo, the argument was that Palestine should be a special case considering the historic longevity and trajectory of the conflict. Recognition of Palestinian statehood was not seen as a substitute for a negotiated peace, but would in fact contribute to one by addressing the asymmetry between the parties and enabling negotiations between two states rather than an occupier and the occupied. Recognition was in many ways an effort to keep the dwindling prospect of a two-state solution alive: "there are those who will argue that today's decision is premature. If anything, I fear it is too late." (Wallström, 2014).

The decision was hotly criticized and debated by the opposition parties. The Conservative, Liberal, and Christian Democrat parties questioned the "moderate" and democratic nature of the Palestinian Authority, pointing to incitement to violence against Israel, praise for terrorists, and violations of Palestinian human rights (Riksdagen, 2014b). In a similar vein, the far-right Sweden Democrats concurred that recognition was tantamount to recognizing Hamas, who had announced their intention to form a unity government with Fatah, and also denounced the Palestinian Authority's support for and payments to terrorists and their families, calling for an end to Swedish aid to the Palestinians (Riksdagen, 2013a). This echoed the criticism that emanated from Israel. Before being recalled for a month, the Israeli ambassador to Sweden commented that the decision would encourage terrorism ("Israel kallar hem", 2014).

Effects of recognition

While there is little evidence to suggest that Swedish recognition has in fact encouraged terrorism, it can hardly be said to have had the desired effect either. According to a September 2017 poll by the Palestinian Centre for Policy and Survey Research (2017), the Palestinian Authority and the Fatah leadership in particular remain deeply unpopular, with 67% of Palestinians polled wanting Abbas to resign. Fifty-seven percent of those polled believe that a two-state solution is no longer practical due to Israeli settlement construction.[3] Much as then-Foreign Minister Bildt noted in 2012, the notion of Palestinian sovereignty remains largely symbolic, with no meaningful change in the asymmetry between the parties and little improvement in the day-to-day lives of Palestinians.

Sweden continues to be a major donor to Palestine, now on a bilateral basis. In conjunction with recognition, the government presented their 2015–2019 development strategy for Palestine, which focuses on democratic development, human rights, environmental issues, and private sector development, to the tune of 1.5 billion SEK ($177 million), a significant increase on previous aid budgets (Ministry of Foreign Affairs, 2014). While considered significant by Palestinian (Interview 3) and Swedish officials (Interview 2), it is a continuation of existing international state-building policy, the effectiveness of which has arguably been limited (Bouris, 2014). It is also noteworthy that while Palestinian diplomatic representation in Stockholm has been upgraded to that of an embassy, Swedish representation to Palestine has not; Sweden maintains a general consulate in East Jerusalem rather than an embassy. In substance, relations are marked by continuity rather than change.

In terms of reviving the peace process, the parties have not returned to the negotiating table and the gaps between the two sides remain as substantial as they have ever been. This deadlock was clearly reflected in the 2016–2017 French international peace initiative which convened in Paris, to which the parties themselves were not invited. Sweden was invited to participate and lead the working group on civil society development, which Swedish officials considered an important vindication of their policy (Interview 2). However, this had little effect on the lives of Palestinians or on the peace process as a whole. The repetition of the same old hackneyed phrases about seizing the opportunity before it is too late without any type of innovative engagement made the exercise, in the words of one journalist, "a damp squib." (Ahren, 2016; Rabbani, 2017) *The Economist* ("An Israel-Palestine peace conference", 2017) has argued that the January 2017 meeting was primarily designed to impact the policy of the new Trump administration, but this too seems to have failed. It continues to prove difficult for the international community to formulate a coherent strategy which harnesses the strengths of different key actors, including the Arab world.

This lack of coherence is also reflected within key actors like the EU. One of the main ways in which recognition was intended to affect the peace process was to impact EU policy towards the conflict, much like Sweden did in 2009. A more unified EU position on Palestinian statehood could serve to strengthen international consensus, protect a two-state solution, and make it possible for some pressure to be exerted on the parties to return to the negotiating table. Despite this ambition, the decision to recognize Palestine was not discussed in-depth with EU representatives, partly out of frustration with the EU's seeming acquiescence to the status quo in the conflict, nor was it discussed with fellow member state governments (Aggestam & Bicchi, 2018). Instead, a broader vision was discussed at party-political level with European Labour parties for Sweden to take the lead on recognition, and for other parties to follow suit when they were in a position of power to do so, including France, Slovenia, and the UK (Interview 1, on France see also Voltolini in this special issue). Ireland, another sympathetic member state, was also thought likely to join such a movement.

However, this did not come to pass. In the UK, Ed Miliband lost the 2015 elections, and even though socialist Francois Hollande was in power, the French sought to leverage recognition in order to produce results at an international peace summit in Paris in 2016, without any success. Many parliaments in Europe, including the British, French, Spanish, and the EU, have passed motions to recognize Palestine, but although the Swedish government has pointed to this as some measure of progress, it has little impact. Further consultation and more in-depth coordination of recognition could perhaps have led to a better outcome. Still, the consensus that, for example, Bildt achieved in the 2009 statement (although watered down) has not been replicated on the issue of recognition due to domestic political reasons in each member state, no doubt amplified by the greater significance of the move, and it is debatable whether these obstacles could have been overcome.[4]

As a major donor to the Palestinian Authority[5] and Israel's most lucrative trading partner, the EU has a tremendous amount of potential economic leverage at its disposal to affect the cost-benefit calculus of both parties. If the EU were to implement its differentiation policy in accordance with EU law, make trade and aid conditional on certain Israeli and Palestinian behaviour respectively, or refuse to continue to subsidize the Israeli occupation and dismantle the Palestinian Authority, this might have a substantial effect on moribund negotiating prospects (Lovatt, 2016). The unity required to make any such moves, however, is severely lacking, and the potential negative humanitarian and political effects of dismantling the Palestinian Authority make this a risky option. Like the EU, Sweden has and continues to invest millions in Palestinian statebuilding efforts, capacity building programmes, and institutional development, which it will not abandon, and certainly not while a two-state solution remains the official goal of the Palestinian Authority. The rationale of recognition was to support the Authority in their own internationalization strategy, and Wallström would not undercut it by calling time on its existence before they do. As a supporter of the two-state solution, Sweden is unlikely to advocate any move perceived to threaten this outcome.

From a normative perspective, recognition can still be considered significant despite the reality on the ground. Persson (2017) argues that both Israelis and Palestinians take European normative power seriously, particularly in the case of recognition of Palestinian statehood, as evidenced by the discourse surrounding the Palestinian bid for UN membership in 2011. Swedish-Israeli relations were negatively affected by recognition, and Israel sent a clear message of diplomatic protest to the rest of the world (Interview 4). The Palestinian leadership considered it a very significant move, and although they wanted more countries to follow the Swedish lead, the fact that this did not materialize does not, in their view, diminish the importance of the Swedish decision (Interview 3). The hope remains that additional states will eventually follow the Swedish example and strengthen the idea that Palestinian statehood is morally and legally correct on the basis of the right to self-determination, not just as an outcome of negotiations with Israel.

Consensus around norms, however, takes time to develop. In the early 1970's, Sweden adopted a normative position on the need for Palestinian self-determination and statehood which came to be widely recognized as legitimate after having been considered controversial for many years. The European Community eventually followed suit in the 1980 Venice Declaration which called for self-determination, and the 1999 Berlin Declaration which called for statehood. Time, however, is not a commodity the Palestinians have in abundance. Each year, settlement expansion diminishes the territory Israel is likely to concede in any peace deal. Moreover, normative power alone is not the main factor which compels action, but the ability of norms to be used to affect tangible interests of the parties.

Ultimately, Israel is correct when it suggests that any resolution to the conflict will need to be negotiated between the two parties. While Wallström is theoretically correct to argue that levelling the asymmetry can be an important contribution to the negotiating process, recognition itself will do little to affect this or bring the parties back to the table; it needs to be anchored in a wider European and international strategy which moves beyond recognition. The extent to which Swedish policy more broadly has any positive effect on this outcome will remain to be seen.

One of the most important roles Sweden can continue to play is to push within the EU for stronger and clearer unified policy towards the occupation. Indeed, Sweden continues to lobby within the EU regarding final status issues, for example when it argued strongly in favour of the January 2016 foreign affairs council resolution condemning Israeli settlement expansion (Beaumont & Rankin, 2016). It also continues to be in favour of differentiation and the labelling of settlement goods (Wallström, 2015). Beyond the EU, Sweden is since 2017 a non-permanent member of the UN Security Council, where the Palestinians are confident that Sweden actively represents their interests (Interview 3). However, this has yet to generate any significant new initiatives towards the Israeli-Palestinian conflict or other tangible outcomes for the Palestinians. At the time of writing, US President Donald Trump's recognition of Jerusalem as the capital of Israel has prompted an emergency meeting, but a US veto would prevent anything significant from emerging from it.

The Swedish decision to recognize Palestine attests to the primacy of politics when recognizing new states in the international system. Although international law featured in the rationale, showing the relevance of the declaratory school, the decision was primarily motivated by political considerations, chiefly the failed peace process. The case thus demonstrates the continued relevance of the constitutive school. Regardless of whether or not Palestine meets the traditional criteria for statehood, this statehood will be incomplete without acceptance by Israel and other key members of the international community, such as the permanent members of the UN Security Council.

Even so, the strength of Israeli objections to the recognition of Palestine suggests that the normative element of recognition remains significant, though insufficient. Similarly, Swedish opposition parties remain staunchly opposed to the government's policy. Christian Democrat, Liberal, Moderate, and Sweden Democrat parliamentarians continue to raise their objections to a policy they deem hostile to Israel and unhelpful to the peace process. In 2016 the Sweden Democrats even called for parliament to withdraw recognition, though unsuccessfully (Söder et al., 2016; Wiechel, Söder, Nissinen, Kronlid, & Skalin, 2017). Although a prominent foreign policy issue, the Israeli-Palestinian conflict is not politically decisive in Sweden. While there is widespread public criticism of the

Israeli occupation, public opinion is not blindly pro-Palestinian; there is also criticism of Palestinian actions, including terrorism, and understanding for the security challenges Israel faces (Bjereld, 2005). In fact, previous generations of Social Democratic foreign policy towards the Palestinians did not necessarily reflect public opinion, but was still accepted (Eriksson, 2015, pp. 77–78). Far from being settled, the issue will undoubtedly continue to feature prominently in political debate and be a source of opposition criticism.

Nonetheless, Swedish officials are confident that history will repeat itself and their stance towards the Palestinians will once again become the new norm (Interviews 1 & 2). This optimism, however, stands in stark contrast to the lack of progress towards widespread European recognition of Palestine. If history is anything to go by, Sweden may once again have to wait many years for others to follow, if indeed they ever do.

Notes

1. On the legal debate about the occupation of Palestinian territories, see Lynk and Azarova in this special issue.
2. It is worth noting that one member of the ruling coalition, the Center party, also argued in favour of recognizing Palestine (Riksdagen, 2013b).
3. These results echo longer term trends observable in an earlier poll (Palestinian Centre for Policy and Survey Research, 2016).
4. On the issue of recognition in Norway, see Pace in this special issue.
5. For specific figures, see Wildeman in this special issue.

Disclosure statement

No potential conflict of interest was reported by the author.

References

Agence France Press. (2014, October 30). Sweden officially recognises state of Palestine. *The Guardian*. Retrieved from http://www.theguardian.com

Aggestam, L., & Bicchi, F. (2018). Breaking away or leading the way? Cross-loading and like-minded groups in EU foreign policy post-Lisbon. Paper presented at the EUIA conference in Brussels, 16-18 May 2018.

Ahren, R. (2016, June 3). Paris summit ends with vague call for international conference by year's end. *The Times of Israel*. Retrieved from http://www.timesofisrael.com

An Israel-Palestine peace conference – without Israel or Palestine. (2017, January 17). *The Economist*. Retrieved from http://www.economist.com

Beaumont, P., & Rankin, J. (2016, January 18). EU adopts resolution criticising Israeli settlement expansion. *The Guardian*. Retrieved from http://www.theguardian.com

Bildt, C. (2008, March 5). Därför erkänner Sverige Kosovo. *Svenska Dagbladet*. Retrieved from www.svd.se

Bjereld, U. (2005, April 25). Svagaste svenska stödet för Israel på 35 år. *Dagens Nyheter*. Retrieved from http://www.dn.se

Bouris, D. (2014). *The European Union and occupied Palestinian territories: State-building without a state*. London: Routledge.

Cabinet office. (2015, February 9). Konstitutionsutskottets granskningsärende 8 – Deklarationen om Palestina i regeringsförklaringen.

Crawford, J. (2007). *The creation of states in international law*. Oxford: Oxford University Press.

Dahlberg, A. (2009, December 6). Bråka på, Bildt!. *Expressen*. Retreived from http://www.expressen.se

Davidovich, J. (2014, October 31). Sweden and Israel: The IKEA wars. *The Times of Israel*. Retrieved from http://www.timesofisrael.com

Eriksson, J. (2015). *Small-state mediation in international conflicts: Diplomacy and negotiation in Israel-Palestine*. London: IB Tauris.

Geldenhuys, D. (2009). *Contested states in world politics*. Basingstoke: Palgrave.

International Crisis Group. (2012, December 20). *Extreme Makeover? (I): Israel's Politics of Land and Faith in East Jerusalem* (Middle East Report No. 134) Brussels.

Interview 1, Swedish official, 9 June, 2016.

Interview 2, Swedish official, 10 June, 2016.

Interview 3, Palestinian official, 17 July, 2017.

Interview 4, Israeli official, 18 July, 2017.

Israel kallar hem Sverige-ambassadör. (2014, October 30). *Svenska Dagbladet*. Retrieved from http://www.svd.se

Löfven, S., Romson, Å, Fridolin, G., Sjöstedt, J., Ahlin, U., Ceballos, B., & Linde, H. (2012, February 12). Sverige bör erkänna en palestinsk stat. *Svenska Dagbladet*. Retrieved from http://www.svd.se

Lovatt, H. (2016, October). EU differentiation and the push for peace in Israel-Palestine. *European Council on Foreign Relations*. Retrieved from http://www.ecfr.eu

McCarthy, R., & Black, I. (2009, December 8). Europe softens Middle East statement after condemnation from Israel. *The Guardian*. Retrieved from http://www.theguardian.com

Ministry of Foreign Affairs. (2014, October 30). Strategy for Swedish international development assistance to Palestine, 2015–2019. Retrieved from http://www.government.se

Montevideo Convention on Rights and Duties of States. (1933). LNTS 165, 19. Retrieved from http://treaties.un.org

Palestinian Central Bureau of Statistics. (2016). Palestinians at the end of 2016. http://www.pcbs.gov.ps

Palestinian Centre for Policy and Survey Research. (2016, December 8-10). Public Opinion Poll #62. Retrieved from http://www.pcpsr.org

Palestinian Centre for Policy and Survey Research. (2017, September 19). Public Opinion Poll #65. Retrieved from http://www.pcpsr.org

Persson, A. (2017). Shaping discourse and setting examples: Normative power Europe can work in the Israeli-Palestinian conflict. *Journal of Common Market Studies*, 55(6), 1415–1431.

Rabbani, M. (2017, January 15). Paris peace conference: a damp squib. *Al Jazeera*. Retrieved from http://www.aljazeera.com

Ravid, B. (2009, December 1). Haaretz Exclusive: EU Draft Document on Division of Jerusalem. *Ha'aretz*. Retrieved from http://www.haaretz.com

Ravid, B., & Reuters. (2009, December 8). EU Foreign Ministers: Jerusalem must be joint capital of Israel, Palestinian state. *Ha'aretz*. Retrieved from http://www.haaretz.com

Riksdagen. (2011, October 25). Parliamentary foreign policy debate. Retrieved from http://www.riksdagen.se

Riksdagen. (2012, February 15). Parliamentary foreign policy debate. Retrieved from http://www.riksdagen.se

Riksdagen. (2013a, December 16). Parliamentary debate. Retrieved from http://www.riksdagen.se

Riksdagen. (2013b, October 14). Parliamentary debate. Retrieved from http://www.riksdagen.se

Riksdagen. (2014a, November 4). Parliamentary debate. Retrieved from http://www.riksdagen.se

Riksdagen. (2014b, November 20). Parliamentary debate. Retrieved from http://www.riksdagen.se

Ryngaert, C., & Sobrie, S. (2011). Recognition of states: International law or realpolitik? The practice of recognition in the wake of Kosovo, South Ossetia, and Abkhazia. *Leiden Journal of International Law, 24*(2), 467–490.

Söder, B., Ahl, J., Nissinen, J., Skalin, J., Wiechel, M., & Gamov, P. (2016). Fredsprocessen i Mellanöstern: Motion till Riksdagen, 2016/17:472 [Parliamentary motion on the Middle East Peace Process]. Retrieved from http://www.riksdagen.se

UN Special Coordinator for the Middle East Peace Process. (2011, September 18). Palestinian state-building: An achievement at risk. Retrieved from http://unispal.un.org

Wallström, M. (2014, October 30). Därför erkänner Sverige idag staten Palestina. *Dagens Nyheter*. Retrieved from http://www.dn.se

Wallström, M. (2015, November 10). From Sweden, looking toward Israel with friendly concern. *Ha'aretz*. Retrieved from http://www.haaretz.com

Wiechel, M., Söder, B., Nissinen, J., Kronlid, J., & Skalin, J. (2017). Fredsprocessen i Mellanöstern: Motion till Riksdagen, 2017/18:3335 [Parliamentary motion on the Middle East Peace Process]. Retrieved from http://www.riksdagen.se

The angel in disguise? Norway's complicity in Israel's continued colonisation of Palestinian territories

Michelle Pace

ABSTRACT
Norway's ambiguous approach towards Israel and Palestine can be traced back to the 1940s when it was the most pro-Israeli of the three Nordic countries. Since then, there has been a change in perceptions of Israel amongst the Norwegian public and at the official government level. The article follows this change through four crucial phases: the first focuses on the period 1978 up until 1993; the second highlights the Oslo Accords period; the third elucidates the Second Intifada phase and the fourth concentrates on the time of the Gaza war of 2014 up to this day. While Middle East events influenced Norwegian public opinion vis-à-vis Israeli occupation of the Palestinian territory, policies of Norwegian governments throughout these periods did not necessarily reflect public opinion. Nowadays, the Norwegian government continues to enhance its economic relations with Israel, in spite of the more pro-Palestinian stance amongst the general public in Norway.

Introduction

This contribution traces the dramatic shifts and turning points over the decades in Norway's approach towards Israel and Palestine, in particular in regard to the former's occupation of Palestinian territory (OPT). It does this through an analysis of the changing perceptions of Israel amongst the Norwegian public first from the period 1978–1993, then at the time of the Oslo accords, followed by another pivotal historical moment – the Second Intifada, as well as through the periods of expansion of Israeli settlements and the 2014 Gaza war. In doing so this contribution traces the impact of these key events on Norwegians' (government and general public) stances on the Israeli occupation of Palestinian lands. It argues that, in spite of what, on the surface, may appear as an ambiguous strategy of balancing relations between Israel and the Occupied Palestinian Territory (OPT), Norway's policies continue to enhance and deepen relations with the occupying power. The article also highlights how the Norwegian government has de-coupled itself from the EU in this regard, although Norway's unilateralism and its independent line from the EU on issues relating to Israel may well, in fact, be a feature of changing governments.

Norway's diplomatic relations with Israel kicked off in 1949 when Norway formally recognized the State of Israel, which in turn contributed to the admission of the latter as a full member of the United Nations. The Norwegian Labour Party (or AP for

Arbeiderpartiet) held power from the first post-war elections in 1945 until the 1961 elections and had a pro-Israeli stance. For the majority of non-socialist and Christian Norwegians the new Jewish state represented the fulfillment of Old Testament prophecies (NOU, 2000). In this context, the sale of Norwegian military equipment to Israel at that time was broadly acceptable to the Norwegian (Israel-friendly) population. During this period, Norway was in fact the most pro-Israeli of the three Nordic countries and, especially throughout the 1950s, there was a close connection between Norwegian and Israeli Social Democratic government parties.

This sympathetic attitude of the Labour Party towards Israel had not been entirely so prior to 1949. In 1945, the creation of a Jewish state was considered by the AP to be neither possible nor fair. The Party's suggestion was a non-Zionist solution: the assimilation of the Jews in their respective European countries. Norwegian historian Waage (2000) explains the change in the AP's position regarding Israel largely in terms of religious repentance. On 20 November 1949 a plane carrying 27 Jewish children from Tunisia who were to transit through Norway while immigrating to Israel, crashed due to bad weather at Hurum. All children – except one – died. The crash was the second deadliest air disaster in Norway at that time. Public sympathy ran high, and the secretary of the AP, Håkon Lie, started a fundraising campaign to build a Norwegian village, the moshav Yanuv, in Israel.

Following the 1956 Suez crisis and until the 1967 war the majority of the Norwegian population remained largely sympathetic towards Israel. But when Knut Frydenlund of the AP became Foreign Minister in 1973, he played a decisive role in promoting the demands of the Palestinians early on in his political career. In fact in 1974 Norway made a controversial move by giving its support for PLO leader Yasser Arafat to speak for the first time at the UN General Assembly (NUPI, 1974) clearly signaling to Israel that Norway couldn't be taken for granted in terms of its support for Israel and its actions. However, in the same year, Norway was one of eight countries that voted against granting the PLO observer status in the UN General Assembly. At the time, 87 of Norway's 157 parliamentarians were members of what was called the Friends of Israel Foundation (Damen, 2013). This attempt to pursue a balanced approach towards both the Palestinians and the Israelis is a trait that marks the historical development of Norway-Palestine-Israel relations, although on the one hand Norway's public opinion has moved towards a more pro-Palestinian position in more recent times and, on the other, Norway's policies have moved in the opposite direction.

Norway and changing perceptions of Israel amongst the Norwegian public 1978–1993

From 1978 Norway's peacekeeping forces in southern Lebanon (as part of UNIFIL) had an impact on the development of Norwegian attitudes towards the country's relationship with Israel. Thousands of Norwegian soldiers serving in UNIFIL had arrived in Lebanon with sympathy for Israel: the perception of Israel of these soldiers however changed to a much more critical one upon their return back home in Norway (Ness, 1989). The image of Israel also changed amongst several Norwegian politicians and journalists who witnessed at first hand the harassment of the Haddad forces. Moreover, Norway's foreign ministry was concerned about the safety of Norwegian UNIFIL members (Damen, 2013).

As Iran experienced its revolution in 1979, sending the oil markets in turmoil, Norway's position came into focus. Having relied on oil supplies from Iran prior to the revolution, the US and Israel looked to Norway as an alternative supplier. Norwegian diplomat Hans Longva discussed the matter with Yasser Arafat who supported the Norwegian plan to guarantee an oil supply to Israel, on condition that the Norwegians would provide a secret back channel to Israel when needed (Olsen, 2012). During the 1980s the AP decided to reassess its views of the PLO: in December 1982 Frydenlund and other AP politicians had an unofficial meeting with Arafat in Tunis. In 1989 foreign minister Thorvald Stoltenberg heralded a drastic shift through official talks with Arafat.

Stoltenberg managed to do this at a time when the public opinion climate in Norway was more pro-Palestinian: times were shifting (Finnanger, 2015). In 1967, Norwegian public debates referred to the ME conflict as one between Israel and the (slightly vaguely defined) "Arab states" and therefore that at this time it was unthinkable for Norway to acknowledge a Palestinian state. However, Norwegians' opinions about the ME conflict, perceptions of what the conflict is about and who the conflict parties involved are changed between the period 1967 to 1984. This can be explained through a connection between these changes and evolving events in the Middle East. During this period press coverage of the ME conflict in Norway changed significantly as well. During the Six Day 1967 war, coverage in VG (a foreign-owned Norwegian tabloid newspaper) and Aftenposten (a moderately conservative newspaper) mainly held more sympathy with Israel than with Egypt. At the time of the Lillehammer affair (21 July 1973) Mossad agents mistook the identity of Ali Hassan Salameh (the target of their operation who had been the chief perpetrator of the terrorist group Black September that had kidnapped and murdered 11 Israeli athletes, officials and trainers at the Munich Olympics in 1972) and killed Ahmed Bouchikhi, a Moroccan waiter and brother of the renowned musician Chico Bouchikhi. The editors of VG and Aftenposten were reluctant to condemn Israel for the murder. Six of the Mossad 15 member team were captured and convicted of complicity in the murder by the Norwegian justice system. The coverage in Aftenposten and VG of the 1973 Yom Kippur war also revealed a greater sympathy for the Israeli side than for how Egyptians and Syrians experienced the war (Ibid.).

These two newspapers changed tone when in October 1978 it was announced that the Nobel Peace Prize was to go to Egypt's President Anwar Sadat and Israeli Prime Minister Menachem Begin. Aftenposten and VG questioned whether the prize should go to Sadat alone given that it was he who had initiated a trip to Jerusalem in November 1977 and thus it was Sadat who had paved the way for the Egypt-Israel peace treaty. Israel was also criticized for its second invasion of Lebanon in 1982 which was (as already mentioned earlier) reinforced by the Norwegian contribution to UNIFIL.

This change of tone also reflected Norwegian public opinion. While in 1967 75% of Norwegians polled reported that they supported Israel, in 1971 67% wanted Israel to retreat to the borders of the pre-Six day war. A December 1973 poll shows that only 12.5% of respondents believed that Norway should support Israel. The late 1970s and early 1980s were in fact marked by an overall decline in support for Israel in Norway (Finnanger, 2015). However, this decline was not necessarily replaced by more sympathy for Palestinians. This was probably due to the negative associations that respondents made with the PLO. Following the 1967 war, press coverage in Norway was dominated by frequent mention of conflicts in the ME region. This led to an impression amongst the public that the conflict level in the ME was on the increase – an impression that reflected in the low percentage of Norwegians that believed in the possibility of a peace agreement.

Stoltenberg's 1989 opening of official talks with Arafat occurred at a time when most Western countries held at a distance from the PLO, as the latter was designated as a terrorist organization by the US and Israel until the Madrid Conference in 1991. While these Norwegian moves signaled an appreciation and understanding of the rights of the Palestinian people, Norway managed to successfully develop and navigate a relationship with *both* Israel and the PLO, thus continuing its balancing act. In this way it created an impression of neutrality which underpinned the basis for the "Oslo Agreement", in which Norway played an important role (or so it was thought).

Norway and the Oslo accords

Norway was the location where behind-the-scenes negotiations between the PLO and Israel that led to the signing of the 1993 Declaration of Principles – also known as the Oslo Accords – were held (Waage, 2002, 2004 and 2005). During this period (1990–1997) Norway had a Labour government. The series of secret meetings in Oslo were led by Terje Rød-Larsen, Mona Juul, Jan Egeland and Johan Jørgen Holst (then Foreign Secretary). With this declaration, which was actually signed in Washington, DC, the government of the state of Israel and the PLO team, representing the Palestinian people, agreed to recognize their mutual legitimate and political rights, and to strive to live in peaceful coexistence and mutual dignity and security. The ultimate aim of this declaration was to achieve a just, lasting and comprehensive peace settlement and historic reconciliation through the agreed political process. The agreement led to the first official recognition of Palestinian peoplehood and Palestinians' rights by Israel. However, there was no recognition of Israel as an occupier. Furthermore, there was no "reference to the Palestinian right to self-determination or statehood" (Abu Amr, 1994, p. 78) in the Accords confirming that these accords were never meant to bring about a sovereign State of Palestine (Milton-Edwards & Alastair, 2004; Pace & Sen, in press; Persson, 2010).

Norway's "crusader diplomacy" in the most intractable conflict in the Middle East gained the country a lot of prestige and fame. Norway built up an image of a country with moral integrity and a great conflict mediator firmly placing the country on the highest levels of the international peace scene. Oslo specifically became known as the world's "capital of peace." Peace mediation became one of Norway's primary export services. Norway's "value-added component" also came to use in peace processes in Sri Lanka, Cyprus, Sudan, Guatemala, Columbia and the former Yugoslavia (Bullion, 2001; Hæglund & Svensson, 2002; Kelleher, 2006; Kelleher & Taulbee, 2006; Moolakkattu, 2005; Skånland, 2010).

However, the view of Norway amongst the majority of Palestinians, but especially amongst the youth, was quite different, as it emerged from interviews and field observations held by the author, October 2014 in Gaza and during May, June and October 2016 in East Jerusalem and the West Bank. Far from being celebrated, Oslo was criticized as the beginning of the end of any hope for meaningful Palestinian sovereignty and as the main set up for the theatrical machinery of the Palestinian Authority as well as the performativity surrounding the notion of a "Palestinian state" (Pace & Sen, in press). These perceptions resonated amongst Palestinians in diaspora, as expressed in interviews held by the author in Copenhagen and London in May 2017.

The Oslo Accords have also been heavily criticized in Norway as raising a false hope for peace in the Middle East. According to Waage (2008) – a renown expert on Norway-Israel-Palestine relations – Norwegians were very naive to believe that through dialogue and a gradual building of trust, an irreversible dynamic of peace would be created that could push the process forward to a solution. Waage's point is that the entire approach missed the core issue at hand: Norway's facilitative role did not address the power asymmetry between Palestinians and Israelis. "In the end," she argues, "the results that can be achieved by a weak third-party facilitator are no more than the strong party will allow (63)."

At the official level, however, Norway continued its balancing act of assisting Israelis and Palestinians in achieving a supposedly "negotiated" agreement fulfilling the vision of two states, Israel and Palestine, living side by side in peace and security. Norway also persisted with its role as chair of the Donor Coordination Group (the Ad Hoc Liaison Committee or AHLC), where both conflict parties participate actively. This can be understood in the context of the political landscape in Norway which generally considers foreign policy as a prerogative of the government, rather than a topic for political parties as such. There is also a long-standing Norwegiantradition of consensus-oriented foreign policy. The general line on the Israel-Palestine issue is just like that of the EU in that a) the occupation is a problem, but the only way to solve it is through direct negotiations between the conflict parties; b) the two-state solution is the only solution c) Norway has an important role through the AHLC and cannot rock the boat because that would undermine that influence.[1]

The Second Intifada, Norway's position on Israel and Norwegian public opinion

In 2002, during the course of the Second Intifada, the IDF launched a large-scale military Operation named "Defensive Shield" in the West Bank. Soon after, *Opinion* conducted an opinion poll for the leading broadsheet newspaper Aftenposten which revealed that 44% of Norwegians felt the most sympathy with the Palestinians in the ongoing conflict while only 9% had the greatest sympathy for Israel. Moreover, 68% of the respondents believed that Israel should withdraw from the occupied territories on the West Bank and Gaza Strip – a sharp increase from the 47% that were noted during a similar survey also conducted by *Opinion* for Bergens Tidende in 1988. Thus events in the Middle East clearly triggered a shift in Norwegians' sympathy towards Palestinians. This was at a time (between 2001 and 2005) when Norway had a centre-right coalition government with the Christian Democrats (KrF or Kristelig Folkeparti), which was the party of the prime minister. The KrF used to be a staunch supporter of Israel but developed a more balanced stance, losing a fraction of the most right-wing supporters to FRP or Fremskrittspartiet, the People's Progress Party because of this), Høyre (Conservative party) and Venstre (Liberal party which is a centre party).

At the official government level, during 2007, when the Norwegian Labour government was in power, and when Jonas Gahr Støre was Foreign Minister, Norway deviated from its constant support for Israel by recognizing the Hamas unity government after Hamas won the 2006 Palestinian elections for the second Palestinian Legislative Council or PLC and the legislature of the Palestinian National Authority (PNA). "It would be the height of hypocrisy," Støre said, "if we saluted the ballot box but refused its result. We must accept the results of the ballot box. But we must also hold accountable any majority which might emerge from elections. Any such majority must abide by international human rights standards... The Palestinians are suffering a double tragedy – the tragedy of living under occupation, and the tragedy of being divided. In 2007, we decided to engage with the Palestinian national unity government. But the European Union made the mistake of deciding not to engage. We in Norway are prepared to talk to all Palestinian groups, including Hamas, even though we do not recognize its charter, which we find deeply disturbing. We are in favour of Palestinian national reconciliation (Seale, 2012)."

This was a monumental moment when Norway proved its independence from other major European interlocutors in the Middle East saga. In fact, it was the only "Western" country, together with Switzerland, to do so at the time. This shift in policy can be explained by Norway's commitment to the principles of democracy. The 2006 elections in the OPTwere deemed to be the most transparent, free and fair elections in the whole Arab world by the European Parliamentary election monitors (Pace & Pallister-Wilkins, 2018). This conclusion effected public sympathy in Norway which also shifted Government policy since the latter was true to reflecting the Norwegian majority's opinion. Støre's policy was to engage with all actors, without necessarily endorsing their policies. To engage was a key principle of the foreign policy of Norway's centre-left government which came to power in 2005 and was re-elected in 2009. During this period, Norway regularly warned Israel that if it refused to move forward with the political process, it would face donor fatigue, and might itself, as the occupying power, have to assume responsibility for the West Bank Palestinians. But Israel continued its relentless seizure of Palestinian land while counting on foreign donors to continue to finance the PNA.

On January 12, 2011, Jonas Gahr Støre (then Norway's Foreign Minister) avowed that Norway "could recognize the Palestinian state" and followed this up on 18 July when he claimed that Norway was to recognize Palestine.

On 21 December 2012, MIFF (Med Israel for fred/"With Israel for Peace") – which keeps a regular track record of sympathy for and against Israel in Norway – quoted an opinion poll (without actually specifying which "poll conducted by one of the major professional Norwegian polling institutes" they had gained access to) and stipulated that only 14 percent of Norwegian youth believed that Israel really wants peace. MIFF also reported that sympathy for Israel and the Palestinians varies across different parts of Norway. In Sørlandet (southern Norway where the Middle East debate is much more polarized), 10% of the population polled had great sympathy for Israel (with a national average of 6 percent) while 9% had greater sympathy for the PA (with a national average of 5 percent) (MIFF, 2012). At the time of the quoted opinion poll (between 2005 and 2013) Norway had a centre left coalition government composed of the AP (Labour party), the Socialist Left party (SV or Sosialistisk Venstreparti) and the centre party (Sp or Senterpartiet). Events in the oPt changed public opinion in Norway. The 2008 and 2012 wars in Gaza as well as the work and reports that emerged from Norway's civil society groups played a role in exposing Israel's continued violations of international law in the oPt which in turn effected Norwegians' opinion about the occupying power.

Settlements, Gaza war 2014 and impact on Norwegian stance on occupation

In a damning report published in 2013 entitled "Dangerous Liaisons. Norwegian Ties to the Israel occupation", the NGO Norwegian People's Aid (NPA) and the Norwegian Union of Municipal and General Employees (Fagforbundet) expose how Norwegian authorities (including municipalities) and companies – through financial investments and trade – are complicit in activities that contribute to Israel's violations of international law and human rights in the occupied Palestinian territories. The said report goes further to reveal how groups in Norway directly support the occupation through money transfers to individual settlements that are illegal under international law. The International Court of Justice (ICJ) has concluded that Israeli settlements in the occupied Palestinian territory including East Jerusalem have been established in violation of international law.

Furthermore, the Government Pension Fund of Norway – Global (or GPFG: Norway's sovereign wealth fund) invested NOK 13,3 million in equities and NOK 11,3 million in fixed assets in Israel (which is the fund's largest investments in the Middle East region) (see also Bahl, 2017). Moreover, the Israeli government, business sector and academia look to Norway to learn lessons in managing oil and gas revenues and building an energy industry. The report details how the Government Pension Fund of Norway – Global (GPFG) and 13 private Norwegian banks and investment funds are implicated in the occupation and related violations. Twelve such companies are considered to be particularly involved in serious violations, including: the building of key infrastructure in the oPt, the provision of essential factors of production for the construction of settlements or the Wall, as well as heavy machinery used to destroy Palestinian homes and infrastructure, the extraction of non-renewable natural resources from occupied areas, and the development and provision of technology and systems contributing to Israeli military control and the restriction of freedom of movement. Israelis journalists have also reported on the working environment legislation which is not enforced in the Israeli industrial zones in the West Bank where many Palestinians work. It is often the case that Palestinian workers receive too little pay. The Mishor Adumim industrial zone on the outskirts of Jerusalem is one of the largest Israeli industrial zones in the West Bank. Mishor is linked to the Ma'ale Adumim settlement, the third largest settlement in the West Bank. The purpose of the project is to cut the link between Jerusalem and the West Bank by expanding the industrial zone/settlement. Mishor has a lot of industry that produces waste that is hazardous to the environment. SodaStream, the producer of home carbonating devices, had its main factory in the Mishor Adumim industrial zone (it moved its production out of Mishor in December 2015). The company sells its products to Norway. Mishor includes other companies that the Norwegian Government Pension Fund Global (SPU) owns shares in: these include Mayer's Cars and Trucks, the official representative of the Volvo Group in Israel and Rami Levy and Shufersal, two supermarket chains (Moa, 2013, p. 22).

The report's authors argue that these companies' activities are in breach of GPFG guidelines. Such reports leave a negative imprint amongst the general public in Norway vis-à-vis Israel and its occupation of Palestinian land.

In July 2014, in a strongly worded message, Jonas Gahr Støre of Norway's Labour Party, Stefan Löfven of Sweden's Social Democrats, Árni Páll Árnason of Iceland's Social

Democratic Alliance and Antti Rinne of Finland's Social Democrats all added their names to a letter which condemned Israel's use of "disproportionate violence" during the 2014 Gaza war and called on Israel to end its blockade of Gaza and occupation of the West Bank. This letter was initially meant to be a unified Nordic message but then Danish Prime Minister (Social democrat) Helle Thorning Schmidt refused to sign (The Local Denmark, 2014).

But this message again exposed the realities on the ground for Palestinians living under Israeli military occupation to the scrutiny of the Norwegian public. It is therefore argued there that Norway is actually de-coupling from itself with regard to Israel and especially on the issue of Israeli settlements. In the main, Norwegian public opinion and civil society would much rather align with and support the EU's differentiation policy, in line with UNSC 2334. (United Nations Security Council Resolution 2334 was adopted on 23 December 2016. It concerns the Israeli settlements in "Palestinian territories occupied since 1967, including East Jerusalem". The resolution states that Israel's settlement activity constitutes a "flagrant violation" of international law and has "no legal validity". It demands that Israel stop such activity and fulfil its obligations as an occupying power under the Fourth Geneva Convention). However, the current Norwegian government, made up of a right of centre coalition and which has been in power since September 2013, has instead enhanced cooperation with Israel with fewer strings attached than what the EU differentiation policy calls for. This applies to new trade deals, gas exploration, etc. This exposes how the Norwegian government's policy no longer reflects the opinion of the majority of the Norwegian public: a worrying trend that shows how even long standing democracies can start to erode from within.

On 16 August 2017 the Palestine Committee of Norway published a report detailing the various political parties' responses to 8 questions set by this committee in cooperation with the Joint Committee for Palestine. The Progress Party did not agree with the premise of the questions and therefore chose to answer the questions without considering the options provided. Their position on the recognition of a Palestinian state is that doing so now will be devastating to the peace process. Moreover, the Frp holds that the areas in which petroleum activities are conducted between Norway and Israel are not contested by the party. The party holds that cooperation with Israel within the petroleum sector is good for Norway. Furthermore the Frp's position on the Government's Global Pension Fund which invests in Israel (including in settlements) continues because it provides a good return for the Fund and thus favourable for the Norwegian economy: clearly the Frp does not follow an ethical foreign and economic policy. Thus, on the one hand, the FrP, the country's third largest political party (a party which used to be highly bourgeois but is now mostly charismatically Christian – an interesting shift given that there is very little by way of overlap between the two groups)[2] and a part of the centre-right government coalitionseem to be home to the pro-Israel lobby.

On the other hand, at time of writing (2018), there seems to be an unequivocal and fairly steady shift in Norwegian public opinion away from supporting Israel towards seeing Israel as the oppressor of Palestinians, and as at least an equal if not more aggressive part in the Middle East context generally. This would point to an increasing disconnect between, on the one hand, the Norwegian government's stance vis-à-vis Israel and, on the other, the Norwegian public's perception of the occupying power in the OPT.

Norwegian government and public opinion on the occupation: a summary analysis

The above being noted, it is important to observe that some differences between the parties actually exist. In terms of the political parties in the Norwegian parliament there is today only one clearly pro-Israel party – the Progress Party (FrP). In fact the FrP (right wing populists), as well as parts of the Christian Democratic party, are even pushing for Norway to follow Trump's example regarding the embassy move to Jerusalem. The two socialist parties, SV and Rødt, advocate on the contrary an economic boycott of Israel. The SV called for a re-evaluation of Norwegian policy towards Israel and Palestine, but the parliament voted against it. Parts of the Labour Party advocate supporting the EU differentiation policy. The Labour Party has gradually moved towards supporting the recognition of a Palestinian state (in 2015) even without the existence of a peace agreement between the parties. This was an important step from the previous position – which was that the recognition of Palestine could only be offered as a result of a negotiated peace agreement with Israel. However, the government coalition, which includes FrP, sustains its support for "the goal of Israel and Palestine as two states within secure and internationally recognized borders" (Government of Norway, 2018).

In terms of differences between some of the Nordic countries today, Sweden has taken the step of recognizing Palestine as a state. As the Israeli government has often refused to meet with Swedish representatives and denied Sweden access to Gaza (cf. Eriksson in this special issue), the Swedish case is often used negatively in Norway as an example of why rocking the boat is negative.

Conclusion

This contribution has sought to present the evolution of Norway's ambiguous approach towards Israel and the OPT.. In doing so it has been important to follow both the position of Norwegian governments, politicians and political parties in power over time, as well as public opinion. The point was made that events in the OPT have had an impact on the change recorded over time in Norwegians' perception about Israel as the occupying power. At the government level, although Norway often deviated from the EU's position – as in 2006 when Norway recognized the Hamas government – what is more noticeable is that Norway's official policy does not always reflect the will of the majority of its population. As has been shown, Norway's public opinion and civil society would prefer their country to support the EU's differentiation policy which states that Israel's settlement activity is a clear violation of international law and demands that Israel stops such activity. Yet, Israel continues to enjoy a very positive diplomatic relationship with Norway, just as it did since its founding in 1948 (Waage, 2000).

In 2014 (one year after leaving office), the Labour Minister Espen Barth Eide declared that alternatives to the EU's much emphasised "two-state solution" should be considered, implying that the solution might indeed be that of a one state (in Omvik & Fjeld, 2014). But the current government from the political right (since 2013) has turned more pro-Israel in its political rhetoric and action.

Another development worth noting is that during its latest congress in May 2017 the Norwegian trade unions, LO, which is very close to the Labour Party, agreed on a boycott of Israel, going against the policy of the Labour party (Grande, 2017).

While seemingly ambiguous and at times contradictory, with Norway recognizing the Palestinian national unity government in 2007 and with the government's pension fund divesting from three Israeli companies due to construction activity in East Jerusalem in 2014, Norway continues to expand its economic relations with Israel, as reports from 2013 and 2017 expose. It can thus be concluded that Norway's unilateralism or its independent line from the EU on issues relating to Israel (as in labelling of goods from settlements) may well be a feature of changing governments, although the political line may change.

Notes

1. Author communications with Jørgen Jensehaugen, 7th June 2018.
2. Discussions held by the author with Iver B Neumann and with Are Hovdenak, 6th June 2018. See also Andersen and Bjørklund (1990).

Acknowledgements

The author wishes to thank the following colleagues who were consulted during the writing of this contribution: Hilde Henriksen Waage, Iver Neumann, Are Hovdenak, Line Khateeb, Egil Bjørnsen, Elin Maria Fiane, Tora Systad Tyssen, Jon Hanssen-Bauer, Mark Taylor, Hilde Berg-Hansen, Henrik Thune, Mari Salberg, Ada Elisabeth Nissen, Jørgen Jensehaugen, Nils A Butenschøn, Dag Henrik Tuastad, Marte Heianengdal, Jon Pedersen and Jonas Finnanger.

Disclosure statement

No potential conflict of interest was reported by the author.

Funding

This work was supported by the Carlsbergfondet [grant number CFtS-0729].

References

Abu Amr, Z. (1994). *Islamic fundamentalism in the West Bank and Gaza: Muslim brotherhood and Islamic Jihad*. Bloomington, IN: Indiana University Press.
Andersen, J. G., & Bjørklund, T. (1990). Structural changes and new cleavages: The progress parties in Denmark and Norway. *Acta Sociologica*, 33(3), 195–217.
Bahl, M. (2017, January 31). Europe's largest pension funds heavily invested in illegal Israeli settlements. *Danwatc*. Retrieved from https://danwatch.dk/en/europes-largest-pension-funds-heavily-invested-in-illegal-israeli-settlements/
Bullion, A. (2001). Norway and the peace process in Sri Lanka. *Civil Wars*, 4(3), 70–92.

Damen, R. (2013). *The Price of Oslo*. Al Jazeera World. Retrieved from https://www.aljazeera.com/programmes/aljazeeraworld/2013/09/2013910121456318891.html

Finnanger, J. (2015). *Endrede meninger om en konflikt i endring: Norske holdninger til Midtøstenkonflikten mellom 1967 og 1984* (Changes in Norwegian public attitudes towards the Middle East conflict from 1967 to 1984). Masters thesis in history. University of Oslo. 15 May. Retrieved from https://www.duo.uio.no/bitstream/handle/10852/45173/Endrede-meninger-om-en-konflikt-i-endring-Jonas-Finnanger.pdf?sequence=1

Government of Norway website: Political platform. Report dated 14.01.2018 https://www.regjeringen.no/no/dokumenter/politisk-plattform/id2585544/#k17 and Israel / Palestine: Peace resolution with two states. Last updated: 08.04.2016. Retrieved from https://www.regjeringen.no/no/tema/utenrikssaker/fred-og-forsoning/land_for_land2/engasjement_midtoesten/id2522237/

Grande, A. (2017, May 12). LO – fler tall for boikott av Israel [More vote for boycott of Israel]. *Dagens Naeringsliv*. Retrieved from http://www.dn.no/nyheter/2017/05/12/1307/Politikk/lo-flertall-for-boikott-av-israel

Hæglund, K., & Svensson, I. (2002). The peace process in Sri Lanka. *Civil Wars*, 5(4), 103–118.

Kelleher, A. (2006). A small state's multiple-level approach to peace-making: Norway's role in achieving Sudan's comprehensive peace agreement. *Civil Wars*, 8(3-4), 285–311.

Kelleher, A., & Taulbee, J. L. (2006). Bridging the gap: Building peace Norwegian style. *Peace & Change. A Journal of Peace Research*, 31(4), 479–505.

MIFF Med Israel for fred. (2012, December 21). Nye tall om nordmenns holdning til Israel. Retrieved from https://www.miff.no/norge-og-israel/2012/12/21nyetallomnordmennsholdningtilisrael.htm

Milton-Edwards, B., & Alastair, C. (2004). Elusive ingredient: Hamas and the peace process. *Journal of Palestine Studies*, 33(4), 39–52.

Moa, I. (2013). *Dangerous liaisons. Norwegian ties to the Israeli occupation*. Oslo: Norwegian People's Aid and Norwegian Union of Municipal and General Employers.

Moolakkattu, J. S. (2005). Peace facilitation by small states: Norway in Sri Lanka. *Cooperation and Conflict*, 40(4), 385–402.

Ness, M. H. (1989). UN peacekeeping operations. UNIFIL - Participants - Defense: Feedback from the first 17 battalions. Oslo: NUPI Report, No. 127. (Original in Norwegian: FNs fredsbevarende operasjoner; UNIFIL - deltakerne -forsvaret: en tilbakemelding fra de første 17 bataljonene). Retrieved from https://forsvaretsforum.no/Sider/Nyhetsarkiv.aspx in Norwegian

Norges offentlige utredninger (NOU). (2000). Lillehammer-saken. Chapter 4 on 'Båndene til Israel styrkes, 1948–1956. (The ties to Israel are strengthened, 1948–1956). Statens forvaltningstjeneste Informasjonsforvaltning. Volume 6. Oslo. Retrieved from https://www.regjeringen.no/no/dokumenter/nou-2000-6/id142668/sec6

Norsk Utenrikspolitisk Institut (NUPI). (1974). *Norsk Utenrikspolitisk Årbok* 1974. Edited by Johan Jørgen Holst. Oslo.

Olsen, D. T. (2012). Secret diplomacy in Lebanon during the Norwegian UN mission in Lebanon. In J. E. Smildens (Eds.), *Norges Forsvar* (No. 3, pp. 40–41). Oslo: Norges Forsvarsforening.

Omvik, O. R., & Fjeld, I. E. (2014, August 17). Barth Eide: Vil diskutere alternativer til to-statsløsning [We will discuss alternatives to the two-state solution] NRK. Retrieved from https://www.nrk.no/urix/vil-drofte-alternativer-i-midtosten-1.11884155

Pace, M., & Pallister-Wilkins, P. (2018). EU–hamas actors in a state of permanent liminality. *Journal of International Relations and Development*, 21(1), 223–246.

Pace, M., & Sen, S. (in press). *The Palestinian authority in the West Bank. The theatrics of woeful statecraft*. Abingdon: Routledge. Routledge Studies in Middle Eastern Democratization and Government series, L. Sadiki (Eds.). Retrieved from https://www.routledge.com/The-Palestinian-Authority-in-the-West-Bank-The-Theatrics-of-Woeful-Statecraft/Pace-Sen/p/book/9781138567399

Persson, A. (2010). Legitimizing a just peace: EU's promotion of the parameters of just peace in the Israeli-Palestinian conflict. JAD-PbP Working Paper Series. Retrieved from http://portal.

research.lu.se/portal/en/publications/legitimizing-a-just-peace(6fa19bc1-5e8f-4a0e-972c-b1beb0738bd8).html
Seale, P. (2012, June 22). 'The Palestinians' best friend. *Gulf News*. Retrieved from https://gulfnews.com/opinion/thinkers/the-palestinians-best-friend-1.1038893
Skånland, Ø. H. (2010). 'Norway is a peace nation': A discourse analytic reading of the Norwegian peace engagement. *Cooperation and Conflict*, 45(1), 34–54.
The Local Denmark. (2014, July 29). Thorning refuses to sign Nordic letter on Gaza. Retrieved from https://www.thelocal.dk/20140729/thorning-refuses-to-sign-nordic-letter-on-gaza
Waage, H. H. (2000). How Norway became one of Israel's best friends. *Journal of Peace Research*, 37 (2), 189–211.
Waage, H. H. (2002). Explaining the Oslo backchannel: Norway's political past in the Middle East. *Middle East Journal*, 56(4), 597–615.
Waage, H. H. (2004). *'Peacemaking is a Risky Business.' Norway's Role in the Peace Process in the Middle East 1993-96. PRIO report 1*, Oslo.
Waage, H. H. (2005). Norway's role in the Middle East peace talks: Between a strong state and a weak belligerent. *Journal of Palestine Studies*, 34(4), 6–24.
Waage, H. H. (2008). Postscript to Oslo: The mystery of Norway's missing files. *Journal of Palestine Studies*, 38(1), 54–65.

Missing the train. International governance gaps and the Jerusalem Light Railway

Mary Martin

ABSTRACT

Since 2005, civil society activism appeared to be the most effective weapon against illegal economic activities in the Occupied Palestinian Territories (OPT). Campaigns such as the Boycott, Divestment and Sanctions (BDS) movement provided a means to disrupt foreign investment, by targeting companies directly and invoking an idea of corporate responsibility for human rights abuses. However, European Union member states and the EU itself have failed to build on civic activism and have been slow to address the potential of the private sector to create new facts on the ground or use the concept of corporate responsibility as a framework for innovative policy approaches towards the occupation. Drawing on the example of the Jerusalem Light Railway (JLR), and the subsequent development of the UN Guiding Principles on Business and Human Rights (UNGPs), the paper examines the effectiveness of a discourse of corporate responsibility in addressing the continuing plight of Palestinian communities under occupation.

1. Introduction

Passengers stepping off morning commuter trains in London in the summer and early autumn of 2005 were greeted by an unusual sight of protesters waving placards calling for a boycott to "Derail Veolia", the train operator. The Palestinian Boycott, Divest, Sanctions (BDS) campaign against Israeli occupation targeted Veolia, not because it operated in the suburbs of south-east England, but because it was part of a consortium to build another rail line linking Israeli settlements in the West Bank.

BDS activists heckled rail passengers, ratepayers whose councils had contracted Veolia to provide water services or clear household rubbish, subway riders in Stockholm, and laid siege to public opinion from Europe to the US and Australia. By singling out international companies, accusing them of discrimination against Palestinian residents and workers, of enabling the spread and ensuring the viability of illegal Israeli settlements, civil activists moved the occupation of the West Bank from an issue of elite international politics and diplomacy and international law, to a narrative of governance and corporate complicity, making this a ground for resistance and activism.

In this article, I look at the idea of corporate responsibility within the context of the Israeli occupation. The case of Veolia and the Jerusalem Light Railway illustrated how business behaviour can be integral to issues of peace and security, and the potential for policies which reflect the salience of corporate activities. However, the case also highlights the difficulties of making companies accountable for actions that create significant impacts in conflict settings, and which may even directly drive conflict. The case points to a persistent governance gap represented by the failure of governments and international organizations to control corporate activities, even where these activities threaten their own policy objectives. In the case of the Israeli occupation of Palestine, I argue that the disconnect between business behaviour, civic mobilization and policy represents a significant and continuing weakness resolving the crisis in the region.

The first part of the article looks back to the events of September 2005. It sets out the challenge the Jerusalem Light Railway presented to international law and to customary law on human rights, and how it ignited a new wave of civil society resistance to the occupation. Opponents of the railway sought to use different means of compliance, based variously on law and civil activism, in order to stop foreign companies participating in the project, with varying degrees of success and failure.

The second part moves to the present and reviews ethical/normative and governance initiatives as contemporary mechanisms for either encouraging corporate responsibility or forcing corporate compliance. Of particular significance is the emerging discourse spearheaded by the UN Guiding Principles on Business and Human Rights (UNGPs), agreed by UN member states in 2011, which provide a framework for government and business responsibility, and which link voluntary forms of responsibility with quasi formal compliance. In this section I look at whether and how the UNGP mechanism has relevance in light of the increased economic/business dimension of the occupation in the last decade, and the continued investment by companies in the disputed territories. The aim is to examine whether the UNGP framework of Protect, Respect and Remedy represents a new opportunity for European member states to address the occupation, and the role of companies within it, and thus fill the gap between the *ad hoc* impact of social activism, as in the Veolia case, and a sustained policy which recognizes the significance of the economic and investment dimension of the occupation. Much has been written from a perspective of international law on the situation of business, and foreign companies in particular, in the expansion of illegal Israeli settlements on the West Bank (Mendes-France, 2006, pp. 213–223). This article does not offer a legal argument. Rather it takes a governance perspective, examining the increasingly dominant concept of corporate responsibility for human rights, protection of citizens and conflict prevention, within global normative discourse, to explore whether and how corporate responsibility is relevant to resolving the crisis of the Occupied Palestinian Territory (OPT).

2. The Jerusalem light railway

The Jerusalem Light Railway (JLR), is a one-billion-euro international transport infrastructure project, which began construction in April 2006, and opened five and a half years later. The railway was designed to link the western – Israeli - part of Jerusalem with the new residential areas developing to the south, north and east of the city in OPT. Although the railway was presented as an essential public good to deal with a growing city within an image of a unified, modern metropolis, it was also a political project, to promote the viability of Israeli settlements and to its critics, a means of discrimination against Palestinians in the OPT (Boycott, Divestment, Sanctions (BDS), 2009).

In this last sense, the railway delivered the Palestinian resistance movement a new focus of opposition to the increase in Jewish settlements and the increasingly economic nature of the Israeli occupation. It created a new set of targets for civil activism among the foreign companies that had been contracted to build and operate the railway. These became the lightning rods for a fresh wave of civil society mobilization. The targeting of foreign investors was indicative of the transformation of resistance from a predominantly internal Israel-Palestinian issue to a transnational movement which engaged non-state actors and created new pressure points of action among European companies.

BDS argued that

> "JLR is considered an integral part of Israel's illegal colonial regime and, therefore, a violation of international law that may amount to a war crime. Companies that participate in building and running the JLR or in constructing, maintaining and servicing Israeli colonies, more generally, can therefore be regarded as 'aiding and abetting' these crimes." (Barghouti, 2009, p. 48).

French environmental and transport group, Veolia became a focus of the new resistance, on account of its 25% stake in the consortium created to build and manage the railway in partnership with the city municipality (The Civic Coalition for Defending Palestinians Rights in Jerusalem, 2009, p. 13) Veolia's consumer businesses relied on public authorities for renewable contracts, meaning that its public profile made it particularly attractive for activists, seeking both impact and visibility.

The campaign produced immediate effects. Veolia's contracts with public authorities were cancelled or not renewed. In 2009 Veolia announced it was seeking a buyer for its stake in the consortium and withdrawing from the 30-year contract. It finally sold the stake six years later (Bar-Eli, 2009). The company denied its decision was linked to the boycott, but the campaign had cost the group an estimated 25 billion euros in lost business.[1] Veolia subsequently sold all its transport operations in the region.[2]

International law provided a second avenue of attempts to make foreign companies accountable for their presence in the OPT. In 2007, the Palestine Liberation Organization (PLO) and the Association France-Palestine Solidarité (AFPS) launched a combined law suit against Veolia and Alstom claiming that the companies had violated international humanitarian law (IHL) in helping Israel to build the light railway. AFPS argued that claim should be examined by French judges, because the companies were headquartered in France.

The case sought to establish a legal principle of corporate responsibility and to clarify relationships of accountability between governments and businesses domiciled in their territory, by testing whether the French government could be held legally accountable for the behaviour of a French company in a foreign country (Cour d'Appel de Versailles, 2013). The French Foreign Ministry (quoted in Mendes-France, 2006) argued: "The fact that Alstom and Connex (Veolia) are private businesses exonerates the French government from this issue and disables any means it may have had with which to act".[3]

The case failed to establish a legal responsibility of either the government in relation to corporate activity, or of the companies themselves, as the court ruled that companies had no legal personality under international law. Only states could be said to have obligations as a result of international agreements (Ahren, 2013).

3. Holding companies accountable: three mechanisms

It has been suggested that responsibility is an established norm within the context of business management, business and human rights and governance agendas on security and development (Bondy, Moon, & Matten, 2012, p. 281). A discourse of corporate responsibility is predicated on an expectation that business has purposes beyond solely (or narrowly conceived) financial gain, and that other imperatives such as social and environmental concerns also shape business decisions (Bondy et al., 2012, p. 283). The commonplace or "almost truism" nature of corporate responsibility (Johnson, 2006) is also suggested by propositions that there should be a specific corporate responsibility for security (Deitelhoff & Wolf, 2010), a political role for corporations (Scherer & Palazzo, 2011), and in ideas such as corporate citizenship (Moon, Crane, & Matten, 2005).

The Jerusalem Light Railway case highlighted three potential mechanisms for regulating corporate actions and aligning business with social objectives. First, a voluntary and self-reflexive mechanism, under which a company itself would view its operations within a responsibility lens, connected either to avoiding human rights abuses and/or ensuring that its activities would not contribute to conflict. This self-responsibilisation[4] (Garland, 2001) is enacted by a company's commitment to global norms on ethical behaviour and human rights due diligence. In the case of Veolia, the company had signed up to governance standards such as the UN Global Compact, and the OECD Guidelines on Multinational Enterprises, which include practices such as social reporting, yet it failed to transmit these norms to the operating level in the context of its JLR contract. Going beyond a basic "do no harm" approach, the idea of conflict sensitivity, defined as "acting to minimize negative impacts and maximize positive impacts of intervention on conflict, within an organization's given priorities/objectives" (Conflict Sensitivity Consortium, n.d.) suggests a higher level of voluntary corporate responsibility, which was also absent in the Veolia case. Veolia opted for a much more limited definition of responsibility when it came to the JLR contract, justifying its involvement in terms of a "legitimate need" for infrastructure projects in Jerusalem, and claiming to have acted responsibly through canvassing community opinion about the tramway, and because the JLR would operate on a non-discriminatory basis for the benefit of all groups, including Palestinians. Both these latter claims are disputed on the grounds that there appears to have been limited consultation or engagement between the company and the community, and that station stops on the line serve predominantly Jewish neighbourhoods (Diakonia, 2009).

The second mechanism for holding companies to account is through international law. This failed in the JLR case because the French courts rejected a legal connection between state and private business actions, on the grounds that companies were not accountable under IHL because they have no legal personality (Cour d'Appel de Versailles, 2013). Subsequent cases in the Netherlands and Canada have raised different legal arguments and reached contradictory views on the issue of whether corporate liability could be adjudicated by a foreign court: in the Dutch case, which concerned whether Shell (Netherlands domiciled) could be held liable for environmental and human rights abuses in Nigeria, the court ruled that any Dutch person and legal entity was responsible for ensuring that they did not in any way infringe international humanitarian law, with even minor incidents capable of triggering prosecution in the courts of the home country (McConnell, 2014; Dutch Association of Investors for Sustainable Development (VBDO), 2014). In a more recent case, which attempted to sue Canadian companies for abetting settlement activity in OPT and alleged specific infringements of rights such as freedom of movement, arbitrary interference with the home, the right to pursue livelihood and the right to enjoy culture, Canadian courts – as in the Veolia case – refused to accept extra-territorial jurisdiction. The action also revealed more practical difficulties associated with legal forms of compliance, such as the limited financial resources of small villages to confront corporations in court, the lengthy legal procedures required to bring such cases and a lack of information about relations between parent companies and their subsidiaries in Israel/Palestine. (Moffat, 2009; Azarov, 2013)

To date, the most successful avenue for corporate responsibilisation remains social activism, and the "naming and shaming" strategies adopted by civil society. This has included quasi-legal initiatives, which may have no formal status in international law (Russell Tribunal on Palestine, 2013), but which frame attempts to enforce corporate accountability for human rights abuses in the OPT in legal terms. The use of pressure points such as other NGOs, investors, lenders and consumer publics is also critical to the success and impact of social activism (Kittrie, 2016; Corporate Watch, 2009).[5]

Amnesty International's campaign to mark the 50th anniversary of occupation, which drew attention to the "multi-million dollar" business of settlement activity, is an example of how NGOs continue to pressure both companies and states to ban imports of settlement goods (Amnesty International, 2017), using one-off public campaigns. The limits to this approach are indicated by the fact of the continuing spread and growth of "settlement business" despite such high-profile initiatives. The success of the Veolia case was partly dependent on the unique set of pressure points, such as local authority contracts and the ability to mobilise consumer opposition among a defined target audience such as railway passengers. The nature of the BDS campaign suggests that activism as a means of enforcing corporate responsibility for the human rights and conflict implications of business in the OPT has its limits, in terms of whether it can be replicated with other foreign investors (Business Conflict and Human Rights Network, 2017).

4. Applying a governance approach

The UN Guiding Principles on Business and Human Rights (UNGPs) are the most ambitious policy initiative to date, which seeks to mitigate the negative impacts of corporate actions and increase the accountability of business for preventing and addressing human rights abuses. The UNGPs were intended to address a governance gap, identified by their author, UN Special Representative John Ruggie (Report of the Special Representative of the Secretary General on the issue of human rights and transnational corporations and other business enterprises, 2010) as "the permissive environment within which blameworthy acts by corporations may occur without adequate sanctions or reparation".

Going beyond the provisions of the OECD Guidelines for Multinational Enterprises, the UNGPs invoke a tripartite framework of "Protect, Respect and Remedy" that affirms the primary duty of states to protect human rights, creates a corporate responsibility to respect human rights, and seeks to provide access to remedy for victims of human rights abuses. This formula defined human rights protection as a mutual and shared enterprise between public, private and civil society stakeholders, stressing the governance aspect of this interactive obligation compared to the existing (unilateral) legal obligations of companies under International Human Rights Law. The UNGPs sought a new alternative to compliance through due diligence, which was neither compulsory as in international law, nor relied on the discretionary good behaviour of companies. Their significance to the case of the OPT lies particularly in the relationship the Principles propose between states and companies. In the specific case of conflict-affected countries, Ruggie (2010) noted a "negative symbiotic relationship" between companies, human rights abuses and conflict, and proposed a heightened duty on states to deploy both assistance and constraint to ensure that companies do not abuse human rights.[6] In a companion report "Business and human rights in conflict-affected regions: challenges and options towards State responses" submitted to the UN Human Rights Council in 2011, the UN Working Group clarified that "home" states, where companies are domiciled, had a particular role in this regard given that conflict is most likely in situations where host states are too weak to enforce responsible business behaviour (Martin, The Guiding Principles on Human Rights and Business – Implementation in conflict affected countries, 2012).[7]

In the context of the Israeli occupation, the UNGPs offer three pillars for responsibilising corporate behaviour and holding companies to account for their impacts on human rights, sometimes described as three legs of a stool, in which each leg depends on the other. Firstly, the Principles provide a framework for foreign governments to "assist and restrain" corporate behaviour through requiring concrete measures such as human rights due diligence,[8] impact assessments, consultation and systematic redress for victims, exercises which recognize that corporate investments entail human rights implications and are intended to deter deliberate or incidental abuses. Secondly, the Principles require companies themselves to determine the potential negative impacts of their operations and take avoiding action. Thirdly, the Principles are intended to support victims of abuse – in this case Palestinians who feel their rights have been compromised by specific corporate actions- to seek redress and remedy. Thus, for example, disruption to homes caused by the Jerusalem Light Railway construction, and discrimination against Palestinian access to the railway, should be actionable under the provisions of the UNGPs, as an instrument of existing legal obligations on both states and companies.

Here we can begin to see the weakness of the UNGPs, for clearly no such means exist to take and enact access to remedy, given the absence of international law jurisdictions, Israel's resistance to the OPT's legal status, the weak or non-existent rights-claiming capacities of Palestinians and Israel's persistence in establishing exceptional forms of control over the West Bank. In a relevant statement, the UN High Commission for Human Rights pointed out that the Guiding Principles were based on existing obligations and responsibilities under international human rights law, but

> "do not create new international law obligations, nor do they limit or undermine any legal obligations with regard to human rights that a State may have undertaken or to which it is subject under international law" (UN High Commission for Human Rights, 2014, p. 3).

While the UNCHR (2014) noted that problems might arise "when companies are in situations where their responsibility to respect human rights is being tested against the state's inability or unwillingness to protect them", it added that the UNGPs made it clear that businesses are still expected to respect human rights, even in areas where the state does not live up to its own responsibilities.

This highlights the circular nature and dilemma of the UNGP's tripartite formula. For neither third-party state duties, nor access to remedy are standalone mechanisms, much less guarantees of corporate accountability. Both are dependent on a state's willingness to exercise its duty to protect human rights in the first place. As Wettstein (2015, p. 166) observes in his critique of the weak normative force of the UNGPs, the Ruggie framework left states in central place within the responsibility discourse, so it ultimately reinforced the problem the Principles were meant to solve – that companies are beyond regulatory purview in a globalized system (Wettstein, 2015, p. 166). As illustrated by the continuing presence of foreign companies in the settlement economy, complicity between an unwilling state and "disrespectful" companies continue to be a feature of the occupation. More fundamentally, the criticism of the UNGPs is that – even setting aside the instrumental weaknesses of the tripartite formula – they offer an insufficiently thick conceptualization of corporate responsibility, which is limited to doing no harm, but does not take account of the specific context of the occupation, or of the impacts that companies have in such a situation (Wettstein, 2015, p. 172). To illustrate this, a 2015 civil society report on the contractual links between French telecoms operator Orange and Partner, which provides telephone services in the West Bank using the Orange brand, pointed to Orange's lack of understanding of the situation in the OPT and how it emphasised a concern for its obligations under Israeli law, rather than acknowledging international law or France's public policy commitments on the illegality of settlements (Pinaud, 2015, p. 6). This suggests that in order to be effective the UNGP framework also requires a shift in corporate culture and/or less leeway in how companies choose to implement the Principles. More than this, the expansion of settlement business has been framed predominantly in commercial terms, which emphasises companies' economic role rather than their immanent social nature. By making responsibility agent-specific, the UNGPs tend to reinforce rather than counter this orthodox view of the salience of business operations. This stifles a more general conversation about rights and duties that companies owe in the context of a specific conflict. Palestinian legal activists have further argued the need for more clarity in what the UNGPs mean by the need for "enhanced due diligence" in situations of conflict and that this should include undertakings by states to criminalize involvement of corporations in unlawful activity and a requirement on companies to terminate investments or not to engage in the first place (Al-Haq, 2015).

5. Using the UNGPs to reframe policies towards the occupation

The relevance of the UNGPs to the politics of the occupation goes beyond simply the possibility to enforce human rights due diligence and shape business behaviour. The UNGP Framework provides European member states with a justification and a code to recognize and reflect the business dimension of the conflict, as part of their core peacebuilding and conflict prevention policies to the region. For example, in the case of Orange referred to above, it has been suggested that the French government could address its own obligations under international humanitarian law as well as fulfil its commitments to implementing the UNGPs by using its 25% stake in the company to establish the principles of business and human rights in the case of the OPT and enforce company compliance (Pinaud, 2015). Other policy options for European member states suggested by the UNGP framework include governments explicitly supporting business and human rights guidelines in international fora such as the UN and taking legislative action to enforce due diligence procedures. In this sense the failure of governments to grasp corporate investment as a lever for addressing the conflict and building peace reflects a gap noted by critiques of the liberal peacebuilding agenda, which reifies free markets and foreign investment but pays less attention to the micro processes and impacts which corporate actors create in the conflict space (Ganson & Wennmann, 2016, p. 77; Millar, 2016, p. 578). Instead there is a taken-for-granted attitude towards foreign investment which regards it as indispensable to peace, without questioning the paradoxes and inconsistencies which foreign business operations give rise to, particularly where local governance is weak or dysfunctional. In other words, governments which otherwise subscribe to an ideology of liberal peace, tend to display a blind spot towards the full implications of corporate activities. (Martin & Bojicic-Dzelilovic, 2017)

An indication that governments failed to grasp the possibility that foreign investments in the OPT presented for a change in policy approach, is that reports by the Heads of Government, while expressing increasing concern with settlement activity , pressures on land use and resources such as water and the implications of this for Palestinian rights (EU Heads of Mission, 2009), make no detailed mention of European corporate involvement in OPT development, beyond brief recommendations to prevent or discourage financial transactions in settlements, or legislation on EU involvement in transactions and settlement products (EU Heads of Mission, 2012). The 2016 HoG report for example proposes closer monitoring of business activity but fails to identify private sector actors as salient counterparties, integral to initiatives to resolve discrimination issues in the OPT (European Parliament, 2012).

Implementing the UNGPs is currently a cornerstone policy initiative by both member state governments and the European Union as an autonomous entity, yet this is routinely disconnected from mainstream peacebuilding initiatives, while these have also been criticised for a lack of engagement with grass roots processes, for example what occurs in the local level political economy (Martin, 2018; Mac Ginty & Richmond, 2013; Jabri, 2013; Lidén, 2009). Implementation of the UNGPs is via National Action Plans to be developed by each UN member state. These can include general orientations as well as detailed guidance. For example, the UK National Action Plans (NAPs) looks into promoting awareness of the diplomatic personnel at foreign missions via a "Business and Human Rights Toolkit" intended to guide staff on how to promote good conduct by UK companies operating abroad. In the case of the OPT, it has been suggested that the NAPs should make specific mention of the relevance of international humanitarian and human rights law as governing business operations (El Haq, n.d.).

As the EU is an independent separate signatory to the Guiding Principles, EU policy provides an additional lever for ensuring responsible business behaviour in the OPT, and explicitly incorporating this into its stance towards the conflict (Pinaud, 2015, p. 36).[9] However, EU policy has been notable for both its reticence to confront companies domiciled in Europe over their settlement activities whether in terms of public rhetoric, or demands regarding financial and social reporting, or even using the Ruggie framework to raise the issue of human rights in the context of settlement businesses and citing international law obligations as a justification for prohibiting settlement business activity.[10]

By way of comparison, the 2014 UN Working Group on human rights and transnational cooperation and other business enterprises, made a clear attempt to use the UNGPs to frame responses to settlement activities. Its report said companies

> "need to be able to demonstrate that they neither support the continuation of an international illegality nor are complicit in human rights abuses; that they can effectively prevent or mitigate human rights risks; and are able to account for their efforts in this regard" (United Nations Human Rights, 2014).

Where companies cannot prevent or mitigate the risks of being involved with human rights violations through their operations and business relationships, the WG suggested companies need to consider termination of operations (United Nations Humans Rights - Office of the High Commissioner, 2011). Richard Falk, while UN special rapporteur on the OPT added:

> "I strongly encourage all business to use the UN Guiding Principles on Business and Human Rights as a guide for how to conduct their business, and to exercise due diligence to ensure they do not contribute to human rights violations and abuse, and in order to avoid responsibility for complicity in breaches of international law" (United Nations High Commissioner for Human Rights, 2013).

EU reticence on this subject stem from a more broad-based failure to either incorporate the private sector as a significant component in crisis management, conflict prevention and peacebuilding policies, or resolve tensions between peace and security objectives and other types of policies (Benraïs & Simon, 2017; Van der Borgh, 2017). The introduction of the Raw Materials Initiative (RMI) is a case in point: it was intended to ensure adequate inputs for European business and food security for European consumers but was seen by critics as incompatible with guidelines limiting resource exploitation in fragile societies (Kublbock, 2013).

However, EU action to encourage member state implementation of the Principles has been slow. By 2016 (five years after adoption of the UNGPs) only eight of 28 EU member states had established NAPs, while efforts at Union level towards mainstreaming the UNGPs into the EU's external relations and developing a programme encouraging business and member states to utilize them have been criticised both internally and externally.[11] In February 2017, Ruggie sent an unprecedented letter of rebuke to EC president Jean-Claude Juncker, in which he accused the European Commission of failing to support responsible business conduct, of stalling, and setting aside the agenda of business and human rights. He claimed that the Commission's draft guidance to companies on their non-financial (i.e. social responsibility) reporting "dilutes and undermines the language of the UN Guiding Principles ... provides negligible guidance ... and fails to reference the UN Guiding Principles Reporting Framework" (Ruggie, 2017).

A report commissioned by the European Parliament Human rights sub-committee in 2016 noted: "The EU has the potential to be an international game-changer when it comes to business and human rights. It also has a specific responsibility, because of the large numbers of European companies involved in global value chains." It called for further implementation of the UNGPs and related instruments, "less declaration and more real political will."

6. Conclusion

Since 2005, the cases of Veolia and other foreign company operations in the OPT have highlighted how the occupation has been re-articulated not only as an abuse of Palestinian human rights, but also as a conflict, which increasingly relies on economic and business complicity between companies and governments, which sustains settlement activity and Israeli control. This was the basis for the civil activism, which succeeded in pressuring Veolia to make highly publicized withdrawals from the OPT. However, the development of institutional mechanisms to restrain business activity and ensure that companies respect the obligations of international humanitarian and human rights law, has been notably weak. Since Veolia, European governments have failed to address a governance gap exposed by the presence of settlement business and foreign investments in the OPT and the absence of regulations on European company involvement or the enforcement of international legal provisions.

Despite the success of the Veolia boycott, in forcing JLR's foreign investors to withdraw, the concept of corporate responsibility as a core trope of the emerging business governance agenda has proved to be largely non-performative, whether in making companies account for their impacts on human rights, or through voluntary actions of self-responsibilisation, or as part of international law or global governance initiatives. Indeed, the continuing presence and investment by European companies, even French companies, in not only settlement activities, but in the JLR itself, suggests that even the headlines and adverse publicity generated in the Veolia case, no longer have the force to deter other business investments (Association France Palestine Solidarité, 2018).[12]

While the campaign against Veolia highlighted the potential for new modes of resistance against the Israeli opposition, this potential has not been realized in the near decade since the BDS boycott in new avenues of conflict resolution by governments, that take account of the grounds and implications of targeting corporate responsibility. Indeed, the boycott of the JLR companies remains a singular example of effective corporate responsibilisation in terms of impact and scale.[13] One reason for the gap between the expectations created by BDS and the failure to reproduce and systematise corporate accountability lies in the weakness of mechanisms such as the UNGP framework. While it was introduced to clarify the requirements on business to apply due diligence to avoid human rights abuses, failure to do so carries no sanction while the underlying notion of responsibility, on which the UNGPs are predicated, is both limited and liable to be defined unilaterally and minimally by companies themselves.

Another reason why the long-term effects of BDS have been limited is suggested by Bicchi's paper in this issue : its account of how groups countered the BDS academic boycott and campaign on UK campuses, using government legislation to fight radicalization, and introducing new "rules of the game" after 2011 raises the question of whether global activism of the kind unleashed in 2005 could have had the same traction in the climate which developed outside Israel after 2011.

Furthermore, in highlighting the limitations of corporate responsibility as a way of managing the emerging conflict dynamics in the OPT, this article has showed how the success of social activism failed to spill over into sustained action by policy-makers to target the private sector and recognize explicitly the economic dimension of the occupation. European governments missed opportunities presented by the emerging business and human rights agenda and frameworks such as the UNGPs to enforce human rights due diligence by companies. leverage their influence over investors, and ultimately interdict business activities.

While global public hostility to the JLR, orchestrated by civil activism provided an opening to regulate the private sector as a means for governments to demonstrate their opposition to settlement growth, inaction and reticence in applying the mechanisms at hand, including examples such as legislation on labelling settlement products (see Voltolini this issue) have kept this particular policy window closed.

Notes

1. The Swedish council said the 3.5 billion euros decision was based on commercial factors.
2. It also ran a bus service in the OPT.
3. Paris, 26 October 2005: Reply of the spokesman of the French Ministry of Foreign Affairs retrieved from the website of the French Ministry of Foreign Affairs (www.diplomatie.gouv.fr) and quoted in Mendes-France, 2006; Mendes-France's legal review of the court proceedings, highlights evidence that the French government had not disregarded Veolia and Alstom's business in the West Bank, but on the contrary, that the companies' involvement was part of a systematic policy of encouraging French contracts in Israel.
4. The idea of "responsibilisation" figures originally in criminology as an approach which places the governance of crimes in the hands of individuals, similarly it has been used in security discourse to involve particular actors beyond the state in efforts to resists threats, natural disasters and man-made catastrophes (see Garland, 2001).
5. Hewlett Packard, Caterpillar and Motorola have been among companies targeted through investors and lenders.
6. See Principle 7 (United Nations Humans Rights - Office of the High Commissioner, 2011, p. 9), The commentaries to Principles 12 and 21 refer to companies' duty to also respect international humanitarian law.
7. See also Martin, 2012.
8. Due diligence arrangements are for example spelled out in Principles 17 and 19 of the UNGPs.
9. In 2014, Germany excluded the Occupied Territories from its support for Israeli tech companies and a bilateral scientific agreement with Israel (Pinaud, 2015, p. 36).
10. See for example: UN Report on database of business activities in settlements paragraph 41 (United Nations, 2018)
11. European states have however proved more active than most in developing NAPs, with slow takeup worldwide. 12 NAPs have been approved to date.
12. Subsidiaries of French transport groups SNCF and RATP alongside Caisse des Dépôts et Consignations, a French public sector financial institution, and ALSTOM are involved in a second phase of the Jerusalem railway, which extends the existing line and creates two new lines, with settlements as endpoints (Association France Palestine Solidarité, 2018)
13. Sodastream faced consumer campaign by BDS, which was similar in its profile to Veolia. The company moved its operation from the OPT to southern Israel in 2014.

Disclosure statement

No potential conflict of interest was reported by the author.

References

Ahren, R. (2013, April 29). French court's Light Rail ruling breaks no legal ground, scholars say. *Times of Israel*.

Al-Haq. (2015, November 19). *Al-Haq presents at the fourth annual forum on business and human rights 2015*. Retrieved from Alhaq.org: http://www.alhaq.org/advocacy/targets/united-nations/994-al-haq-presents-at-the-fourth-annual-forum-on-business-and-human-rights-2015

Amnesty International. (2017, June 7). *States must ban Israeli settlement products to help end half a century of violations*. Retrieved from Amnesty.org: https://www.amnesty.org/en/latest/news/2017/06/states-must-ban-israeli-settlement-products-to-help-end-half-a-century-of-violations-against-palestinians/

Association France Palestine Solidarité. (2018, June 13). *Israeli settlements in East Jerusalemn 3 French companies involved in Light Rail*. Retrieved from www.france-palestine.org: http://www.france-palestine.org/Israeli-settlements-in-East-Jerusalem-3-French-companies-involved-in-light-rail

Azarov, V. (2013, May 1). Backtracking on responsibility: French court absolves veolia for unlawful railway construction in occupied territory. *Rights as Usual*.

Bar-Eli, A. (2009, September 13). *Dan to buy 5% stake in Jerusalem Light Rail From Veolia*. Retrieved from Haaretz: https://www.haaretz.com/1.5491693

Barghouti, O. (2009). Derailing injustice: Palestinian civil resistance to the "Jerusalem light rail". *Jerusalem Quarterly, 38*, 46-75.

Benraïs, L., & Simon, J. (2017, March 24). Review of EU policy towards conflict prevention and peacebuilding.

Bondy, K., Moon, J., & Matten, D. (2012). An institution of corporate social responsibility (CSR) in multi-national corporations: Form and implications. *Journal of Business Ethics, 111*, 281–299.

Boycott, Divestment, Sanctions (BDS). (2009, November 19). *Jerusalem Light Railway: Effects & legal implications*. Retrieved from https://bdsmovement.net/news/jerusalem-light-railway-effects-legal-implications

Business Conflict and Human Rights Network. (2017). Remarks. *Business conflict and human rights network annual conference*. Geneva.

Conflict Sensitivity Consortium. (n.d.). *An Introduction to conflict sensivity*. Retrieved from http://www.conflictsensitivity.org: http://www.conflictsensitivity.org/an-introduction-to-conflict-sensitivity-3/

Corporate Watch. (2009). *Profiting from the occupation, UK and international companies complicit in Israeli war crimes against Palestinians*.

Cour d'Appel de Versailles. (2013, March 22). *Arrêt n° contradictoire du 22 mars 2013. Association France-Palestine Solidarité "AFPS" c/ Société Alstom Transport SA*. Retrieved from http://www.france-palestine.org/IMG/pdf/decision_de_la_cour_d_appel.pdf

Deitelhoff, N., & Wolf, K. (2010). *Corporate security responsability? Corporate governance. Contributions to peace and security in zones of conflict*. Basingtoke: Palgrave Macmillan.

Diakonia. (2009, January 20). *Diakonia press statement*. Retrieved from Diakonia: www.diakonia.se/en/IHL

Dutch Association of Investors for Sustainable Development (VBDO). (2014, February). Dutch Institutional Investors and Investments related to the Occupation of the Palestinian Territories.

El Haq. (n.d.). *"Language to be included in a template for states' National Action Plans (NAPs) for the implementation of the United Nations Guiding Principles on Business and Human Rights (UNGPs)*. Retrieved from El Haq: http://www.alhaq.org/images/stories/PDF/2012/Al-Haq_Template_for_States_National_Action_Plans.pdf

EU Heads of Mission. (2009, November 23). Report on East Jerusalem.
EU Heads of Mission. (2012, February 10). *EU Heads of mission, report on East Jerusalem, Jerusalem, 10 February 2012 (excerpts)*. Retrieved from www.palestine-studies.org/sites/default/files/jps-articles/jps.2012.xli_.3.223.pdf
European Parliament. (2012, July 5). Resolution on EU policy on the West Bank and East Jerusalem. *(2012/2694(RSP))*.
Ganson, B., & Wennmann, A. (2016). *Business and conflict in fragile states: The case for pragmatic solutions*. London: Routledge.
Garland, D. (2001). *The culture of control*. Oxford: Oxford University Press.
Jabri, V. (2013). Peacebuilding, the local and the international: A colonial or a postcolonial rationality? *Peacebuilding, 1*(1), 3–16.
Johnson, P. (2006). Whence democracy? A review and critique of the conceptual dimensions and implications of the business case for organizational democracy. *Organization, 13(2)*, 245–274.
Kittrie, O. (2016). *Lawfare*. Oxford: Oxford University Press.
Kublbock, K. (2013, September). The EU raw materials initiative - scope and critical assessment. *Austrian Research Foundation for International Development*.
Lidén, K. (2009). Building peace between global and local politics: The cosmopolitical ethics of liberal peacebuilding. *International Peacekeeping, 16(5)*, 616–634, (online).
Mac Ginty, R., & Richmond, O. (2013). The local turn in peace building: A critical agenda for peace. *Third World Quarterly, 34*(5), 763–783(online).
Martin, M. (2012, October 29). The guiding principles on human rights and business - implementation in conflict affected countries. *Private Sector and Conflict*. Retrieved from http://www.eplo.org/civil-society-dialogue-network.html
Martin, M., & Bojicic-Dzelilovic, V. (2017). 'It's not just the economy, stupid'. The multi-directional security effects of the private sector in post-conflict reconstruction, *Conflict, Security & Development, 17*, 361–380.
Martin, M. (2018). Private partnerships, public peace: The role of the private sector in second generation human security. In M. Kaldor, I. Rangelov, & S. Selchow (Eds.), *EU global strategy and human security. Rethinking approaches to conflict* (pp. 195–212). Abingdon: Routledge.
McConnell, L. (2014). Establishing liability for multinational corporations: Lessons from akpan. *International Journal of Law and Management, 56(2)*, 88–104.
Mendes-France, M. (2006). The Jerusalem light railway: Symbolic issue or international responsibility of the French state? *Guild Practitioner, 63*, 213–223.
Millar, G. (2016). Local experiences of liberal peace: Marketization and emergent conflict dynamics in Sierra Leone. *Journal of Peace Research, 53(4)*, 569–581.
Moffat, S. (2009). Bil'in and beyond - prosecuting corporate complicity in war crimes under Canadian law. *Graduate Department of Law thesis*. University of Toronto.
Moon, J., Crane, A., & Matten, D. (2005, July). Can corporations be citizens? Corporate citizenship as a metaphor for business participation in society. *Business Ethics Quarterly, 15(3)*, 429-453.
Pinaud, B. E. (2015, May). *Orange's dangerous liaisons in the occupied palestinian territory*. Retrieved from fidh.org: https://www.fidh.org/IMG/pdf/rapport_orenge-eng.pdf
Ruggie, J. (2010). *Report of the special representative of the secretary general on the issue of human rights and transnational corporations and other business enterprises*. United Nations General Assembly.
Ruggie, J. (2017, February 24). *Letter to European commission president Jean-Claude Juncker*. Retrieved from https://www.shiftproject.org/media/resources/docs/Ruggie_LettertoPresidentJunckerFeb2017.pdf
Russell Tribunal on Palestine. (2013, March 16–17). *Russell Tribunal hearings on Palestine*. Retrieved from http://www.russelltribunalonpalestine.com/en/full-findings-of-the-final-session-en
Scherer, A., & Palazzo, G. (2011, June). The New political role of business in a globalized world: A review of a New perspective on CSR and its implications for the firm, governance, and democracy. *Journal of Management Studies, 48(4)*, 899–931.
The Civic Coalition for Defending Palestinians Rights in Jerusalem. (2009, December). *The Jerusalem Light Rail train*. Retrieved from Civic Coalition: https://www.civiccoalition-jerusalem.org/uploads/9/3/6/8/93682182/the_jerusalem_light_rail_train.pdf

UN High Commission for Human Rights. (2014, June 6). Statement on the implications of the guiding Principles on business and human rights in the context of Israeli settlement in the Occupied Palestinian Territory.

United Nations. (2018, February 1). *UN 2018 report on database of business activities in settlements. A/HRC/37/39.* Retrieved from United Nations Human Rights: http://ap.ohchr.org/documents/dpage_e.aspx?si=A/HRC/37/39

United Nations High Commissioner for Human Rights. (2013, October 31). Corporate complicity in international crimes related to Israeli settlements in occupied Palestine.

United Nations Human Rights. (2014, June 6). *Statement on the implications of the guiding principles on business and human rights in the context of Israeli settlements in the occuopied Palestinian Territory.* Retrieved from Office of the High Commissioner for Human Rights: https://www.ohchr.org/Documents/Issues/Business/OPTStatement6June2014.pdf

United Nations Humans Rights - Office of the High Commissioner. (2011). *UN guiding principles on business and human rights.*

Van der Borgh, C. (2017). Final research report whole of society conflict prevention and peacebuilding. www.woscap.eu.

Wettstein, F. (2015). Normativity, ethics, and the UN guiding principles on business and human rights: A critical assessment. *Journal of Human Rights, 14,* 162–182.

OECD principals or World Bank guidance? EU development aid in the occupied Palestinian territories

Jeremy Wildeman

ABSTRACT
The European Union (EU) and its member states shoulder a significant part of the aid devoted to the Palestinian Authority (PA) and Palestinians in Occupied Palestinian Territory (OPT). They do so according to a development aid model that is driven intellectually by the World Bank, under US political oversight. This article locates European aid in the World Bank-led approach and analyses its shortcomings. It starts with an overview of how such an approach came to characterize economic development in the Oslo Peace Process. It highlights its fundamental ambiguities when it comes to analysing the occupation and settlements. It then focuses on the issue of settlement-building and de-development in the Occupied Palestinian Territory (OPT) that punctuates the failure of the aid model. It concludes by analysing current thinking in aid effectiveness and how it could be adopted as an alternative approach by the Europeans.

Introduction

All donors in a conflict situation become de facto actors in the conflict itself (Anderson, 1999), as well as ethically responsible for the well-being of the people for whom they are intervening. This article looks at the case of donor development aid spending in the occupied Palestinian territory (OPT) in support of the 1993 Oslo Accord. It is a process dominated politically by the United States, with an aid model structured for international donors by the World Bank. There the EU and its individual member states have though provided the largest amount of funding to sustain the model (Le More, 2008, p. 109), spending a combined 4.360 billion $USD from 2012 to 2016 (OECD QWIDS concatenated, 2012 to 2016 [Dataset], 2018), and covering as much as 40% of the Palestinian Authority's (PA) 2012 to 2014 budget (Tartir & Wildeman, 2017, p. 17) This aid model and aid provision were meant to foster Palestinian economic and institutional development, and represented an investment in peace (The World Bank, 1993), meant to nurture conditions favourable to the political process of peacebuilding with Israel. However, as we are going to see, the disconnect between the aid model and political realities on the ground does not mean that aid provision is politically neutral or grounded in strong analysis, and in fact the Europeans, as main donors to the PA, are towing a fine line between denouncing the occupation through their declarations, on the one hand, and contributing to its further entrenchment by following the World Bank's flawed development model, on the other.

The EU considers itself the most important donor for the Palestinian people, and "a reliable and predictable partner" (EEAS, n.d.). The EU has in particular been aiming to build up the PA's institutions to have a "democratic, independent and viable Palestinian State living side-by-side with Israel in peace and security" (EEAS, 2016). As Table 1 shows, the Europeans have invested significant funds in the OPT. There the EU institutions work alongside member national authorities, providing the PA with resources to support not only its activities, but its very existence. At the same time, Europeans have adopted a standard response to excuse a lack of political protagonism in the so-called Peace Process by highlighting their contribution to the PA, their role in keeping the PA afloat and therefore in contributing to sustain a "partner for peace" with which the Israelis could potentially dialogue.

Using OECD data, from 2012 to 2016 the EU institutions gave 45% of the total funds spent on the OPT from EU sources. Those funds are provided by the EU through a number of organizational units – particularly the European External Action Service (EEAS) and the Directorate-General for International Cooperation and Development (DEVCO) – under a number of budget lines, funding the payment of PA civil servants' salaries and pensions, social allowances by the PA for the poorest and most vulnerable

Table 1. Total EU and EU member funding.

Donor(s)	Total ODA by year by EU Donor 2012 to 2016 (in 2018 July 13 $USD millions)					
	2012	2013	2014	2015	2016	Totals
EU Institutions	315.72	357.89	481.26	406.26	417.04	1978.17
Austria	4.8	6.35	8.2	4.78	6.1	30.23
Belgium	33.45	33.54	20.66	24.23	34.76	146.64
Bulgaria	..	..	0.07	..	..	0.07
Croatia	..	..	..	..	..	0
Cyprus	..	0.01	0.08	0.49	..	0.58
Czech Republic	1.68	0.81	0.7	1.24	0.42	4.85
Denmark	25.72	40.33	30.41	25.79	5.58	127.83
Estonia	0.08	0.13	0.52	0.32	0.14	1.19
Finland	14.74	14.17	15.24	13.41	10.06	67.62
France	71.53	66.06	57.45	42.78	40.43	278.25
Germany	136.74	117.38	124.8	92.34	137.42	608.68
Greece	5.14	0.78	1.52	0.71	0.16	8.31
Hungary	0.06	0.01	0.11	0.27	0.49	0.94
Ireland	5.87	7.66	7.54	6.38	5.63	33.08
Italy	7.27	12.13	20.2	31.27	18.84	89.71
Latvia	..	..	..	..	..	0
Lithuania	..	..	0.04	0.01	0.03	0.08
Luxembourg	4.32	5.23	4.38	8.33	7.03	29.29
Malta	..	..	0.13	0.01	..	0.14
Netherlands	31.91	20.22	31.5	22.52	22.79	128.94
Poland	0.47	0.77	1.02	1.03	1.21	4.5
Portugal	0.01	0	0.27	0.13	0	0.41
Romania	0.2	0.29	0.32	0.44	0.49	1.74
Slovak Republic	0.12	0.17	0.23	0.16	0.08	0.76
Slovenia	0.2	0.21	0.16	0.24	0.35	1.16
Spain	23.02	16.88	19.45	16.75	18.71	94.81
Sweden	62.77	61.02	67.16	54.61	53.15	298.71
United Kingdom	67.96	108.63	137.24	78.58	30.67	423.08
All EU Institutions and EU Member Totals						4359.77

Note: In million $USD at 2018 July 13 values. Data calculated by the author using the OECD QWIDS data-set. *(OECD QWIDS concatenated, 2012 to 2016 [Dataset],* 2018).

Palestinian families; as well as, infrastructure projects, judicial and financial reform initiatives, and programmes supporting Palestinian security, health and education systems (EEAS, n.d.). Separately as member states Germany, traditionally considered close to Israeli interests (see Busse in this special issue), is by far the biggest contributor to the PA, delivering nearly 50% more in aid than the next donor, the UK. Moreover, Germany's contribution is more than twice France's contribution, despite the popular perception of France as a champion of Palestinians' rights (See Voltolini in this special issue). Meanwhile, Sweden has consistently provided more aid than France in spite of having about 10% the population of France. Notably, Sweden, Denmark, Belgium and the Netherlands contributed significantly more per capita than other more populous states like the UK and France, and more in total than either Italy or Spain. From a per capita perspective, Luxembourg and Finland are particularly generous donors.

As these figures show, aid to the Palestinians has mobilized significant amounts of money from Europeans' taxpayers.[1] This article scrutinizes the aid model embraced by European actors. It starts by providing an overview of how the Oslo development aid process came into being, before then analysing the key aspects and the main weaknesses of the policy approach charted by the World Bank. It further delineates the deterioration in the Palestinian economy, upon which political peace had been meant to be built, and the indicators that could have predicted the result. The article concludes that Europeans could choose to plot a different course in search of Israeli-Palestinian peace, based on principles for aid effectiveness and for aid giving in a fragile and conflicted state, and by taking full account of the political context of Israeli settlement policies as the key element undermining any chance for Palestinian statehood, development or peace.

The Oslo development aid model

Liberal "idealists" in international affairs (and neoliberals) extol the virtues of cooperative interaction between states. This is built upon a classical liberal enlightenment faith in the innate goodness of the individual, the capacity of political institutions to promote social progress and the idea that states are capable of meaningful cooperation leading to positive change and progress. This cooperation is characterized by trade, where every participant state contributes their strengths to the world economy, altogether benefitting from the overall gains. Cooperation in turn leads to a connectedness defined by open markets and global economic integration, which makes it too costly for states to turn away from, and this helps preserve peace (Keohane & Nye, 1998, p. 84). In such a world, the primary path to prosperity and leadership on the global stage is through peaceful interaction and law. Rosecrance described this as a major crossroads in international affairs where the military option for states to seize territory for growth became much more costly than cooperation and trade (Rosecrance, 1986, p. 39). In the liberal perspective, this vision of peace and progress goes hand in hand with liberal and capitalist states, which in turn are assumed to be naturally predisposed towards peace (Doyle, 1983, p. 213).

These ideas have informed the approach taken by international policy makers engaged in Israeli and Palestinian peacebuilding. There, in support of the Oslo Peace Process, they have sought to enhance cooperation between Israelis and Palestinians for mutual beneficial economic gain. Essentially proposing peace by economics, they believed that the international community could give peace a boost by engaging in institution building to catch the underdeveloped Palestinians up to their liberal and capitalist Israeli counterparts' standards. This could be done by investing in development programmes, which would have the benefit of incentivising Palestinians to abandon violence and cooperate with Israel in building peace. Thus, Western – and particularly European – donors decided to instil liberal democracy into Palestinian state-building, in order to create conditions for peace to take hold (Amundsen, Giacaman, & Khan, 2004; Hanieh, 2016).

To develop the aid model, the US quickly pushed for the World Bank to play a lead role in 1993, trusting the Bank to represent the American viewpoint, given that the US remained the biggest shareholder of the World Bank (Le More, 2008, p. 110). Further, the US administration always choses the President of the Bank, and that person has always been an American. The World Bank is so closely linked to the US that rival states in fact consider it an extension of American foreign policy (*Inside Story - China banking checkmate?*, 2015).

The World Bank first laid out the conceptual model for Palestinian aid in its 1993 paper *An Investment in Peace* (The World Bank, 1993). It had been developed coincidentally as a six volume report in 1993 at the request of the organizing group behind the separate 1992 Madrid negotiations between Israelis and Palestinians (Schiavo-Campo, 2003, p. 4). Together with other Western donors, the Bank optimistically chose to classify the OPT as a post-conflict scenario (Schiavo-Campo, 2003, p. 4). As a consequence, Palestinian poverty was categorized as a "technical problem", which could be considered separate from politics and addressed through well-constructed and "non-political" policies. This reflected a popular neoliberal development belief that aid policy can be "neutral, rational and objective" (Mosse, 2004a, pp. 3–4). It also fit within a larger donor vision – advocated by the Bank – that a political resolution through negotiations would take place separate from development, but that positive conditions for that political resolution would be established by eliminating Palestinian poverty as a driver for violence through development. That is, Palestinian poverty could begin to be addressed separate of, and irrespective of the political context,

> The focus instead is on policies, institutions and investments-where optimal choices are largely invariant to the eventual political arrangements that may emerge from the bilateral negotiations (The World Bank, 1993, p. 1).

This led to a blue-print approach to Palestinian development centred upon: financial liberalization, open markets, economic growth through trade, and liberal mechanisms like regional institutions, regional economic integration, economic integration with Israel, good governance, democratization, mutual recognition of national rights, and fostering mutual trust through cooperation (Hanieh, 2016; Rynhold, 2009).

For this blue-print to be carried out, a strong central authority would be required to strike a balance between free markets and state intervention (Brinkerhoff, 1996, p. 1498). Like other neoliberal development interventions, existing institutions would need to be strengthened or whole new ones created, requiring nothing short of the wholesale managed reorganization of state and society (Mosse, 2004b, p. 642). Thus, institutional development was put at the top of the Bank agenda from its first mission to the OPT in October 1993 (Schiavo-Campo, 2003, p. 10). Since the Palestinians were in theory leaving behind oversight by the Israeli state, the Bank became deeply involved in building the semi-autonomous PA to be a "good" government that could manage the balance between free markets and state intervention, and to fully implement donor/Bank development advice to build the right kind of state. In this role, the Bank set a legal framework for Palestinian economic activity and their economic relations with Israel (Roy, 1999, p. 68). Some aspects were even codified into Palestinian law, like PA Basic Law Article 21 stating that, "the economic system in Palestine shall be based on the principles of a free market economy" (Bolstad & Viken, 2008).

In this context, donors exercise a preponderance of power over the occupied Palestinians. This includes not only providing large sums of money according to their chosen funding priorities, but also withholding funds from the aid-dependent Palestinians for taking actions that donors do not approve of, like the embargo on the PA after Hamas won the 2006 January 25 Palestinian election. Further, there is profound influence exercised by countless European and other international specialists working closely with and directing Palestinians on how to build institutions for good governance. That included there being in charge of the PA from June 2007 to June 2013 an unelected, donor-backed Prime Minister, Salam Fayyad, who had long worked at both the World Bank and IMF, and collaborated closely with the World Bank and British Department for International Development (DFID) to produce a Palestinian national development plan in 2007 (Hanieh, 2008; Khalidi & Samour, 2011).

Thus, the Oslo development aid model that emerged thanks to the World Bank and was embraced by the Europeans was premised on the separation between political and economic considerations. In line with mainstream popular thought in the 1990s, it was a one-size-fits-all model built around Western neoliberal normative values and imposed on the recipient peoples. There efficient "non-political" economic policies and institution building were expected to contribute positively to an effective and progressive transformation in the political sphere. As the experience world-wide has also shown, politics and economics cannot be separated, while attempting to do so in a conflict situation can easily make a conflict worsen.

Problems in the aid model

As a general rule, for aid to be effective it should respect local leadership and expertise in the development process (OECD, 2008). Providing aid in a conflict situation is particularly complex. Aid can reduce human suffering, and support greater economic and social security in conflict settings (Anderson, 1999, p. 67). However, it can very easily have unintended negative impacts. While aid does not create conflicts, it does influence whether they worsen or abate, and whether new steps towards peace can be found (Anderson, 2005, p. 152). This is likely to be made worse if given in a partisan manner, choosing sides in a conflict. Furthermore, international interventions that lack strong conflict analysis without appropriate safeguards designed to account for the context can inadvertently cause harm in fragile environments (Karlstedt, Abdulsalam, Ben-Natan, & Rizik, 2015, pp. 15–16; OECD, 2011, p. 25). It is therefore essential that international actors understand the specific context in the region they intervene in,

> Sound political analysis is needed to adapt international responses to country and regional context, beyond quantitative indicators of conflict, governance or institutional strength.

International actors should mix and sequence their aid instruments according to context, and avoid blue-print approaches (OECD, 2007, p. 1).

So, sound logic holds that donors wanting to engender development in the OPT should first take account of the greatest problem impacting and undermining Palestinian daily life: the settlements and Israel's colonial policies behind them.

One of the main reasons the humanitarian situation in the OPT never improved, and only got worse was the premature initial classification of the OPT as post-conflict (Sayigh, 2007, p. 9). While limited successes at PA institution building have taken hold in pockets of the OPT, economic growth and peace did not occur. Through 25 years and $30+ billion in spending (Tartir, 2016), there has been no tangible progress on the core political issues first identified by the World Bank in 1993. The report at the time indicated priorities such as, "the allocation of land and water resources, the disposition of Israeli settlements, the future status of expatriate Palestinians, the territorial issues surrounding Jerusalem and, most importantly, the nature of the proposed 'self-governing' arrangements" (The World Bank, 1993, p. 1). In fact, in many cases these priorities have regressed during a period characterized by extremes of pronounced misery and decline, while the OPT economy became dependent on aid to pay for an enormous trade deficit with Israel (Hever, 2010, 2015). By the end-of-the 1990s the OPT was in a much worse condition than prior to Oslo (The World Bank, 2000, p. 14), and the economic situation so poor that the Oslo years have been the worst since the beginning of occupation in 1967 (Taghdisi-Rad, 2010, p. 56). Conditions have become so acute in Gaza the UN has warned it could become uninhabitable by 2020 (UNCTAD, 2015, p. 11).

Settlements

A number of politically driven obstacles have stood in the way. The key issue driving the deterioration in the OPT has been Israel's appropriation of Palestinian resources and land to build colonies, in flagrant violation of international law (Lynk, 2017, p. 3) (see also Lynk and Azarova in this special issue). These settler colonial processes began in 1967 (Khalidi, 2008; Pappe, 2006), as Israel extended its control over Palestinian land and other natural resources exclusively for the benefit of Israelis (Kanafani & Ghaith, 2012). This was accompanied by practices that make Palestinian daily life difficult and unsafe. Such practices include severe restrictions on Palestinian movement, home demolitions, deliberately exposing Palestinians to toxic waste, the destruction of livelihoods, settler violence and denying Palestinians access to clean water (Hart & Forte, 2013, p. 632).

The settlements are an ideological/political enterprise with no solid economic base that justifies their existence (Kanafani & Ghaith, 2012). They are sustained by an infrastructure of roads, checkpoints and the Separation Wall. Settlement growth has been rapid as Israeli citizens are incentivised by government subsidies to move to settlements (Amit, 2017). Since 1995, the population of Jewish settlers in the West Bank has grown four times faster than Israel's (Ferzinger, 2018). When Oslo was signed in 1993 there were approximately 110,000 settlers living in the West Bank and Gaza, and another 146,000 in East Jerusalem ('Israel's settlement policy in the occupied Palestinian territory', n.d.). By 2002, the total living in the OPT stood at 380,000 (B'Tselem, 2002) and increased to nearly 600,000 by 2015 (B'Tselem, 2017).

The expansion of settlements is facilitated by the fact that 61% of the land in the West Bank (Eddin, Massimiliano, & Niksic, 2014, p. 1), labelled Area C in the Oslo Process, remains under full Israeli control. Area C is richly endowed with natural resources and includes almost all the West Bank agricultural land. Less than 1% of Area C is designated by Israel for Palestinian use, while the remainder is heavily restricted or off-limits to Palestinians: 68% for Israeli settlements, 21% for closed military zones and 9% for nature reserves (Eddin et al., 2014, p. 13). By 2018, the majority of Area C was made up of Israeli settlers, intricately integrated into and inseparable from Israel proper. As Secretary of State John Kerry pointed out, Area C is effectively restricted from Palestinian development (Redden, 2015). In a 2014 report, the World Bank estimated the direct benefits Palestinians could derive from access to their land would equal a sum equivalent to 23% of GDP in 2011 figures (Eddin et al., 2014).

Palestinians now mostly live in densely populated "Bantustans" between Israeli settled areas. Palestinian territorial contiguity has been totally undermined and, as Lynk points out in his contribution to this special edition, this process shows no sign of abating, as every Israeli government has since 1967 committed significant resources to the continuous growth of settlements. While the World Bank does not go without acknowledging these settlements, they play a largely secondary part because of the Bank's "non-political" analysis. Development critics argue that non-political approaches bereft of context distracts attention away from the real cause of poverty: the unchecked power of the state against poor people without rights (Easterly, 2014).

Analysis bereft of context

The position of the World Bank on settlements emerges in 18 biannual reports issued over the period 2009-2017. The reports, which span more than 500 pages, are addressed to bilateral donors on the Ad Hoc Liaison Committee (AHLC), where the World Bank acts as Secretary. Tellingly, a keyword count shows that not only does the Bank go entire reports without mentioning the words "settler" or "settlements," but the trend across time is towards mentioning the issue less and less.

In fact, the word "settler" only appears 16 times in just 4 reports out of 18: 4 times in May 2009, 4 times in September 2009, 3 times in September 2010 and 5 times in September 2012. The word "settlement" appears more often at 66 times but combined across only half the reports: 14 times in May 2009, 6 times in September 2009, 1 time in June 2010, 13 times in September 2010, 5 times in March 2012, 22 times in September 2012, 2 times in June 2014 and 2 times in September 2017. Settlements are also mentioned 1 time in April 2011 as an "important employer" of Palestinians (The World Bank, 2011, p. 17). In a 239-page assessment of its work in the OPT covering the decade 2001-2009, the Bank only mentions "settlers" 3 times and "settlements" 2 times (Garcia-Garcia et al., 2009). Further, the trend is that over time the Bank acknowledges the presence of settlers and settlements less-and-less, while they became an ever-larger presence disrupting life in the OPT.

The Bank and other donors also shy away from the use of contextually accurate and broadly accepted terminology. Thus, the Bank only rarely refers to the "occupation" or "occupied", the internationally accepted definition of Israeli rule, as per UN Security

Council Resolutions 298 (1971), 446 (1979) and UN General Assembly resolution 32/5 (1977 October 28).

In the World Bank's 18 reports to the AHLC 2009 to 2017, the word "occupation" is only mentioned 19 times and "occupied" 35 times. Clear references to the occupation occur 7 times in 2 reports: 5 times in September 2011 and 2 times in September 2012. The word "occupied" is mentioned clearly 11 times in 3 reports: 2 times in April 2011, 3 times in March 2012 and 6 times in September 2012. While "occupation" is mentioned 6 times in September 2009, 4 are to a PA plan "Palestine: Ending the Occupation, Establishing the State" and the other 2 references mention the occupation in footnotes. In other reports the mentions are more secondary and equivocal, such as referring in June 2009 to a report by UNRWA, "Prolonged Crisis in the Occupied Palestinian Territory: Socio-economic Developments in 2007"; to programmes, like in September 2009 citing the PA plan "Palestine: Ending the Occupation, Establishing the State"; and to organizations, like in September 2010 referencing the "Office for the Coordination of Humanitarian Affairs, Occupied Palestinian Territory" (UN OCHA oPt). Meanwhile, references to the occupation completely disappear after 2012, even though the occupation very much exists and defines every aspect of Palestinian existence.

Astonishingly, in the 239-page evaluation of its work in the OPT 2001-9, the Bank uses "occupation" only 2 times, as a reference to the PA plan "Palestine: Ending the Occupation, Establishing the State." In the same report, the word "occupied" is mentioned 16 times, but of these only 3 are clear references to the phenomenon with the other 13 being secondary citations. Meanwhile, although the Oslo development model is premised on the establishment of a democratic Palestinian state – particularly for European donors – the words "democracy" and "democratic" are never mentioned in the Bank's 18 reports to the AHLC, outside of a 2010 June report to the AHLC referring to the governance of NGOs.

Partly out of fear of upsetting Israel, the Bank has defended its position as an effort to appear neutral and apolitical, focusing instead on what they consider positive dialogue and avoiding "deconstructive recriminations" about past actions by Israel (The World Bank, 2012). However, evidence also suggests a hypothesis that the World Bank is complicit in expunging not only the expression and the concept, but also the political and legal relevance of the occupation from the reality of global affairs.

The World Bank's extreme reluctance to refer to the occupation clashes with the more outspoken policy of the Europeans, who have been issuing declarations and reports addressing the occupation (cf. Bicchi, 2014, pp. 248-50). In fact, the European Community already in 1980 recognized the Palestinian right to self-determination and challenged Israel's rule and annexation of the occupied territories stating that settlements are illegal under international law and a serious obstacle to peace (European Council, 1980). Moreover, the EU is itself the official author of a number of reports on the OPT. In them it has been more willing to use contextually appropriate analysis. For example, in a 2014 evaluation of its aid to the OPT one EU report mentions settlements 55 times, occupation 49 times, occupied 158 times and democracy 115 times – in just 114 pages (Development Researchers' Network, European Centre for Development Policy Management, & Ecorys Research and Consulting, 2014). Yet regardless of these differences, the EU and its member states ultimately pay into and sustain the 25-year old Oslo framework maintained, under US oversight, maintained by the World Bank.

De-development

Alongside its refusal to address and emphasize the role of settlements and of the occupation, a second analytical shortcoming in the World Bank's model is represented by the adoption of a popular but flawed theory that under Israeli occupation Palestinian services and infrastructure improved, industry developed and the OPT thrived generally (Starr, 1989, p. 30). Thus, the Bank wrote,

> The economy of the OT grew rapidly between 1968 and 1980 (average annual increase of 7% and 9 per- cent in real per capita GDP and GNP, respectively), triggered by a number of factors, including the rapid integration with Israel and the regional economic boom (The World Bank, 1993, p. 4).

This growth was said to be the natural occurrence of a poorer state integrating, "with a larger, richer, and more technologically advanced neighbour" (Diwan & Shaban, 1999, pp. 2–3). Further, World Bank policy-makers seemingly operated on an assumption that governments consider it in their best interest to provide public goods and open markets for all the people they govern, and considered Israel to have been incurring expenditures in the OPT for the Palestinians (The World Bank, 1993, p. 18). This is because, they assume, Israel naturally wanted to see the Palestinians do well economically (The World Bank, 1993, p. 1), including for its own strategic interests (The World Bank, 2005, p. 3).

However, while Israel has at times had a strategic interest in allowing some form growth in the Palestinian economy, or to prevent total economic collapse, this is fully compatible with an equally strong interest in not only maintaining the occupation but profiting economically from it while colonizing and annexing OPT lands. When conducting research on the Gazan economy in the 1980s, Roy showed that Gaza was becoming poorer because the Israeli occupation had been structurally designed for the sole benefit of Israel. Palestinians provided cheap labour to propel forward Israeli economic growth, while their earnings bought Israeli goods in a captive Gazan economy unable to trade freely with the outside world. By absorbing Palestinian labour into its workforce, Israel was also able to free Jewish labourers from menial jobs to further develop Israeli advanced industry (Tamari, 1988, p. 25). Moreover, Palestinians could not develop their own economic sectors, as Israeli policy specifically undermined sectors that might compete with any Israeli equivalent. Roy coined the term "de-development" to describe this economic relationship, a "deliberate, systematic deconstruction of an indigenous economy by a dominant power" (Roy, 1995, p. 4). As Salim Tamari would argue this was also part of long-standing Israeli government policy to reinforce its rule over and integrate the OPT into Israel (Tamari, 1988). It was a process Roy linked to settler colonialism, because its goal was to "rob the native population of its important economic resources – land, water and labour – as well as the internal capacity and potential for developing those resources (Roy, 1995, p. 5).

As a result, by the 1980s the OPT had become Israel's most important export market; a market that was tariff-free, non-competitive and from which Palestinian goods were prevented from entering Israel. With the gross trade imbalance that resulted from this economic relationship, the OPT economy came to rely first in the 1970s on external remittances from Palestinian labourers in Israel and family members working abroad in the oil rich Gulf states, and later in the 1980s on "sumud" solidarity funds coming from the Arab world. After Oslo, foreign aid replaced Arab funds and work remittances, further helping Israel to offset costs and make the occupation profitable (Hever, 2010, 2015), without having to surrender OPT land or allow Palestinian freedom of movement for labour and commerce (Anderson, 2005, p. 144). In fact, aid helped turn a once private sector-led OPT economy into an economy dependent on aid (Tartir, 2011), achieving the exact opposite economic goal donors had set out to do. All the while, led by the World Bank, they kept encouraging the PA to engage and integrate with Israel, reinforcing a grossly unequal relationship (Gerster & Baumgarten, 2011, p. 11).

Conclusion

Since the 2000s agreements and norms have been adopted within the international donor community that could be used to chart a different course in the OPT. For instance, it is now widely acknowledged that for aid to be effective, stakeholders like the Palestinians need to play a leadership role in designing and implementing their own aid. The Paris Declaration (2005) on Aid Effectiveness states that developing countries should "set their own strategies for poverty reduction, improve their institutions and tackle corruption" and that "donors and partners are accountable for development results" (OECD, 2008). Further, the Accra Agenda for Action (2008) emphasizes that stakeholder countries need to have "more say over their development processes through wider participation in development policy formulation, stronger leadership on aid co-ordination and more use of country systems for aid delivery" (OECD, 2008). Further, as argued in a recent report by the Swedish International Development Cooperation Agency (SIDA), an important step in the OPT would be to combine the so-called "fragile state principles" (FSP) with the aid effectiveness principles to support constructive donor engagement while minimizing unintentional harm. There the first of ten principles is to start with strong analysis to understand the context well (Karlstedt et al., 2015, pp. 15–16), to be effective and not cause harm.

By contrast, since 1993 donors have imposed a radically transformative and one-size-fits-all model upon the Palestinians, remodelling OPT society from the top-down, with basically no accountability to the Palestinians. Were donors to reflect the aid effectiveness principles that have emerged in the last decade and fully adopt Palestinian analysis and leadership, Palestinian aid policy would look radically different (Abu Zahra, 2005). For instance, a poll of Palestinian public opinion conducted 2018 June 25 to July 1 found that: 43% of Palestinians consider their first most vital goal to be to end the occupation, 29% the right of return of refugees to their 1948 towns and villages, 14% to build a pious society and 13% to establish a democratic political system respecting freedoms and rights. Meanwhile, 27% consider the most serious problem confronting Palestinian society to be the continuation of the occupation and settlement activities, 25% poverty and unemployment, 22% the siege on Gaza and 21% the spread of corruption in public institutions (Survey Research Unit, 2018). For Palestinians, any effective aid would have to start by taking account of the realities of occupation and settlement building.

After 25 failed years of Oslo, contributing to a harmful status quo, EU donors are even more ethically responsible to Palestinians than ever before. They are powerful actors with substantial financial and political clout. As new ideas about aid effectiveness and local ownership become more widespread, it is time for them to revise their thinking behind aid provision, in order to help build peace and improve Palestinian lives. To do this, however, they would need to plot a path separate from the World Bank, starting with sound political analysis, respect for both democracy and Palestinian leadership over the aid process, and a willingness to directly address hard political issues like Israeli settlements.

Note

1. It has also attracted the attention of the European Court of Auditors, *European Union direct Financial Support to the Palestinian Authority*, Special Report n.14, 2013.

Disclosure statement

No potential conflict of interest was reported by the authors.

Funding

This work was supported by Economic and Social Research Council followed by the grant number [grant number ES/P009883/1].

ORCID

Jeremy Wildeman http://orcid.org/0000-0003-3460-5473

References

Abu Zahra, N. (2005). No advocacy, no protection, no 'politics': Why aid-for-peace does not bring peace. *Borderlands E-Journal*, 4(1). Retrieved from http://www.borderlands.net.au/vol4no1_2005/abu-zahra_aid.htm

Amit, H. (2017, November 20). Israeli Government Allocates Disproportionate Aid to Settlements, Study Finds. *Haaretz*. Retrieved from https://www.haaretz.com/israel-news/business/israel-allocates-disproportionate-aid-to-settlements-study-finds-1.5466853

Amundsen, I., Giacaman, G., & Khan, M. H. (2004). *State formation in Palestine: Viability and governance during a social transformation*. London: Routledge.

Anderson, M. B. (1999). *Do no harm: How aid can support peace - or war*. Boulder, CO: Lynne Rienner Publishers.

Anderson, M. B. (2005). 'Do no harm': The impact of international assistance to the occupied Palestinian territory. In M. Keating, A. L. More, & R. Lowe (Eds.), *Aid, diplomacy and the facts on the ground: The Palestinian experience of disconnection* (illustrated edition, pp. 143–153). London: Royal Institute of International Affairs.

Bicchi, F. (2014). Information exchanges, diplomatic networks and the construction of European knowledge in European Union foreign policy. *Cooperation and Conflict, 49*(2), 239–259. doi:10.1177/0010836713482871

Bolstad, E., & Viken, T. M. (2008, February). 2003 Amended Basic Law [Legal - it presents a collection of various drafts and amendments related to the Basic Law.]. Retrieved from http://www.palestinianbasiclaw.org/basic-law/2003-amended-basic-law

Brinkerhoff, D. W. (1996). Coordination issues in policy implementation networks: An illustration from Madagascar's environmental action plan. *World Development, 24*(9), 1497–1510. doi:10.1016/0305-750X(96)00046-0

B'Tselem. (2002). *Land Grab: Israel's Settlement Policy in the West Bank, May* 2002. Retrieved from http://www.btselem.org/publications/summaries/200205_land_grab

B'Tselem. (2017, May 11). *Statistics on Settlements and Settler Population.* Retrieved from http://www.btselem.org/settlements/statistics

Development Researchers' Network, European Centre for Development Policy Management, & Ecorys Research and Consulting. (2014). *Evaluation of the European Union's Cooperation with the occupied Palestinian territory and support to the Palestinian people* (No. Volume 1). European Commission.

Diwan, I., & Shaban, R. A. (eds.). (1999). *Development under adversity: The Palestinian economy in transition.* Washington, DC: Palestine Economic Policy Research Institute (MAS) and The World Bank.

Doyle, M. W. (1983). Kant, liberal legacies, and foreign affairs. *Philosophy & Public Affairs, 12*(3), 205–235.

Easterly, W. (2014, March 10). The New Tyranny. *Foreign Policy.* Retrieved from http://www.foreignpolicy.com/articles/2014/03/10/the_new_tyranny

Eddin, N. N., Massimiliano, C., & Niksic, O. (2014). *Area C and the future of the Palestinian economy. (No. 89370)* (pp. 1–99). The World Bank. Retrieved from http://documents.worldbank.org/curated/en/2014/07/19798093/area-c-future-palestinian-economy

EEAS. (2016, April 11). Political and economic relations [Government]. Retrieved from http://eeas.europa.eu/delegations/westbank/eu_westbank/political_relations/index_en.htm

EEAS. (n.d.). West Bank and Gaza Strip, UNRWA and the EU [EU Government]. Retrieved from https://eeas.europa.eu/delegations/palestine-occupied-palestinian-territory-west-bank-and-gaza-strip/1887/west-bank-and-gaza-strip-unrwa-and-eu_en

European Council. (1980). *Venice declaration.* Venice. Retrieved from http://eeas.europa.eu/archives/docs/mepp/docs/venice_declaration_1980_en.pdf

Ferzinger, J. (2018, March 22). Quicktake Israeli Settlements. *Bloomberg.* Retrieved from https://www.bloomberg.com/quicktake/israeli-settlements

Garcia-Garcia, J., Atanesyan, K., Farah, J., Polenakis, G., Kotb, T., Gopal, G., ... Willoughby, C. (2009). *The World Bank Group in the West Bank and Gaza, 2001–2009: Evaluation of the World Bank Group program (No. 100011)* (pp. 1–239). The World Bank. Retrieved from http://documents.worldbank.org/curated/en/144151467998201026/The-World-Bank-Group-in-the-West-Bank-and-Gaza-2001-2009-evaluation-of-the-World-Bank-Group-program

Gerster, K., & Baumgarten, D. H. (2011). *Palestinian NGOs and their cultural, economic and political impact in Palestinian society. By Karin Gerster and Prof. Dr. Helga Baumgarten.* Rosa Luxemburg Foundation. Retrieved from http://www.palestine.rosalux.org/news/38136/palestinian-ngos.html

Hanieh, A. (2008, July 15). Palestine in the Middle East: Opposing Neoliberalism and US Power Part 1. *The Bullet, E-Bulletin No. 125.* Retrieved from http://www.socialistproject.ca/bullet/bullet125.html

Hanieh, A. (2016). Development as struggle: Confronting the reality of power in palestine. *Journal of Palestine Studies, 45*(4), 32–47. doi:10.1525/jps.2016.45.4.32

Hart, J., & Forte, C. L. (2013). Mandated to fail? Humanitarian agencies and the protection of Palestinian children. *Disasters, 37*(4), 627–645. doi:10.1111/disa.12024

Hever, S. (2010). *The political economy of Israel's occupation: Repression beyond exploitation* (1st ed.). London: Pluto Press.

Hever, S. (2015). How much international aid to Palestinians ends up in the Israeli Economy? *Aid Watch*.

Inside Story - China banking checkmate? (2015). Retrieved from https://www.youtube.com/watch?v = yioaSWu3fUY&feature = youtube_gdata_player

Israel's settlement policy in the occupied Palestinian territory. (n.d.). Retrieved from https://afsc.org/resource/israel%E2%80%99s-settlement-policy-occupied-palestinian-territory

Kanafani, N., & Ghaith, Z. (2012). *The economic base of Israel's colonial settlements in the West Bank*. Palestine Economic Policy Research Institute (MAS). Retrieved from http://www.lacs.ps/documentsshow.aspx?att_id = 5061

Karlstedt, C., Abdulsalam, W., Ben-Natan, S., & Rizik, H. (2015). *Effectiveness of core funding to CSOs in the field of human rights and international humanitarian law in occupied Palestine - final report* (Sida Decentralised Evaluation No. 2015:25). Stockholm: Sida. Retrieved from https://www.sida.se/English/publications/139125/effectiveness-of-core-funding-to-csos-in-the-field-of-human-rights-and-international-humanitarian-law-in-occupied-palestine---f1/

Keohane, R. O., & Nye, J. S. (1998, September 1). Power and Interdependence in the Information Age. *Foreign Affairs*, (September/October 1998). Retrieved from http://www.foreignaffairs.com/articles/54395/robert-o-keohane-and-joseph-s-nye-jr/power-and-interdependence-in-the-information-age

Khalidi, R. (2008). Sixty years after the UN partition resolution: What future for the Arab economy in Israel? *Journal of Palestine Studies*, 37(2), 6–22.

Khalidi, R., & Samour, S. (2011). Neoliberalism as liberation: The statehood program and the remaking of the Palestinian national movement. *Journal of Palestine Studies*, 40(2), 6–25. doi:10.1525/jps.2011.XL.2.6

Le More, A. (2008). *International assistance to the Palestinians after Oslo*. London: Routledge.

Lynk, M. (2017). *A/HRC/34/70 report of the special rapporteur on the situation of human rights in the Palestinian territories occupied since 1967* (thirty-fourth session 27 February-24 march 2017 No. A/HRC/34/70)*. Geneva: UN General Assembly Human Rights Council.

Mosse, D. (2004a). *Cultivating development: An ethnography of aid policy and practice*. London: Pluto Press.

Mosse, D. (2004b). Is good policy unimplementable? Reflections on the ethnography of aid policy and practice. *Development and Change*, 35(4), 639–671. doi:10.1111/j.0012-155X.2004.00374.x

OECD. (2007, April). *Principles for good international engagement in Fragile states and situations*. Retrieved from http://www.oecd.org/dac/incaf/38368714.pdf

OECD. (2008). *The Paris declaration on aid effectiveness and the Accra Agenda for Action*. Retrieved from http://www.oecd.org/dac/effectiveness/34428351.pdf

OECD. (2011). *Conflict and Fragility - International Engagement in Fragile States - Can't We Do Better?* Retrieved from https://www.oecd.org/countries/somalia/48697077.pdf

OECD QWIDS concatenated, 2012 to 2016 [Dataset]. (2018). EU Institutions and Member State ODA disbursements to the West Bank and Gaza. *OECD*. Retrieved from https://stats.oecd.org/qwids/

Pappe, I. (2006). *A history of modern palestine: One land, two peoples* (2nd ed.). Cambridge: Cambridge University Press.

Redden, K. (2015, December 6). Kerry: Israel 'imperiling' two-state solution. *Maan News Agency*. Retrieved from http://www.maannews.com/Content.aspx?ID = 769192

Rosecrance, R. N. (1986). *The rise of the trading state: Commerce and conquest in the modern world*. New York: Basic Books.

Roy, S. (1995). *The gaza strip: The political economy of De-development*. Washington, DC: Cambridge: Institute for Palestine Studies.

Roy, S. (1999). De-development revisited: Palestinian economy and society since Oslo. *Journal of Palestine Studies*, 28(3), 64–82. doi:10.2307/2538308

Rynhold, J. (2009). Liberalism and the collapse of the Oslo peace process in the Middle East. *Journal of Diplomacy - School of Diplomacy and International Relations - Seton Hall University*. Retrieved from http://blogs.shu.edu/diplomacy/files/archives/05%20Rynhold.pdf

Sayigh, Y. (2007). Inducing a failed state in Palestine. *Survival, 49*(3), 7–39. doi:10.1080/00396330701564786

Schiavo-Campo, S. (2003). *Financing and aid management arrangements in post - conflict situations* (CPR Working Papers No. 6). Social Development Department, World Bank. Retrieved from http://documents.worldbank.org/curated/en/967011468777577384/pdf/266890Conflict0prevention0wp0no-06.pdf

Starr, J. (1989). *Development diplomacy* (Policy Papers 12). Washington Institute for Near East Policy. Retrieved from http://www.washingtoninstitute.org/policy-analysis/view/development-diplomacy-u.s.-economic-assistance-to-the-west-bank-and-gaza

Survey Research Unit. (2018). *Press release: Public opinion poll (68) (No. 68)*. Ramallah: Palestinian Center for Policy and Survey Research (PSR). Retrieved from http://www.kas.de/wf/doc/kas_26218-1442-2-30.pdf?180704142051

Taghdisi-Rad, S. (2010). *The political economy of aid in Palestine: Relief from conflict or development delayed?* London: Routledge.

Tamari, S. (1988). What the uprising means. *Middle East Report*, (152), 24–30. doi:10.2307/3012098

Tartir, A. (2011). *The role of international Aid in development: The case of Palestine 1994–2008*. Lambert Academic Publishing. Retrieved from http://documents.worldbank.org/curated/en/1999/01/1561492/promise-challenges-achievements-donor-investment-palestinian-development-1994-1998

Tartir, A. (2016, December 2). How US security aid to PA sustains Israel's occupation. *Al Jazeeera*. Retrieved from http://www.aljazeera.com/indepth/features/2016/11/security-aid-pa-sustains-israel-occupation-161103120213593.html

Tartir, A., & Wildeman, J. (2017). *Mapping of Donor Funding to the occupied palestinian territories 2012–2014/15: Limited, Disorganized and Fragmented Aid Data Undermining Transparency, Accountability and Planning*. (Research Study). Aid Watch Palestine. Retrieved from https://alaatartir.com/2017/11/10/mapping-of-donor-funding-to-the-occupied-palestinian-territories-2012-2014-15/

UNCTAD. (2015). *TD/b/62/3 report on UNCTAD assistance to the Palestinian people: Developments in the economy of the occupied Palestinian territory* (Sixty-second session No. TD/B/62/3)*. Geneva: United Nations Conference on Trade and Development.

The World Bank. (1993). *Developing the occupied territories: An investment in peace*. Washington, DC: The World Bank.

The World Bank. (2000). *Aid effectiveness in the West Bank and Gaza*. Government of Japan and World Bank.

The World Bank. (2005). *The Palestinian economy and the prospects for its recovery: Economic monitoring report to the Ad Hoc liaison committee (No. 40462) (pp. 1–55)*. The World Bank. Retrieved from http://siteresources.worldbank.org/INTWESTBANKGAZA/Data/20751555/EMR.pdf

The World Bank. (2011). *Building the Palestinian state: Sustaining growth, institutions, and service delivery - economic monitoring report to the Ad Hoc liaison committee (No. 76019) (pp. 1–32)*. The World Bank. Retrieved from http://documents.worldbank.org/curated/en/2011/04/17451464/building-palestinian-state-sustaining-growth-institutions-service-delivery-economic-monitoring-report-ad-hoc-liaison-committee.

The World Bank. (2012). *Towards economic sustainability of a future Palestinian state: Promoting private sector - Led growth* (Report No. 68037-GZ). Retrieved from http://siteresources.worldbank.org/INTWESTBANKGAZA/Resources/GrowthStudyEngcorrected.pdf

Index

Abbas, Mahmoud 71, 75, 76
Ad Hoc Liaison Committee (AHLC) 86, 114–115
Aftenposten 84
anti-Semitism 42, 63, 66; definition of 65–66
Arab-Israeli conflict 61–62
Arafat 37, 84–85
Articles on the Responsibility of States for Internationally Wrongful Acts (ARSIWA) 20–22, 24

Ben-Naftali, O. 8
Benvenesti, E. 8
bilateral dealings 20, 24, 28, 38–39
bilateral relations 2, 23, 35, 49–51
Bildt, C. 75
Boycott, Divest and Sanction (BDS) movement 2, 42, 53, 61–62, 64–65, 94, 96, 103; groups countering 60, 64–66
Bundestag 54

Chirac, Jacques 37
conflict 2–6, 13, 36, 38, 41, 59–60, 62, 66, 72–76, 78, 84, 97, 99–101, 103, 112
conflict parties 84, 86
Conseil Représentatif des Institutions Juives de France (CRIF) 37, 42
cooperation 23–24, 27, 35, 40, 89, 110–111
corporate responsibility 2, 95–98, 100, 103
Crawford, J. 21, 23, 29, 72

Direction Générale de la Concurrence, de la Consommation e de la Répression des Fraudes (DGCCRF) 39–40
discrimination 42, 94, 96, 99
due diligence, enhanced 100

EU-Israeli relations 20, 23, 25, 28; revisions to 19–20, 26
European Commission 13, 52, 102
European Council 6, 50–51, 115
European Council on Foreign Relations 27–28

European External Action Service (EEAS) 24–25, 109–110
Europeanization, strategy of 49
European member states 95, 100–101
European Union 5–6, 19, 24, 27, 29, 34, 49, 51–53, 74, 101, 108
EUROPOL 26–27

Federal Foreign Office 52–53, 55
foreign investments 101, 103
France 2, 34–42, 62, 77, 96, 100, 110; and Israeli occupation 34–42
France-Israel Foundation 37
Fremskrittspartiet 86
French foreign policy 34, 36, 41–42
French-Israeli cooperation 35–36
French-Israeli relations 35, 37

Gaza war 88–89
Geldenhuys, D. 71–72
German government 47–55
German-Israeli Foundation 51
German-Israeli special relationship 48, 50
Germany 2, 47–55, 62; and Israeli occupation 47–55
Government Pension Fund 88
government policies 47–48
Gross, A. 8

Hollande, François 37–38
human rights 2, 5, 8, 12, 27, 66, 73, 75–76, 88, 95, 97–103

illegal situation 20–22, 24–25, 27
institutional practices 24, 28
international actors 20–22, 29, 112–113
international community 5–8, 13, 38, 41, 49, 74–76, 78, 111
international governance gaps 94–104
international law 4–29, 37–38, 40–41, 51–52, 64, 71–73, 75, 78, 87–90, 94–100, 102–103, 113, 115; obligation of non-recognition in

INDEX

19–20; peremptory norms of 21; violations of peremptory norms of 20–21
international law obligations 23, 27, 102
international lawyers 20, 22, 29
interstate dealings 22, 29
Israel 2, 4–13, 19–20, 23, 25–28, 34–42, 47–55, 61–62, 64–66, 71–75, 77–78, 82–91, 96, 108–109, 111–117; occupation 2, 8, 12, 21, 34–35, 38, 48, 54; security 48; settlement activity 89–90; settlements 50, 94–95, 110; sovereignty 25–26
Israel Apartheid Week 62, 64–65
Israeli and Palestinian peacebuilding 110
Israeli authorities 19, 26–27
Israeli entities 19, 25–27, 39
Israeli government 10, 26, 38, 47–48, 55, 88, 90, 114
Israeli government policies 48
Israeli military occupation 89
Israeli occupation 7–8, 10, 13, 34–35, 38, 40, 47, 53, 55, 77, 79, 82, 94–96, 99; addressing 2; condemned 41; France and 34–42; ongoing 72
Israeli-Palestinian conflict 2, 4–6, 23, 34–36, 38, 41, 60–61, 63, 66, 78; on UK campuses 63
Israeli-Palestinian peace 110
Israeli policies 4, 42, 54, 116
Israeli settlements 2, 4–6, 26, 28, 35–36, 38–42, 49–54, 82, 88–89, 96, 113–114, 118; activities 52; construction 76; enterprise 7; German position on 49; Green Line and 2; policies, criticizing 55
Israeli universities 59, 61; boycott of 61–62
Israel occupation 88
Israel-Palestine conflict 48–50, 54–55
Israel-Palestine peace conference 76
Israel/Palestine portfolio 49
Israel's occupation: condemning 36; and French policy practice 41
Israel's Settlement Policy 113
Israel's sovereignty, non-recognition of 25–26

Jerusalem Light Railway (JLR) 94–104

Kattan, V. 5
Kosovo 75

land 7, 11, 113–114, 116–117
Leber, Hubert 50
legalization 49, 53, 55
legislation 26, 39–40, 52–53, 61, 101, 104
Lieberman, Avigdor 71

Michaeli, K. 8

néocons à la français 37
Netanyahu 51, 54–55

Netherlands 97, 110
non-recognition à la European Union 19–29
non-recognition of Israeli settlements 35, 41, 51
Norway 2, 82–91; complicity in Israel 82–91
Norway-Israel-Palestine relations 86
Norway-Palestine-Israel relations 83
Norwegian governments 82, 90

occupation 2–13, 35, 37, 39–42, 47–49, 55, 59–64, 66, 73–74, 86–90, 94–95, 100, 103, 108, 113–117; laws of 4, 9–10, 12
occupied Palestinian territories (OPT) 2, 4, 21, 23, 25, 74, 82, 87–90, 95–96, 98–103, 108–118
OECD 108–118
Oslo Accords 5, 82, 85–86, 108
Oslo development aid model 110, 112
Oslo Peace Process 4, 37, 50, 108, 110

Palestine, Swedish recognition of 71–79
Palestine Liberation Organization (PLO) 5, 36, 50, 84–85, 96
Palestinian Authority (PA) 13, 50, 60, 75–77, 85, 87, 108–110, 112, 117
Palestinian poverty 111
Palestinian self-determination 38, 49–50, 73, 78
Palestinian statehood 51, 72, 74–77, 110
Palestinian Territories 2–13, 19–29, 35–41, 48–55, 59–65, 72–79, 82–91, 95–103, 109–117
peace process 4–7, 38, 48–49, 51–52, 71–73, 75–76, 78, 85–87, 89, 101–102, 108–113, 115, 118
peremptory norms 20–21
Persson, A. 77

radicalization 59, 61, 63
Ruggie, J. 99

Sarkozy, Nicolas 37
Second Intifada 59, 82, 86–87
self-determination 2, 4, 6, 10, 12, 21, 34, 36, 50, 77–78, 85
settlement activities 6, 37, 98, 101–103, 117
settlement products 13, 26, 47, 49, 52–53, 101
Shafir, G. 10
special relationship 28, 38, 48–50, 54–55
special responsibility 2, 12, 53
state intervention 111–112
Sweden 71, 73–79, 90, 110
Swedish government 71, 75, 77

Talmon, S. 23
territories 9–10, 12, 19, 25–26, 36–37, 39, 41, 51–52, 72–75, 96, 110; acquisition of 4, 9–10, 72
terrorism 4, 12, 63, 75, 79
treaties, bilateral 41

two-state solution 6–7, 34–35, 37–38, 41–42, 48, 52, 55, 73–77, 86, 90

UK 2, 53, 59–63, 65–66, 77, 110; occupation of Palestinian territories on 59–66
UN Guiding Principles on Business and Human Rights (UNGPs) 95, 98–104
United Nations Security Council (UNSC) 5, 8–10, 12–13, 89

violence 42, 75, 111

Waage, H. H. 83, 86
Wallström, M. 75, 77–78
West Bank 7, 9–11, 34, 39–40, 50, 52, 74–75, 85–86, 88–89, 94–95, 99–100, 113–114
Wettstein, F. 100
World Bank 2, 11, 75, 108–118